KT-167-413

R. H. Blyth: Haiku, Vol. II

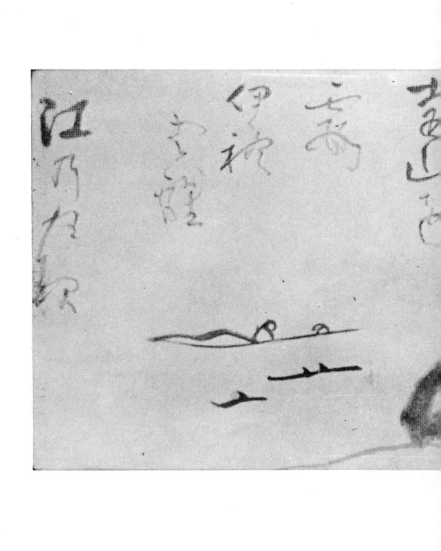

江の月夜 遠山を 月波玉屑
いれたり
霞

A moonlit night over the creek,
The distant mountains
Hidden in the haze.

Gyokusetsu

(The picture also is by the poet, d. 1826)

HAIKU

BY

R. H. BLYTH

Volume Two: Spring

(Pp. 345–640)

(Reset in paperback edition)

1981

THE HOKUSEIDO PRESS

Tokyo

Haiku, Volume Two © by R. H. Blyth 1950, 1981
Paperback edition, first printing 1981
fourth printing 1992

Complete set ISBN 4-590-00571-9
Vol. II ISBN 4-590-00573-5

Published by The Hokuseido Press
3-32-4, Honkomagome, Bunkyo-ku, Tokyo

VOL. II SPRING

SEASONAL INDEX

THE NEW YEAR

SPRING

The Season

Sky and Elements

Fields and Mountains

Gods and Buddhas

Human Affairs

Birds and Beasts

Trees and Flowers

ILLUSTRATIONS

HAIKU

IN FOUR VOLUMES

VOL. II

SPRING

野のなかに
蝶の飛けり
夕日影　　　　　北枝

No no nakani   chō no tobikeri   yūhikage

In the midst of the moor
Flutters a butterfly
In the rays of the evening sun.　　　Hokushi

GRATEFULLY

DEDICATED

TO

SAKUO HASHIMOTO

THROUGH WHOSE PATRIOTIC GENEROSITY

THE PUBLICATION OF THESE VOLUMES

WAS MADE POSSIBLE

PREFACE

This volume, Spring, and the two succeeding volumes, Summer, and Autumn and Winter, contain all the good haiku that I could find from the beginnings up to and including Shiki, 1866–1902. No doubt some good verses have been omitted by oversight; I hope to include such in any future edition.

The reader will see that the seasonal arrangement provides a rough kind of index for finding any verse of which he remembers the subject. Some verses have two seasonal subjects, some none, but these are very few indeed. (As for authors, an index will be given at the end of the last, the fourth volume). I would like to add here a short note on the history of this arrangement of haiku according to seasons and subjects.[1]

In Palgrave's *Golden Treasury*, "the most poetically-effective order has been attempted," but this is combined, very skilfully, with the chronological. There are in English, what are hardly to be found in Japanese literature, special anthologies of poems, for example about birds, flowers, the sea; but few seasonally arranged anthologies. We come across some haiku that can hardly be included in the ordinary classification, such as congratulatory verses or those describing famous places; these are usually put in a "miscellaneous" group, 雑. Otherwise, up to modern times, there were no verses outside the seasonal classification. This insistence on the seasons has been explained in various ways; for example, by the brevity of haiku, the climate of Japan, the influence of waka, and all these no doubt had a concerted effect. Above all it should be noted that the hokku, the first verse of renku, chain-poems, was a verse indicating the season. But we must go farther back, to the very beginnings of Japanese poetry to find the *vital* reason for the deep consciousness of the seasons which the Japanese have not yet lost.

In the *Manyōshū*[2] we see the Japanese love of nature already deep and wide, and in the following, two of the seasons are

---

[1] This was already treated, somewhat more superficially, in Vol. I, Section V, 8. [2] c. 750.

consciously distinguished. It is part of a Long Poem by Yamabe
Akahito of the 8th century, composed when he climbed up Mount
Kannabi and thought of the Capital (at Asuka) of the Emperor
Temmu, 673–686.

明日香の古き都は山高く河遠白し、春の日
は山し見がほし、秋の夜は河しさやけし、
朝雲にたづはみだれ、夕霧にかはづはさわぐ。

I would gaze upon the ruined Palace of Asuka:
The hills are high, the river far-flowing.
In the days of spring the mountain is fair to see;
In autumn nights the waters are clear.
Together through the morning clouds fly the cranes;
In the evening mists the frogs are loud.

From the time of the *Manyōshū* onwards, spring with the
uguisu, the cherry blossoms, wistaria flowers; summer with the
cuckoo, the pink,[1] the summer grasses; autumn with the Milky
Way, the autumn breeze, the red foliage, the deer's cry; winter
with the snow on the pine-tree, frost on the thickets of bamboo
grass; all these were distinctly realized and with a separate and
integral interest. However, the *Manyōshū* itself is not divided
simply into spring, summer, autumn, winter. Book I, for ex-
ample, is chronologically arranged, but Book VIII into miscel-
laneous poems and epistolary (amatory), each under the heads
of the four seasons.

For the Japanese of Manyō times, man and nature were still
indistinguishable. We cannot say that Nature was not loved
for its own sake, but rather that nature was suffused with man,
man was interpenetrated with nature, and the distinction of
love poems and miscellaneous poems was still stronger in their
minds than the seasonal one. When therefore the modern
Japanese or the emulous foreign student reads the *Manyōshū*,
it is with a very different eye from that of the writers of
the verses.

During the hundred and fifty years between the *Manyōshū*
and the *Kokinshū*, Chinese poetry flourished in Japan and many
collections appeared. Among these there are few nature poems,
and no seasonal arrangement, until we come to the late *Wakan*

---

[1] The lily suddenly disappears as a subject after the *Kokinshu*.

Rōeishū,[1] 和漢朗詠集, the first part of which is divided into spring, summer, autumn and winter, but the second according to subjects, wind, clouds, wine, mountains, etc., in more or less indiscriminate order. This was the result of the beginning of a return to the ideals and aims of waka. From such Chinese poets as Tōenmei and Hakurakuten, however, the Japanese feeling of nature was deepened, and with it, though indirectly, the feeling of the difference of the seasons.

In the *Kokinshū*, completed in 922, we find the seasonal classification clearly made for the first time, but it must be noted that with this very virtue comes the lack of spontaneity, the beginning of the artificiality that is ultimately to be the death of all poetry. The art which alone gives meaning to life yet smothers and strangles it. It is the penalty we pay for the expanding of our vision, for seeing a world in a grain of sand, instead of seeing the sand itself alone; for seeing the plum blossom as the spring, instead of seeing simply its own beautiful form and colour. From this point of view we may look at the history of Japanese poetry as consisting of two great movements. The *Manyōshū* gives up its spontaneity and unselfconsciousness to the *Kokinshū*. The genius of Bashō restores a certain enriched simplicity to it, and this again, two hundred years later, is brought to its end at the hands of Shiki.[2]

However, in the *Kokinshū* the real subjects are not those of insects, grasses and flowers, but the feelings of the poets; these things are used as symbols of human thought and emotion. With the *Shinkokinshū*, first compiled in 1205, we get objective poems of nature, the sky, the voices of insects, the dusk of evening, and this is partly the effect of the deepening consciousness of the meaning of the seasons.

Coming to haikai, one of the things which distinguished it from renga, the linked poems from which it arose, was the insistence upon not merely the advisability,[3] but the *necessity* of having a season word in the hokku, or first verse. Even in the other verses, the idea of the season was never absent from the mind of the poet, though the verse itself might be "mixed."

[1] See Vol. I, page 103, for description and examples.

[2] In Shiki's monumental *Complete Classified Collection of Haiku*, 分類 俳句全集, there is such an excess of system that the poetry is swamped by it. For example, there are no less than fifty classes of fans alone.

[3] As expounded by Abutsu-ni, 阿佛尼, who died 1283.

In 御傘, *Gosan*, by Teitoku, 1570–1653, things are very carefully assigned to their seasons. For Bashō, 1644–94, the season was the most important element of haikai, not as a principle, but as a mode of intuition, a vaster way of seeing particular things. As we look more carefully at the object we see in it the whole world working out its perfect will. And this comes from the historical, the accumulated experiences of the Japanese race during more than a thousand years.

In a recent number of the Times Literary Supplement,[1] the reviewer quotes the following haiku of Bashō:

> On a leafless branch
> A lonely crow is perching
> On an autumn eve.

He then ·makes a rather enigmatic comment:

> It is for use rather than beauty.

This I think is a just "criticism" of the original also, and of all haiku. They are for you to use in your own poetic experience. You are not to be a mere observer of literature, but to play your part in its dynamic re-creation. Reading haiku is more exhausting then, than ordinary poetry, but I know of nothing more worth while. It alone can give meaning to life, and "justify the ways of God to men."

---

[1] April 9, 1949.

新　　年

THE NEW YEAR

The New Year is a season by itself. When the Lunar Calendar was in vogue, January the First was what is now about the beginning of February. Plum was blooming in sheltered places, and the spirit of spring was already in the air. Especially New Year's Morning was felt to be the morning, not only of this day, but the morning of the whole year. The rejuvenation of nature coincided with a fresh trust in humanity, in one's own and other people's goodness, in the Buddha nature. And not only the world of human beings, but the sight of clouds, the blue sky and green grass, the sound of running water and the wind in the pine-trees,—all these familiar things had on this day a new significance. All things are the same, yet all is new. The sameness and the difference; in the unity of these two lies an unnameable, ineffable meaning which the following verses rejoice to express.

新 年 **THE NEW YEAR**

元朝や神代の事も思はるゝ　　　　　　守　武
Ganchō[1] ya　kami-yo no koto mo　omowaruru

It is New Year's Morning;
I think also of the Age
Of the Age
Of the Gods.　　　　　Moritake

Moritake was a High Priest of the Shrine of Ise. When he
wrote this verse and when we read it, we are in

that blessed mood
In which the burthen of the mystery,
In which the heavy and the weary weight
Of all this unintelligible world
Is lightened...
While with an eye made quiet by the power
Of harmony, and the deep power of joy,
We see into the life of things,[2]

even the life of the Gods. Our state of mind is one in which
the Gods are as real as the characters of Shakespeare, as unreal
as are we ourselves; with gentle thankfulness we are one with
those bright beings that live far away and long ago, yet are
alive for evermore in our deepest hearts.

The Gods are happy;
They turn on all sides
Their shining eyes,
And see below them
The earth and men.[3]

日の光今朝や鰯のかしらより　　　　　蕪　村
Hi no hikari　kesa ya iwashi no　kashira yori

A day of light
Begins to shine
From on the heads of the pilchards.　Buson

[1] Note that ん, n, is a syllable in Japanese.　[2] *Tintern Abbey.*　[3] *The Strayed Reveller.*

This verse, the one exception to Buson's rule of inserting a season word in each poem, has been included by some under *Setsubun*, the last day of winter, but the spirit of it belongs rather to the New Year. The pilchards are hanging from the eaves.

This verse is conventional and has no specially deep meaning, other than the real waking of light and life, but illustrates the tendency to bring down the spiritual and majestic into the material rather than glorify the insignificant. It does not matter where the light comes from, whether it is from the finger-nail of Richard Jefferies or the heads of pilchards. Light is light whenever seen, but especially bright on New Year's Day.

大旦昔吹きにし松の風   鬼　貫
Ōashita   mukashi fukinishi   matsu no kaze

　　The Great Morning:
　Winds of long ago
　　　Blow through the pine-trees.   Onitsura

"The Great Morning" is the morning of New Year's Day; apparently a rather uncommon expression, it is peculiarly appropriate here. It associates itself naturally with the past, a past which is still present. In the following verse, the poet has taken only the present moment, by which the here and now is thus weakened:

元日のこゝろや峰の松のかぜ   都　山
Ganjitsu no   kokoro ya mine no   matsu no kaze

　　The wind
　In the pine tree on the peak,—
　　　The very being of New Year's Day.   Tozan

There is a line of Matthew Arnold, in *Resignation*, which is very near in meaning to Onitsura's verse; it is somewhat different, however, in emotional tone:

　　　　　in his ears
　　The murmur of a thousand years.

Ruskin also says something that reminds us strongly of Onitsura's verse:

The orange stain on the edge of yonder western peak
reflects the sunsets of a thousand years.

元日を天地和合のはじめかな　　　　　　　　子　規
Ganjitsu wo　tenchi wagō no　hajime kana

New Year's Day:
The beginning of the harmony
Of Heaven and Earth.　　　　　　　　　Shiki

There is another verse by Shiki which may be quoted here:

元日は是も非もなくて衆生なり
Ganjitsu wa　ze mo hi mo nakute　shujō nari

New Year's Day;
Nothing good or bad,—
Just human beings.

On New Year's Day, all things are once more in their original
state of harmony. There is no distinction between higher and
lower, respectable and criminal, men and animals. All are
united in the ceaseless activity of their Buddha nature, without
any distinction whatever, all happy today and happy ever after.

元日の見るものにせむ富士の山　　　　　　　宗　鑑
Ganjitsu no　miru-mono ni sen　fuji no yama

For this New Year's Day,
The sight we gaze upon shall be
Mount Fuji.　　　　　　　　　　　　　Sōkan

The excellence of this poem has caused many to doubt whether
Sōkan, whose other haiku fall far below this, is really the author.
In Sōkan's time haiku were chiefly concerned with conceits and
puns. However, it is possible that the author meant the verse
in a shallower sense than we now take it.

On New Year's Day we have all kinds of delicacies for our
stomachs, the music of the *koto* and the *biwa* for our ears; with
what shall we gratify our eyes, the most potent source of
poetical pleasure? Let us sit on the verandah and gaze out at

Mount Fuji, seen every day, but on New Year's Day more august and sublime than ever.

There is a verse by Meisetsu which expresses the feelings of most Japanese about Japan on this particular day:

元日や一系の天子不二の山
Ganjitsu ya   ikkei no tenshi   fuji no yama

> The First Day of the Year:
> One line of Emperors;
> Mount Fuji.

それも應是も應なり老の春   涼菟
Sore mo ō   kore mo ō nari   oi no haru

> That is good, this too is good,—
> New Year's Day
> In my old age.   Ryōto

This reminds us of Unmon's

> 日日是好日   （碧巖録第六）
> Every day is a good day,

and of Wordsworth's

> Years that bring the philosophic mind,

the word "philosophic" being used here in its broadest sense. Of the same feeling, but more subdued, is the following:

元日も鐘聞く暮に及びけり   白 起
Ganjitsu mo   kane kiku kure ni   oyobikeri

> New Year's Day also
> Has come to its close,
> With the sounding bell.   Hakki

More similar still is the following:

元日や誰貌見ても念のなき   詩 玉
Ganjitsu ya   taga kao mite mo   nen no naki

> New Year's Day;
> Whosoever's face we see,
> It is care-free.   Shigyoku

元日や思へば淋し秋の暮　　　　　　　芭 蕉
Ganjitsu ya   omoeba sabishi   aki no kure

The First Day of the Year:
I remember
A lonely autumn evening.　　　　　Bashō

This is a little like Wordsworth's

In that sweet mood when pleasant thoughts
Bring sad thoughts to the mind.

This was written *In Early Spring,* and ends with lines that may
or may not express what reminded Bashō of a melancholy
autumn evening:

Have I not reason to lament
What man has made of man?

春立や愚の上にまた愚にかへる　　　　一 茶
Haru tatsu ya   gu no ue ni mata   gu ni kaeru

Spring begins again;
Upon folly,
Folly returns.　　　　　　　　　　Issa

This was written when Issa had reached his sixty-first year,
the sexagenary cycle being thus completed. The wheel has
turned full circle, the original folly of childhood now being
replaced by the enriched folly of the aged. Issa is laughing at
himself, but means what he says.

The children of this world are wiser than the children of
light,

and the true poetical, religious life can never, by any accident,
lead a man to an archbishopric or a baronetcy. In the foreword
Issa says that in his getting a house of his own to live in, his
pleasure is really greater than that of a blind turtle that finds
by accident a floating log (a Zen simile). 實に實に盲亀の浮木に
逢へるよろこびにまさりなん。
A verse in which the subjective is replaced by the objective,
is the following:

無爲庵樗良

うぐひすの
古聲
したふ
初日かな

Uguhisu no   furugoe shitau   hatsuhi kana

The First Day of the Year;
I long for the voice of the uguisu
Of past times.　　　　Chora

　　The *haiga* is by the poet himself. He was known as Mui-an
Chora, since he lived in this "Do-nothing-hermitage."

元 日 や 反 古 も 机 も 去 年 の 儘　　　　松　尾
Ganjitsu ya   hogo mo tsukue mo   kozo no mama

New Year's Day:
The desk and bits of paper,—
Just as last year.　　　　Matsuo

元 日 や 草 の 戸 越 し の 麦 畑　　　　召　波
Ganjitsu ya   kusa no togoshi no   mugi-batake

The First Day of the Year;
Through the door of my hut,
A field of barley.　　　　Shōha

The poet is sitting in his hut on New Year's morning. The world is reborn, all things made new. How shall he celebrate this auspicious time in "tuneful numbers"? As he sits there, though it is still cold, the door is open, and the sea of blue-green barley outside expresses for him the resurgent life that looks forward to hot summer suns and the tranquil autumn moon.

元 日 や さ れ ば 野 川 の 水 の 音　　　　來　山
Ganjitsu ya   sareba nogawa no   mizu no oto

The stream through the fields,—
Ah, the sound of the water!
It is New Year's Day.　　　　Raizan

Today everything tastes different, looks different, sounds different. Is everything really the same, or different? Everything is the same, everything is different. Everything has a meaning that comes from the contradiction of the everyday and the wonderful. Whitman says in *Crossing Brooklyn Ferry*,

Crowds of men and women attired in the usual costumes, how curious you are to me!

家内にも客ぶりのあり今朝の春   惟　艸
Kanai ni mo   kyaku-buri no ari   kesa no haru

Even my wife
Acts like a visitor,
This morning of Spring.   Isō

This verse comes perilously near to being a senryu, but the aim of the verse is not the humour of the wife's formal, slightly self-conscious behaviour on this morning of New Year's Day, but the poet's feeling of newness and rebirth of everything on this one day. Even such a thing as his wife, than whom is nothing more unstimulating and flat, in her dress, her manner, her suppressed excitement appears like a new creature. How much more so all the sights and sounds of this New Year's Morning.

目出度さも中位なりおらが春   一　茶
Medetasamo   chūgurai nari   ora ga haru

A time of congratulation,—
But my spring
Is about average.   Issa

This verse is the first in Issa's poetical essay *Ora ga haru*, which takes its title from the last five syllables of the haiku. There is here a subdued feeling, an unsentimental grimness which gives us Issa's mature view of life, his experience of the thusness of things. "This," he tells us, "is life as I see it." It is not what he tells us (for fundamental questions have no answers) but *how* he tells us, what he does not say, that expresses the effect on him of a lonely childhood, a fifty years' struggle with poverty and relatives, the death of his wife and of so many children in their babyhood. We feel in this verse the commiseration and compassion of the poet with the greatness and pitifulness of mankind.

Another verse which says the same thing less abstractly, but which is not to be taken in any way symbolically:

ぬかるみへ杖つツぱつて初日かな
Nukarumi e tsue tsuppatte hatsuhi kana

Planting my stick
In the quagmire,—
The First Sun of the Year.

Issa worships the new sun, standing in front of his house

元日も立のまんまの屑家哉　　　　　　　一 茶
Ganjitsu mo tachi no manma no kuzu-ya kana

New Year's Day:
My hovel,
The same as ever.　　　　　　　　　　Issa

"My hovel" is in the original "a rubbish house." It is interesting
to note that we do not wonder whose house it is; it is clearly
Issa's. "Hovel" is perhaps too serious a word. There is neither
contempt nor self-pity in the *bottom* of Issa's mind.

There is another, much weaker, explanatory version of this
verse:

元日も別條のなき屑家哉
Ganjitsu mo betsujō no naki kuzu-ya kana

New Year's Day:
Nothing different
About this hovel!

The former with its third line, literally, "It stands as it is,"
shows us the real house, the thing as it is. It is the house and
the house only. "Nothing different" is comparative, intellectual,
第二念, an after-thought. Contrast the following, which is much
better:

あばら屋の其身其まゝ明の春
Abaraya no sono mi sono mama ake no haru

This ramshackle house,
And me just the same as ever,—
The first day of Spring.

元 日 や 晴 れ て 雀 の 物 が た り   嵐 雪

Ganjitsu ya   harete suzume no   monogatari

New Year's Day:
The sky is cloudless;
Sparrows are gossiping.   Ransetsu

Sparrows twitter all the year round. Fine, cloudless days also
are many. How is it that just on this particular day, the first
day of the year, they should attain their real significance, their
poetic life?

元 日 や 上 々 吉 の 淺 黄 空   一 茶

Ganjitsu ya   jōjōkichi no   asagi-zora

New Year's Day:
What luck! What luck!
A pale blue sky!   Issa

This is Issa's unaffected joy in the clear sky and fine weather
of the first day of the new year. Issa, at this moment is man
the relative, "What luck!" that rejoices and weeps; at the same
time he is God the absolute, "the pale blue sky." Welling up
in him is a joy which is as deep as life itself.

The words of Spengler may seem too heavy for the simplicity
of Issa's experience, but that is only because we undervalue the
simple, primitive, sensational experiences, and fail to see that
all our profundity of thought and feeling come out of them:

> Blue...always stands in relation to the dark, the unillu-
> mined, the unactual. It does not press in on us, it pulls us
> out into the remote.... Blue and green—the Faustian
> monotheistic colours—are those of loneliness, of care, of a
> present that is related to a past and a future, of destiny
> as the dispensation governing the universe from within.

There is another verse by Issa which is similar to the above,
but inferior, for in this one Issa and the spring are separated:

我 春 も 上 上 吉 ぞ 梅 の 花

Waga haru mo   jōjōkichi zo   ume no hana

> My spring too,
> What luck! What luck!
> The plum blossoms!

這へ笑へ二つになるぞ今朝からは   一 茶
Hae-warae futatsu ni naru zo   kesa kara wa

> Crawl,—and laugh!
> From today
> You are two!   Issa

According to Japanese reckoning, everyone is one year older every New Year. So this child, which was born the year before, in May, is now counted as two, though actually not more than seven months old. Issa was at this time, 1819, fifty six years old, and though two boy-babies had died already, this was the first girl, Sato-jo.

The poetic merit of this verse lies in the energy of the language. (It reminds one of Bertha's expression of love to her baby in Katherine Mansfield's *Bliss:* "I like you!") Behind it, but nowhere evident, is the joy of the father that the child has lived as long as she has. Six months afterwards, on the thirty fifth day after the death of Sato-jo, Issa wrote another verse on the child; she had died about a year old, of smallpox:

秋風やむしりたがりし紅い花
Akikaze ya   mushiritagarishi   akai hana

> The autumn wind;
> The red flowers
> She liked to pluck.

The red flowers are those that the child saw and wanted to hold in her tiny hands.

元日や雪を踏む人憎からず   也 有
Ganjitsu ya   yuki wo fumu hito   nikukarazu

> New Year's Day;
> I do not hate
> Those who trample on the snow.   Yayu

On ordinary days, Yayu had a feeling of irritation against those people who trod on a beautiful expanse of white snow, spoiling its smooth uniformity. Today, however, the first day of the year, he can rise above such pettiness and feel no rancour whatever against any who sin aesthetically. He is no longer a highbrow, but a man. He has magnanimity enough to transcend such things without the slightest effort.

正 月 の 子 供 に な つ て 見 た き か な   一 茶
Shōgatsu no   kodomo ni natte   mitaki kana

> Ah! to be
> A child,—
>   On New Year's Day!   Issa

The unstained, unconfined happiness of childhood has such a deep meaning to those who have lost it for ever. Just as the gratitude of men causes us to mourn more than their ungraciousness, so this pure joy is far more pathetic and moving than tragedy.

年 玉 や ふ と こ ろ の 子 も 手 々 を し て   一 茶
Toshidama ya   futokoro no ko mo   tete wo shite

> New Year's presents;
> The baby in the bosom also
>   Holds out her tiny hands.   Issa

Why on earth should this be so affecting? In those small hands is seen the desires of Antony and Cleopatra, the ambition of Napoleon.

元 日 や 家 に ゆ づ り の 太 刀 佩 か む   去 來
Ganjitsu ya   ie ni yuzuri no   tachi hakan

> New Year's Day;
> I will gird on this sword,
>   Heirloom of my house.   Kyorai

The feeling of elation which possesses the poet is felt by him to be something more than pride of lineage, general well-being, successful life. He is not proud of himself, nor does he resist any feeling of false modesty. It is a sensation of the past continuous with this present, expressed also in W. S. Blunt's *The Old Squire:*

> I like the hunting of the hare,
>> New sports I hold in scorn;
> I like to be as my fathers were
>> In the days ere I was born.

梅提げて新年の御慶申しけり　　　　　　子　規
Ume sagete   shinnen no gyokei   mōshikeri

> In my hand a branch of plum-blossoms,
> I spoke the greetings
>> Of the New Year.　　　Shiki

There is a delight in self-consciousness, when one is aware of the (momentary) perfect fitness of all one is doing and saying. We are then what the plum-blossom would be if it were human; the plum branch seems to speak through our lips.

新年の枢にあひぬ夜中頃　　　　　　子　規
Shinnen no   hitsugi ni ainu   yonaka goro

> I met a coffin,
> At midnight,
>> In the New Year.　　　Shiki

It is only with some effort that this can be read as poetry and not sentimentality. If the mind is kept absolutely steady, if the grimness on the one hand, and the (intellectually speaking) perfect ordinariness of the occurrence exactly balance each other, there is poetry. But if we are overbalanced either way we have melodrama or cynicism.

蓬莱や唯三文の御代の松   一　茶
Hōrai ya   tada sammon no   miyo no matsu

Elysian fields be mine!
O age of glory!—
For a three-halfpenny pine-branch.   Issa

On the first day of spring, that is, on New Year's Day, on a
small table, 三方臺, were placed the following: some dried per-
simmons, a mandarin orange, a bigarade (bitter orange), a *tokoro*,[1]
a *kaya*,[2] a small orange, a *kōji*,[3] dried chestnuts, dried plums,
a devil's apron,[4] *noshi*,[5] a craw-fish; and other things. According
to Chinese tradition there are three islands in the Chinese Sea,
Hōrai, Hōjō, 方丈, and Eishu, 瀛州. The inhabitants are sages,
immortal and unaging, living in golden, crystal, ruby, and jade
palaces. In the distance, they look like clouds; close to, they
appear under the water. It is to these islands that the above
offerings are dedicated, but to such lofty beings Issa offers only
his miserable little pine-branch, with humour, and *in so far as
it is humour*, with sincerity, with natural piety no less than we
see in the following verse, where the pine-branch is those put
on either side of the gate.

松立つて見にくき門はなかりけり   月　羅
Matsu tatte   minikuki kado wa nakari keri

Setting up the pine-branch,
None of the gates
Look so bad!   Getsura

蓬莱になんむなんむという子かな   一　茶
Hōrai ni   nammu nammu to   iu ko kana

The child says
"Namu, Namu,"
To the Hōrai.   Issa

"Hōrai" means here the emblems placed on the stand, de-
scribed above. The child, not knowing that these things have

---

[1] 野老, A kind of vine folded up in paper of a certain shape. [2] 榧,
Torreya nucifera. [3] 柑, a kind of orange. [4] A kind of sea-weed. [5] A
thin strip of sea-ear.

nothing to do with Buddhism, crawls forward and says, "Namu, Namu" (short for "Namuamidabutsu") before them. Those watching her feel a disagreeable contrast, but, seeing her smile, dimly and unconsciously realize that this "not knowing" of the child is not different from "knowing" that all emblems of respect and veneration are of one essence. In other words, underneath this "cuteness" of the child is a deep realization in her and Issa and us of the fact that

差 別 即 平 等、平 等 即 差 別。
Difference is identity;
Identity is difference.

But Issa does not leave us with this thought. His verse, in the original, ends with the child; it is she upon whom our eyes are fixed, it is her living of our intellectual paradox that means so much to us. We cannot help thinking of Coventry Patmore's *The Toys*, with that collection of things by which the child had forgotten his grief:

A box of counters and a red-veined stone,
A piece of glass abraded by the beach,
And six or seven shells,
A bottle with bluebells,
And two French copper coins, ranged there with careful art,
To comfort his sad heart.

元 日 や 昨 日 に 遠 き 朝 ぼ ら け   移 竹
Ganjitsu ya kinō ni tōki   asaborake

The dawn of New Year's Day;
Yesterday,
How far off!   Ichiku

This is a very simple verse, but it expresses well the distance of the two worlds, the world of today and the world of yesterday. Only a few hours ago and everything was paying bills, work, quarrels, greed; now all is peace and smiles.

追羽子にまけし美人の怒かな　　　　子 規
Oibane ni　makeshi bijin no　ikari kana

Beaten at battledore and shuttlecock,
The beautiful maiden's
　　　Anger!　　　　　　　　　　　Shiki

Poets are the true psychologists, the only psychologists; they alone deal with mental life as it is lived, as it is *being lived*. So-called psychology treats of notions, associations, apperceptions, —all dead mechanisms, instead of the will dominant or thwarted, passions of infinite variety, pains and pleasures of profoundest subtlety. Music is the only perfect expression of the *psyche*. In Bach and Mozart everything felt or willed by man is expressed once and for all. In poetry, great heights and depths have been reached, but much remains to be done in this direction. In the present verse, a whole world of the human soul is revealed in that beautiful, scowling face.

初芝居見て來て晴着未だ脱がず　　　子 規
Hatsu shibai　mite kite haregi　mada nugazu

The first theatre of the year;
Coming back, and not yet taking off
　　　Her gala dress.　　　　　　　Shiki

A young girl, invited by her friends, goes and sees the play at the theatre. She wears her very best clothes, a long-sleeved kimono and a splendid *obi*. She is so excited and pleased by this visit to the theatre for the first time this New Year, that when she reaches home, instead of taking off her fine clothes and putting on her ordinary ones, she sits there talking and talking, with flushed face and animated gestures, telling her mother and other people of the house how wonderful it all was. In her not changing the clothes there is also something pathetic; she wishes to keep herself under the spell, she wishes to live in that dream world as long as possible, before, like Cinderella, she becomes once more the ordinary girl of every day.

畫 に 書 い た や う な 雲 あ り 初 日 の 出   周　齋
E ni kaita   yō na kumo ari   hatsu hi-no-de

The first sunrise;
There is a cloud
Like a cloud in a picture.   Shusai

This inverted simile is found often in Shelley, where things
of nature are described and expressed by means of comparisons
with those of art and artificiality.

初 空 を 今 こ し ら へ る 煙 か な   一　茶
Hatsuzora wo   ima koshiraeru   kemuri kana

The smoke
Is now making
The first sky of the year.   Issa

No smoke, no sky; no sky, no smoke. But Issa does not
think this. He knows, somehow or other, that the smoke rising
up and forming the first sky of the year has a meaning that
can be expressed only by *pointedly* saying nothing about it.

書 き 賃 の み か ん み い み い 吉 書 か な   一　茶
Kakichin no   mikan mii mii   kissho kana

How he looks and looks at the prize
For the first calligraphy of the year,—
That orange!   Issa

The people round the child, father and mother, grandfather
and grandmother, elder brother and elder sister, are doing their
best to encourage him to write something, the first writing of
the year. To persuade him, he is promised an orange, which
is actually produced and placed within reach. With one eye on
his writing and one on the orange the child laboriously traces
the characters. This

longing with divided will

is a painful pleasure for all the family, and for us, too, to watch.

名代にわか水浴る烏かな   一　茶

Myōdai ni   wakamizu abiru   karasu kana

As a representative,
The crow bathing
In the first water of the year.   Issa

This verse appears in *Ora ga haru*, which was published in 1819. The year before, in his *Seventh Diary*, 七番日記, we find:

名代の寒水浴る雀かな

Myōdai no   kanmizu abiru   suzume kana

The sparrow,
As representative,
Bathing in the icy water.

名代の若水浴る雀かな

Myōdai no   wakamizu abiru   suzume kana

The sparrow
As representative,
Bathing in the first water of the year.

It seems clear that these were the originals of ths present verse. Issa seems to have thought the crow a stronger, more humorous "proxy" than the timid sparrow. In front of the house runs a small stream, and there he sees a sparrow (afterwards he finds he made a mistake and *should have seen* a black, glossy crow), having a bath in its icy waters. This is Issa's own "first water of the year."

痩馬を飾り立てたる初荷哉   子　規

Yaseuma wo   kazaritatetaru   hatsuni kana

The first load of the year;
Decorations
On the emaciated horse.   Shiki

At the beginning of the year all newly starting boats and carts used to have small flags attached to them. Even now, in some places, horses have them stuck in the harness.

影法師もまめ息災でけさの春　　　一　茶
Kageboshi mo　mame sokusai de　kesa no haru

　　Even my shadow
Is safe and sound and in the best of health,
　　This first morning of spring.　　　Issa

This verse has a slight Münchausen flavour about it. The shadow is felt, as once by all primitive men, to have an independent existence that is nevertheless vitally and fatally related to that of the man.

初東風の厠の灯うごきけり　　　大江丸
Hatsu kochi no　kawaya no akari　ugoki keri

　　The first wind of spring;
The light in the lavatory
　　Trembles.　　　Ōemaru

This flickering light in the lavatory at the end of the house has a deep meaning; physically it signifies the material bonds with which our life is tied. The darkness beyond is full of the ghosts of the past, cold and distant. The first wind of spring blows, and the uncertain light of the oil lamp flutters and bows and re-erects itself.

Darkness and light, stillness and movement, body and spirit, —all are one in the troubled mind of the poet.

初夢や秘めて語らず一人笑む　　　松　宇
Hatsu yume ya　himete katarazu　hitori emu

　　The first dream of the year;
I kept it a secret,
　　And smiled to myself.　　　Shō-u

This is like the smile on the face of Mona Lisa. This secret everyone understands more or less fully, but when the dream is told, and the meaning of the smile is made known, all is obscure and misunderstood. Everyone knows our secret self. When we begin to explain ourselves, fools are confounded and

the wise shut their ears. Shō-u was cleverer than Takuchi,[1]
澤雄, who says:

あまりよき初夢うそと云れけり
Amari yoki hatsu yume uso to iware keri

It was such a fine first dream,
They said
I had made it up.

---

[1] One of Bashō's circle.

春
SPRING

In spring, mist and haze hang over fields and hills, both morning and evening. Days are long, compared to those of winter, and there is much wind in the day-time, wind that is motion itself and the cause of motion in others. Winter is the season of silence, but when spring comes, not only waters in fields and valleys but skylarks in the blue heaven and birds in the groves fill the air with cheerful sounds. The *uguisu*, or Japanese Bush-Warbler is a small bird, about the size of a sparrow, brown, with a whitish breast. Its song is heard as, *ho-hoh, hokekkyō*. For this reason it is called "Sutra-reading-bird," 經よみ鳥. It is called also "Yellow bird," 黄鳥; "Spring-foretelling bird," 春告鳥; "Poem-reading bird," 歌よみ鳥; "Sweet-smelling bird," 匂ひ鳥. In art it is connected with the plum-blossoms, as sparrows are with the bamboo.

Frogs are a solemnly cheerful, ungainly tribe that add to the gaiety of at least one nation, but the strangest subject of haiku is that of the loves of cats. Here haiku shows its origins, and its connection with senryu.

The flowers of spring are the camellia, the plum, the peach and the cherry. The white or red, rose-like flowers of the camellia bloom in early spring. The leaves are beautiful and the branches very suitable for flower-arrangement. The peach is not a common subject for haiku, but the plum comes only second to the cherry-blossoms, and by some poets, for example Issa, is preferred to them. The cherry-blossoms are almost synonymous with Japan itself, and they are suffused with an astounding range of thought-feeling.

時 候 **THE SEASON**

春立つや静に鶴の一歩より　　　　　　　召 波
Haru tatsu ya   shizuka ni tsuru no   ippo yori

Spring begins
Quietly,
    From the stork's one pace.　　　Shōha

This verse almost defies explanation, though it is easy enough
to understand. The spring used to begin in February, with the
New Year of the Lunar Calendar. The stork, as a symbol of
longevity, is closely associated with the New Year, and as it
quietly lifts up one foot and quietly places it down again, it is
in harmony with our feeling of tranquillity and new-born nobility.

門々の下駄の泥より春立ちぬ　　　　　　一 茶
Kado-gado no   geta no doro yori   haru tachinu

At every gate,
Spring has begun
    From the mud on the clogs.　　　Issa

To see the beginning of spring in the black mud that sticks
to everyone's *geta*,—this especially belongs to Issa. Up to the
present, the mud has seemed only something dirty and unwanted,
but as the harbinger of spring the mud now is not seen as an
inconvenient and ugly thing, but as a delicate happiness for
everybody.

春の日や庭にすゞめの砂あびて　　　　　鬼 貫
Haru no hi ya   niwa ni suzume no   suna abite

A day of spring;
In the garden,
    Sparrows bathing in the sand.　　　Onitsura

This verse gives us the happy feeling of Nash's *Spring*, but
here expressed through the clean mobility of the sand, the

cheerfulness and convulsive movements of the sparrows.

鶏 の 土 に 身 を す る 春 日 か な　　　　　　闌　更
Niwatori no　tsuchi ni mi wo suru　haru-hi kana

> The fowls
> Putting themselves in the earth;
> A day of spring.　　　　　　　　　　Rankō

Such a verse as this may be taken on the one hand with the emphasis on the fowl itself, its nature and habits. But if it ends there, it is little more than ornithology, however interesting and pleasant that may be. On the other hand, we may take the fowl covering itself with the dry, warm earth as a sign and symbol of the spring, the spring day. The truth is, however, that we are to take the verse differently,—both simultaneously, so that in the fowls we see at one and the same time the fowl in its fowlishness, its fowlhood; and the fowl as the whole of the spring and all it means as spring. Only thus, in actual fact, can we really understand the fowl, by seeing it as spring embodied; and only thus can we really understand the spring, by seeing it as the spirit of the fowl. The same applies to such verses as the following by Shiki:

低 き 木 に 鳶 の 下 り 居 る 春 日 か な
Hikuki ki ni　tobi no oriiru　haruhi kana

> A kite
> Down on a low tree;
> The spring day.

宿 の 春 何 も な き こ そ 何 も あ れ　　　　　素　堂
Yado no haru　nanimo naki koso　nanimo are

> In my hut this spring,
> There is nothing,—
> There is everything!　　　　　　　　Sodō

This is poetry only when we take it as a spontaneous gush of feeling at some particular, fresh expression of the infinite meaning of *things*. A mouse runs over the tatami, and the whole Zoological Gardens cannot manifest more of life. Mildew covers an old piece of leather, and the mystery and power of Nature are revealed. The "philosophy" of the verse may be illustrated by a poem of Hakurakuten:

夏　日

東 牕 晚 無 熱、北 戸 凉 有 風。
盡 日 坐 復 臥、不 離 一 室 中。
中 心 本 無 繋、亦 與 出 門 同。

Λ Summer Day

The Eastern window is not hot at dusk;
Through the Northern door comes a cool breeze.
Sitting here, reclining there,
I have not left the room all day;
But if the mind is in its essence attached to nothing,
At home or abroad is just the same.

This thought comes from Rōshi, Chap. 47. Of the sage, he says:

不 出 戸 以 知 天 下、不 窺 牖 以 見 天 道。
其 出 彌 遠 其 知 彌 少。是 以 聖 人 不 行
而 知、不 見 而 名、不 爲 而 成。

Without going out of his door, he knows everything in the world; without looking out of his window, he knows the Way of Heaven. The farther we go, the less we learn. Thus it is that the wise man knows by not-going, perceives by not-seeing, does by not-doing.

The Zen expression of Sodō's verse is terser and better:

本 來 無 一 物。

Not a thing exists of its own nature.

This Mugaku, 無學, expresses in the following whimsical but profound way:

何 に も の か さ し あ げ た く は 思 へ ど も
達 磨 宗 に は 一 物 も 無 し

I thought
I would like
To give you something,—
But in the Daruma Sect,
We have not a single thing.

大佛のうつらうつらと春日かな   子 規
Daibutsu no   utsura-utsura to   haruhi kana

    The Great Buddha,
Dozing, dozing,
    All the spring day.   Shiki

    The seated image of Buddha (at Kamakura or Nara) is the
ostensible but not the real subject of Shiki's verse. The ponder-
ous figure, impassive and with almost shut eyes, seems as if
asleep, only half alive. It thus expresses in its own way some-
thing of a calm day of spring, its length and quietness, its
immobility and benignancy. This again comes from the state
of mind of the poet himself, whose lethargy and tranquillity,
in harmony with that of the spring day and the Buddha, are
expressed through them, they through him.
    The Buddha is sometimes spring, sometimes summer, some-
times autumn, sometimes winter, and thus is the subject of
every verse, of every conversation.

小舟漕で大船めぐる春日かな   子 規
Kobune koide   ōbune meguru   haruhi kana

    The spring day:
A small boat going round
    A great vessel.   Shiki

    Here, as in the previous verse, the size of the great ship,
brought out by the tiny boat, the slowness of this boat, the
cheerfulness and quiet animation of the scene, all express some-
thing of the nature of spring and of man.
    Less successful, because stating more in words what should
be apprehended despite the words:

春の日や人何もせぬ小村かな
Haru no hi ya   hito nanimo senu   komura kana

    A day of spring;
Not a soul stirring
    In the hamlet.

Contrast this with the following:

三尺の庭をながむる春日かな
Sanjaku no niwa wo nagamuru haruhi kana

Gazing
At a three-foot garden,
One spring day.

A very small Japanese garden, such as used to be found every where in all the big cities of Japan, expresses the completeness, the monotony, the stillness, the public privacy of a spring day. Thus Shiki has stated the meaning of spring, what it really is, through the great image of Buddha, two boats, a village, and a miniature garden. Though everything is itself, and itself alone, yet its essence can only be expressed by something else, by all other things.

あつさりと春は來にけり淺黄空　　　一　茶
Assari to haru wa ki ni keri asagi-zora

Spring has come
In all simplicity:
A light yellow sky.　　　　　　Issa

We are constantly astounded at the simplicity and complexity of Nature. An infinite number of phenomena, and we call it by a single word, spring. Spring, in all its variety, is contained in a single phenomenon, the thinness of the colour of the yellow sky. This colour is commonly found in the evening sky; it is to be seen in a well-known colour-print by Hiroshige, small billowing clouds on the horizon. This "yellow" is probably the "green" of Coleridge's verse:

The green light that lingers in the west.

春の日や水さへあれば暮れ殘り　　　一　茶
Haru na hi ya mizu sae areba kure nokori

The spring day closes,
Lingering
Where there is water.　　　　　Issa

Even when the day is done and the sky seems darkened, light still remains on pools and rice-fields, wherever there is the smallest patch of water. This verse is unusually objective for Issa, but there is as always in the most purely objective verse a suggestion of human feeling, a sense of the painfulness of the passing of time.

三味線をかけたる春の野茶屋哉　　　　　　子　規
Samisen wo　kaketaru haru no　nochaya kana

A samisen[1] hung up
In the tea-shop on the moor:
　　　Spring.　　　　　　　　　Shiki

There is a harmony of spring, the samisen with its silent suggestion of joyful relaxation of mind and body under the cherry blossoms, the tea-shop with its coyly bold fair charmers, the moor outside with its new leaves and flowers. Besides this there is a feeling of the unexpected refinement and civilization in the midst of nature. This is much more explicit in another verse of Shiki's, written beside a picture painted by himself, of an oblong pot of flowers:

草花の鉢並べたる床屋かな
Kusabana no　hachi narabetaru　tokoya kana

Pots of flowers
In a row
　At the barber's.

It has the prescript,

昨日床屋ノ持テ來テクレタ盆栽

A potted plant brought yesterday by the barber.

Shiki, as a poet, feels most deeply the poetry, not of things, not of nature, but of man, of other people, and particularly where least expected. The barber, a man of scissors and comb, of flattery and local gossip, also has his divine weakness for significant form.

---

[1] A kind of rectangular banjo, but with silk strings, and more expressive.

眞中に富士聳えたり國の春   松 宇
Mannaka ni fuji sobietari kuni no haru

In the centre,
Mount Fuji towers up:
Spring in our country.   Shō-u

Poetry, like charity, begins at home, and if we do not love
that country which we have seen, how shall we love that
country which we have not seen? For various reasons, excellent
patriotic poems are rare in the literature of every country.
Every nation has its own peculiar love of country, inexpressible
save obliquely as in the above verse. It cannot be explained
and hardly be imagined by anyone unless born and bred in that
country, imbibing in the most trivial affairs of daily life some-
thing which sees, for example, in Mount Fuji an embodiment
of his most secret origins and aspirations.

The love of country here, that is identified with the spring-
time of that country, is rightly felt by Issa to be something of
living value:

> A symbol endures, but everything beautiful vanishes with
> the life-pulsation of the man, the class, the people or race
> that feels it as a specific beauty in the general cosmic
> rhythm.[1]

Thus the symbol (Issa's verse) remains with us, but the
Japanese soul, intuition, poetical life, lives with the Japanese
race, to be lived by us of other races in so far as we are able
to identify ourselves with them, dying as one nationality to live
as another. Elsewhere Spengler tells us that the racial life of
culture which truly lives only at the moments of creation is
difficult enough to express by the people of that race, let alone
the comprehension of its mummified form by those of other
times and places:

> Every culture possesses a proper conception of home and
> fatherland which is hard to comprehend, scarcely to be
> expressed in words, full of hard, metaphysical relations, but
> nevertheless unmistakable in its tendency.[2]

---

[1] Spengler, Appolonian, Faustian, and Magian Soul.
[2] The Form of the Soul.

あたゝかに白壁並ぶ入江哉   子 規
Atataka ni   shirakabe narabu   irie kana

    In the warmth,
  The white house-walls
      Ranged along the creek.   Shiki

    White is a peculiar colour. It can suggest extreme cold and
extreme heat. In this verse, it is used to express the warmth
of spring that is to be felt in a small inlet of the sea, where
boats are moored along the shore, and the white walls of the
houses reflect the afternoon sunshine. This white colour, though
arising from dead clay, has something as living in it as the
greenest of groves, and more purposeful and dynamic than they.

長閑さや早き月日を忘れたり   太 祇
Nodokasa ya   hayaki tsukihi wo   wasuretari

    Calm days,
  The swift years
      Forgotten.   Taigi

    The world is still and quiet; the sea is calm, the forest
motionless, the voices of men afar off; the river flows on, yet
is ever the same. It seems that time is no more, eternity at
last begun. And this is not an illusion, a temporary forgetful-
ness of never-ceasing change. It is the perception of eternity
in time, of timelessness in time, of the absolute in the relative.

長閑さや垣間を覗く山の僧   一 茶
Nodokasa ya   kakima wo nozoku   yama no sō

    A calm sunny day;
  The monk of a mountain temple
      Peeps through a part of the fence.   Issa

    The monk, an old man, has come out in the warm spring
sunshine and stands in the garden looking through the hedge
at the world outside, not yet green, but with the promise of it
in the warmth of the air. The place, the man, his calm gaze,
give the meaning of the serenity of a quiet day of spring.

Another of Shiki's, expressing the same tranquillity, but more subjective:

長閑さの獨り行き獨り面白き
Nodokasa no   hitori yuki hitori   omoshiroki

> Tranquillity:
> Walking alone;
> Happy alone.

Yet another of his, of grimmer import, with the proscript, 起病, Getting up after Illness:

長閑さや杖ついて庭を徘徊す
Nodokasa ya   tsue tsuite niwa wo   haikai su

> Peace and quiet:
> Leaning on a stick,
> Roaming round the garden.

長閑さや一の鳥居は麥の中   子 規
Nodokasa ya   ichi no torii wa   mugi no naka

> Tranquillity:
> The first torii in the middle
> Of the barley field.   Shiki

The first *torii*, the sacred archway of a Shintō shrine, is sometimes quite close to it, but sometimes a mile or so away. There are usually three torii, the third one right in front of the shrine. In the present case, the first torii is in the middle of a field of barley, and from a distance seems quite isolated in it.   It is a picture of the quietness of spring.

Shiki is often called objective, only an artist, non-mystical, and this is to a certain extent true.   He did not dig deep into his poetical nature, as Wordsworth did, and kill the plant by the examination of its roots.   This verse is a picture, but it is also a picture of tranquillity, not a physical or psychological quietness, but a spiritual one.   The torii is not merely two vertical lines and a horizontal one. It has, or let us rather say, it could have, a religious meaning. The field of barley with its freedom of each leaf and ear stands in serried ranks, betokening the law in the mind of man.   There is nature and religion

together, different and opposed, yet *together* expressing the
peaceful calm of a spring day, without a single thought of God
or of natural history.

のどかさや浅間のけむり書の月　　　一　茶
Nodokasa ya   asama no kemuri   hiru no tsuki

Peacefulness:
The smoke from Mount Asama;
The midday moon.　　　　　　　　　　Issa

The thin line of smoke rising up from the volcano, the pale
transparent moon in the blue sky are dissolved into one calm
feeling that belongs to the advent of spring. The moon is cold,
indifferent and dead; the volcano is violent and destructive; but
in our inmost minds, these two things become one with our
serenity and that of the season.

辻談義ちんぷんかんも長閑かな　　　一　茶
Tsuji dangi   chinpunkan mo   nodoka kana

A sermon at the cross-roads;
A lot of gibberish,—
But this also is spring tranquillity.　　　Issa

A monk is giving a sermon to some people at the cross-roads.
He is telling them of Amida's vow, carried away with his own
eloquence. The peasant people listen respectfully, saying "*Na-
muamidabutsu*" at appropriate places. Issa also stands there
and listens. What the priest says is all nonsense. The people
stand there half-hypnotised with it. But Issa feels no contempt
for them at all, no self-superiority. This also, these good people
and the perspiring monk, are part of the calmness of the spring
day. He feels a warm, peaceful love of them and the stone
Jizō standing by, the clouds sailing in the sky, the breeze that
occasionally ruffles their hair and garments.

長 き 日 や 目 の つ か れ た る 海 の 上   太　祇
Nagaki hi ya   me no tsukaretaru   umi no ue

The long day;
My eyes are wearied,
Gazing over the sea.   Taigi

It is not so much the physical as the mental eye that is tired
with looking out over the boundless ocean. There is, as Emerson
says, a systole and dyastole in the spirit of man, which makes
him desire the finite after he has been satiated with infinity.
Taigi uses this weariness of soul to express the length of the
spring day (long by contrast with those of winter) on the sea-
shore. The sense of the passage of time, bound up with the
feeling of the evanescence of things is inborn to the Japanese,
but intensified by the Indian thought that remained in the
Buddhism introduced to Japan. This feeling underlies a great
many poems where it is not mentioned explicitly. Raleigh's

Even such is Time,

can be felt behind most, if not all haiku.

遅 き 日 の つ も り て 遠 き 昔 か な   蕪　村
Osoki hi no   tsumorite tōki   mukashi kana

Slow days passing, accumulating,—
How distant they are,
The things of the past!   Buson

Thinking of long ago, all one spring day—this day, too, now
belongs to the old, forgotten, far-off things. It is as remote,
as irrevocable, as the most distant ages.

O Death in Life, the days that are no more!

The bitterness of the feeling comes out in the onomatopoeia:

Osoki hi no   tsumorite   tōki   mukashi kana

The k and the t sounds express the painfulness of time. Another
verse of Buson in which the k sounds are also used, is the
following:

遅き日や谺聞ゆる京のすみ
Osoki hi ya　kodama kikoyuru　kyō no sumi

> The slow day;
> Echoes heard
> In a corner of Kyōto.

Spengler says of memory, that it is

> a perfectly definite kind of imagining power which enables
> experience to traverse each particular moment *sub specie
> aeternitatis* as one point in an integral made up of all the
> past and all the future, and it forms the necessary basis
> of all looking backward, all self-knowledge and all self-
> confession.[1]

Memory is thus a poetical faculty with its differing degrees
of power and subtlety, ranging up to this experience of time as
such. The things of the past are seen so profoundly that the
"pastness" of things, the distance of them is perceived as a
form of self-knowledge, of life.

遅き日や雉子の下り居る橋の上　　　　　蕪　村
Osoki hi ya　kiji no oriiru　hashi no ue

> The slow day;
> A pheasant
> Settles on the bridge.   Buson

The pheasant is a timid bird and avoids the haunts of men.
But today the day is so long that the pheasant is beguiled into
coming down and settling on the wooden bridge. This verse
is probably not an experience of Buson but a purely artificial
and literary verse constructed by the association of ideas upon
the basis of the subject, "The slow day." Nevertheless, the
association of ideas is a poetical one, in that Buson is using his
poetical unconscious and not his rational faculty in its creation.

---

[1] Physiognomic and Systematic.

砂濱に足跡長き春日かな 子 規
Sunahama ni ashiato nagaki haruhi kana

On the sandy beach,
Footprints:
Long is the spring day. Shiki

These have not the terror of Crusoe's footprint on the sand, but share its mystery. This long wavering line of footprints from out of the distance, away into the distance, has the power of intensifying the length of the long day. Space and time are here one. The following verse of Buson has a similar tone, but the subject of footprints is used to emphasize shortness, not length of time:

短夜や足跡浅き由井ケ濱
Mijika yo ya ashiato asaki yui-ga-hama

A short night of summer:
Faint footprints
On the shore of Yuigahama.

百人の人夫土掘る日永かな 子 規
Hyakunin no nimpu tsuchi horu hinaga kana

A hundred labourers
Digging earth:
The long day. Shiki

This verse does not mean that the day is long for the labourers, though it may well be so, and this fact will reinforce the significance of the poem. Shiki is watching the making of a road, or the digging of a culvert, from a distance. The labourers seem hardly to be moving, and there is no appreciable progress in their work. The words "a hundred," not "hundreds," gives definiteness to the picture. It shows that the poet can see all the men, but their labours are swallowed up in, and yet expressive of, the long day. The warmth of the earth and the heat of their bodies, the suggestion of some new enterprise and the ambition of man, the pathos of man who sows where he does not reap, the group of ant-like men under the great expanse of sky,—all these things are now part of this day of spring.

There is another verse in which Shiki has expressed the length
of the spring day by the length of the river and the unfulfilled
expectation of the poet. Like the day itself, the river winds on
and on, bridgeless however far he goes:

川に沿うて行けど橋なし日の永き
Kawa ni sōte   yukedo hashi nashi   hi no nagaki

> Following the river,
> No bridge appears;
> How long the day!

A similar but weaker verse is the following, also by Shiki:

汽車道にならんで歩く日永かな
Kisha-michi ni   narande aruku   hinaga kana

> Walking in single file
> Along the railway track;
> A long, long day.

老いぬれば日の永いにも涙かな   一 茶
Oinureba   hi no nagai ni mo   namida kana

> As we grow old,
> Even the length of the day
> Is a cause of tears.   Issa

In the mere length, the extra length of the spring day, all
the woe of humanity is contained. Issa's tears are for himself,
for his dead children, his dead parents, but also for death, for
that which is essential for life itself, for *time*, without which
eternity has no existence. This deep grief at the nature of
things is near to the joy in the suchness of everything, near
to that strange region where laughter and tears are mingled.

鐘一つ賣れぬ日はなし江戸の春   其 角
Kane hitotsu   urenu hi wa nashi   edo no haru

> These great temple bells—
> There is no day when one's not sold:
> Springtime in Edo.   Kikaku

There are two poetical currents in this poem, one of hyperbole, the other of self-identification, and these two are one stream. Of hyperbole, that expression of a state of mind in which the river of thought-feeling suddenly overflows its banks and floods the mind, Nesfield condescendingly says:

> This figure is usually a fault, but may be resorted to at times, provided that the departure from fact does not give too great a shock to one's sense of truth.

In the sutras, the Indian mind, which has a natural tendency in that direction, has used hyperbole to outdo the intellect, and induce a state where all things are seen as possible. For example in the *Yuimakyō*, at the beginning of the sixth section, Shari-hotsu (Sariputra) thought to himself, noticing there were no seats in Yuima's room,

斯 の 諸 菩 薩、大 弟 子 中、當 に 何 に 於 て 座 す る を 見 る。
"How will all the Bodhisattvas and disciples be able to sit in here?"

Yuima orders thirty two thousand seats, each one as large as Mt. Sumeru. All the visitors are accommodated in Yuima's one small room, nine feet square. This leads the reader of the sutra towards a timeless, spaceless, transcendental region in which life is working through time and space.

Sōshi (Chuangtze), who shares in this Indian mysticism, begins his work in the same spirit and with the same object:

北 冥 有 魚。其 名 爲 鯤。鯤 之 大 不 知。其 幾 千 里 也。
化 而 爲 鳥。其 名 爲 鵬。鵬 之 背 不 知。其 幾 千 里 也。
怒 而 飛 其 翼 若 垂 天 之 雲。

> There is a fish in the Northern Ocean called the Kon; countless thousands of leagues it is in size. It metamorphoses into a bird, named the Hō; I know not how many leagues its back is across. In power it arises and flies, its pinions covering the sky like clouds.

He shows that this gigantic fish-bird is only like a mote in a sunbeam, thus leading to a kind of cosmic *reductio ad absurdum*.

We can find examples of hyperbole in many writers of haiku, but there is something in it foreign to the nature of haiku, which prefers understatement rather. The following of Buson is a not very successful example:

湖へ富士をもどすや五月雨

Mizuumi e   fuji o modosu ya   satsuki-ame

> The summer rains
> Will return Mount Fuji
> Into the lake?

This means that the summer rains are so violent that they seem as if they will wash back the earth of Mount Fuji into the lake (Lake Biwa) supposed to have been formed by its eruption. One more example, from Shiki:

寒垢離や不動の火焔氷る夜に

Kangori ya   fudō no kaen   kōru yo ni

> Winter lustration;
> The flames of Fudō
> Are freezing tonight.

During the period of *Kan* (the coldest season), every evening after ablution, temples and shrines are visited and worshipped at, especially by apprentices. Anciently, they ran naked, nowadays in white kimonos with *hachimaki* and bells tied to the waist. It is so cold that the red flames of the halo of Fudō, the God of Fire, may freeze.

暮れんとす春の狂や霰ふる   几董

Kuren to su   haru no kurui ya   arare furu

> It begins to grow dark;
> Hail falls,—
> The insanity of spring!   Kitō

Not only spring but all things are a tale

> Told by an idiot, full of sound and fury,
> Signifying nothing.

Buson has a verse in which spring and madness are related:

晝舟に狂女のせたり春の水

Hiru fune ni   kyōjo nosetari   haru no mizu

> The mad girl
> In the boat at midday;
> The water of spring.

The girl, her hair dishevelled, oblivious of the peeping passengers, leans over the edge of the boat, trailing her fingers in the current, staring down with unseeing eyes into the depths of the secret, swelling waters of spring.

鳥 の 羽 に 見 そ む る 春 の 光 か な   樗 良
Tori no ha ni   misomuru haru no   hikari kana

I fell in love
With the wings of the birds,—
The light of spring on them!   Chora

In Marvell's *Thoughts in a Garden* we have a verse somewhat similar but with an artificial flavour that spoils the comparison:

> Here at the fountain's sliding foot
> Or at some fruit tree's mossy root,
>
> Casting the body's vest aside
> My soul into the boughs does glide;
> There, like a bird, it sits and sings,
> Then whets and claps its silver wings,
> And, till prepared for longer flight,
> Waves in its plumes the varied light.

One is pure poetry; the other is poetry stiffening into literature, statuesquely beautiful, but frozen music.

And for the meaning of light we may quote the words of Dionysius the Areopagite in *Divine Names:*

> Let us now extol the spiritual name of Light, under which we contemplate the Good; and declare that he is called spiritual Light because he fills every supercelestial mind with spiritual light—as fontal Ray and overflowing stream of light, shining out of its fulness upon every mind above, around, and in the world, renewing all their powers, and embracing them in its span.

思 ひ 出 て 庭 掃 く 春 の 夕 か な   大 魯
Omoidete   niwa haku haru no   yūbe kana

> Suddenly thinking of it,
> I went out and was sweeping the garden:
> A spring evening.   Tairo

What a peculiar thing poetry is, coming and going like the wind. The most momentous concatenation of important events, long-awaited with hope or fear,—and it

> leaves not a wrack behind.

Valueless, fortuitous things, the mere trivia of life suddenly sink down to the very essence, the soul of existence. One of such moments of vision the poet describes in the above verse. All we can say is that in the very uselessness, the unpremeditatedness, the casual inevitability, lies the secret of the mystery, the connection between the sweeping of the garden and the evening of spring.

燭 の 火 を 燭 に 移 す や 春 の 夕   蕪 村
Shoku no hi wo   shoku ni utsusu ya   haru no yū

> Lighting one candle
> With another candle;
> An evening of spring.   Buson

The original means "lighting one light with another," probably a candle. There is here some mysterious meaning, like that in the propagation of the species. The torch of life is handed on from parent to child in a way which everyone knows but no one understands. The transmission of fire is equally obvious, yet is an eternal mystery. Beyond this, in the moment of suspense when the flame of one candle gives birth to that of another, the inner meaning of spring, of the spring evening, is apprehended. There is something passing from here to there, a glow, a steadiness in the warm dusk, something so deep and delicate that we feel it to be life itself trembling and intangible, yet strong and apparent to all the senses.

等閑に香たく春の夕かな　　　　　　蕪村
Naozari ni　kō taku haru no　yūbe kana

> Indifferent and languid,
> I burned some incense:
> An evening of spring.　　　　　Buson

Without thinking of its meaning, with no feeling of offering
it to the Buddha, the poet lights some incense upon the altar.
The smoke trickles upwards. Outside there is the mild warmth
and calm of a spring evening. The mood of the poet, the curling
smoke, the dusk of spring are all in harmony with one another.
At the hour of twilight there is a momentary balance in things:

> Night eliminates body, day soul.[1]

Body and soul are at their lowest ebb. The smoke rises with
a feeble inevitability in the air.

春の夜や主なきさまの捨車　　　　暁臺
Haru no yo ya　nushi naki sama no　suteguruma

> An evening of spring;
> Ownerless, it seems,
> This abandoned hand-cart.　　　Gyōdai

The cart has been left by someone at the roadside, among the
new grasses. It is not without an owner, of course, but looks
so. And in some remote way we feel that this spring evening
is abandoned and ownerless, and we ourselves, as we glance for
a long moment at this uselessly-useful cart. It epitomises the
spring evening in its melancholy waywardness.

山鳥の尾をふむ春の入日哉　　　　蕪村
Yamadori no　o wo fumu haru no　irihi kana

> Treading on the tail
> Of the copper pheasant,
> The setting sun of spring.　　　Buson

[1] Spengler, Appolonian, Faustian and Magian Soul.

The number, difference and quality of the explanations of this verse are surprising, Meisetsu says that the copper pheasant treads on the shadow of its own tail. Another commentator suggests that some person treads on its tail. Kyoshi says that the verse is subjective, and expresses the length of the spring day. Shiki, concurring, says the head of the pheasant implies the beginning of the day, and the tail the end of the day. The verse seems to me to need no explanation, if we read it as if it were written by Milton or Crashaw. For example:

> While the cock, with lively din,
> Scatters the rear of darkness thin.

This is the reverse of Buson's "metaphor."

春の夜や妻なき男何をよむ　　　　　子 規
Haru no yo ya　tsuma naki otoko　nani wo yomu

A spring evening;
What is the bachelor
Reading?　　　　　　　　　　　Shiki

On a spring evening everyone feels a little restive and un-settled. If a man is married he can talk about trivial matters of interest to both, or quarrel with her, if so disposed. An unmarried man looks out of the window, looks around the room. The only thing to do is to read something, but what shall it be? Grave books are wearisome, light literature a waste of time; what kind of book can arouse and hold his attention?

This verse is a haiku, or senryu according to where we put the emphasis. If it is on the bachelor and his book, he shares with cuckolds and mothers-in-law a not altogether deserved ridicule. If we put it on the spring evening, the feeling of growth, of lack of maturity and balance, of yearning and obscurity is brought out in the solitary man's passivity and loneliness.

春 の 夜 や 籠 人 ゆ か し 堂 の 隅   芭 蕉
Haru no yo ya   komoribito yukashi   dō no sumi

One evening in spring:
In a corner of the Hall,
A mysterious suppliant.   Bashō

This was composed at Hase, 初瀬, In Yamato, what is now
Nara Prefecture, at the temple known as Hasedera, or Kwan-
nondō, or Chōkokuji. In the *Genji Monogatari* and the *Tsure-*
zuregusa we find frequent references to pilgrimages to this
temple, especially by women to the Kwannon enshrined there.

One night Bashō went to the temple to worship, and looking
round saw in one corner of the great hall a man or woman
kneeling there in supplication before the image of Kwannon.
A few candles burning here and there, the hall is full of
shadows. Outside, the cherry blossoms are falling through the
darkness; here in the dusk, the silent, motionless form of the
suppliant.

カ ナ リ ヤ は 逃 げ て 春 の 日 暮 れ に け り   子 規
Kanariya wa   nigete haru no hi   kure ni keri

Our canary escaped:
The spring day
Is at its end.   Shiki

This dejection, arising from some comparatively trivial loss,
or failure to meet circumstances, these

Airs and floating echoes that convey
A melancholy into all our day,

this is the inevitable concomitant of attachment, the (at least)
temporary cessation of which is the essential for poetry. But so
subtle are the ways of life, that the description of the unpoetical
may itself be poetry. Further, in the harmony of transitory
mood and the drawing near of dusk, the poet is able to perceive
what he dimly hints at, the faintly tragic nature of every
evening, every nightfall. From the commonsense point of view,
we may say this is the coloration of a perfectly neutral fact,
the ending of a solar day, as a melancholy thing, by a mind so

predisposed from a trifling circumstance, the loss of a canary. This is true enough. But deeper insight makes us realise that this experience is a perception of the *destiny* in life, a perception made possible by the accidental attuning of the mind to the tragic meanings inherent in so-called neutral, ordinary things.

草臥れて寝し間に春は暮れにけり   几　董
Kutabirete   neshi ma ni haru wa   kure ni keri

> While I slumbered,
> O'er-wearied,
>   Spring drew to its close.   Kitō

The poet felt a passage of time greater than that which actually elapsed while he was sleeping. Compare a similar verse by Kyoshi:

旅せんと思ひし春も暮れにけり
Tabi sen to   omoishi haru mo   kure ni keri

> This spring also,
> When I thought to go on a journey,
>   Has drawn to its close.

The journey he intended to make is like a barren woman's dream of children. But the point of the poem is not so much that of unfulfilled desire as of the passage of time. Time and its passing is here deeply perceived, destiny overriding the will of the individual. The triviality of the matter and the casualness of the treatment conceal a profound depth of life that will not allow itself to be dragged forth into the hard light of our intellectual day.

ゆく春やおもたき琵琶の抱ごゝろ   蕪　村
Yuku haru ya   omotaki biwa no   dakigokoro

> As spring departs,
> How heavy
>   This biwa feels!   Buson

As a result of some odd, secret relation between man and

nature, we feel low-spirited and languid at the end of spring. The poet, seeking to reanimate himself, takes down the *biwa*[1] and puts it on his knees against his breast. It feels unaccountably heavy,[2] and this heaviness is both physical and spiritual.

ゆ さ ゆ さ と 春 が 行 ぞ よ 野 邊 の 草　　　　一　茶
Yusa-yusa to   haru ga yuku zo yo   nobe no kusa

Spring departs,
Rustle, rustle,
In the grasses of the field.　　　　Issa

A light wind blows across the fields. The grass, weak but aspiring, quivers as the wind passes; into the distance the wind departs and with it spring also departs. It sighs away through the stems and leaves, never to return.

行 く 春 の 尻 べ に 掃 ふ 落 葉 か な　　　　蕪　村
Yuku haru no   shiribe ni harau   ochiba kana

Sweeping up the fallen leaves
In the train
Of departing Spring.　　　　Buson

When one comes to think of it, from our cold and intellectual, modern point of view, this personification of spring is an extraordinary, even a fanciful, a superstitious and uneducated thing. But if we explain it as a convention of poets, if we attribute it to the animistic character of primitive thinking and dismiss it as such, we are making a mistake, a deadly and fatal one. For be it in its animistic origins or conventionalized literary form, it is a record of the realization that all things are mind, everything, wind, rain and dead leaves, is animate, is one. The personalizing of the seasons is thus comparable to the persons of the Trinity, different names and manifestations of one Essence, which however (in Buddhist thought) exists in so far as rain and wind and leaves exist.

[1] A musical instrument, most beautiful in shape, but not very expressive.　[2] Time is felt as a weight.

春をしむ人や榎にかくれけり   蕪　村
Haru oshimu   hito ya enoki ni   kakurekeri

    Grieving for spring,
He disappears
    Among the enoki trees.   Buson

    Buson stands looking at nature in its passing phase between
spring and summer, sighing at the youth that cannot stay but
must become lusty manhood. As he does so, someone who, by
his manner also grieves for spring, enters the grove of nettle-
trees and is no more to be seen. As in Keats' *Autumn*, this
man is a symbol of the passing of spring, yet not a mere symbol,
since he too feels in himself the irresistible movement of the
seasons, he too can remain nowhere but must leave, and the
place thereof know him no more. There are other verses of
Buson which give this feeling of the movement of man together
with that of nature:

歩行歩行ものおもふ春の行衛哉
Ayumi ayumi   mono omou haru no   yukue kana

    Walking on and on,
    Lost in thought;
    Spring is departing!

行春のいづち去りけんかゝり舟
Yuku haru no   izuchi sariken   kakari-bune

    A moored boat;
    Whither
    Has spring departed?

ゆく春や眼に逢はぬめがねうしなひぬ
Yuku haru ya   me ni awanu megane   ushinainu

    Spring departs;
    Glasses that did not suit my eyes,
    Have disappeared.

ゆく春や逡巡として遅ざくら   蕪　村
Yuku haru ya   shunjun to shite   osozakura

    Departing spring

Hesitates

       In the late cherry-blossoms.   Buson

The word "hesitates" as applied to nature seems at first sight
a strange one. It expresses the double quality of things in virtue
of which they are never to alter; things wish also to change
and grow, to be different. Spring wishes to be an eternal spring;
but it wishes also to become summer. This is the nature of all
things, but it is especially evident in the indolent vacillation,
the indecisions of late spring.

手燭して庭ふむ人や春おしむ   蕪　村
Teshoku shite   niwa fumu hito ya   haru oshimu

    Candle in hand,

He paces the garden,

       Grieving for spring.   Buson

It is the end of spring, the beginning of summer. The night
is windless, the flame hardly flickers as he walks through the
garden. Enormous shadows move round him. The simplicity,
the youth of Nature is a thing of the past. The candle burns
solemnly, heavily.

行燈をとぼさず春を惜しみけり   几　董
Andon wo   tobosazu haru wo   oshimi keri

    Not lighting the paper lantern,

I grieved

       For spring.   Kitō

Lighting or not lighting seems to have a deep connection with
the nature of spring and its departure. To sorrow at the passage
of time, the falling of the cherry-blossoms, the hopes and fears
of spring, it is necessary to have the absence of light, to express
the feeling of loss and desolation. According to the Lunar

Calendar, spring began in February and ended in April on a
certain day on which the passing of spring was most keenly felt.

行春や撰者をうらむ歌の主   蕪　村
Yuku haru ya　senja wo uramu　uta no nushi

Spring is passing;
The rejected poet feels resentment
Against the selector.   Buson

Here again Buson is seeking that which both harmonizes with
spring's passing, and expresses it. Summer is almost here, there
is to be a change of aspect and mood; we wish spring to linger
a little while with us, but it cannot be. The length of the day
draws out this feeling and deepens it. "How is it that my verse
was not accepted? What is there so fine about his?" thinks
the poet whose verse was rejected. His mood fits in with the
nature of passing, and in doing so, expresses it. Things have
no meaning without man, and man exists *simply* to give them
that meaning.

洗足の盥も漏りてゆく春や   蕪　村
Senzoku no　tarai mo morite　yuku haru ya

This leaks too,
The tub for washing the feet:
Departing spring.   Buson

This has some humour in it, which must not, however, be
emphasized. The leaking of the old tub and the departing of
spring are in obvious harmony. But the fact that the tub may
leak at any season of the year gives this verse a living quality,
that accidental, wilful, wanton element that life always has and
which art must never lose. In the background of the mind also
is the fact that this tub has been used to wash the feet after
coming back from flower-viewing, but this obvious connection
with spring and its departing is kept subservient to the arbitrary
leaking of the tub.

けふのみの春をあるいて仕舞けり　　　　蕪　村

Kyō nomi no　haru o aruite　shimaikeri

Today only
Walking in the spring,
And no more.　　　　　　　　　　　　Buson

How the older haiku poets relished their poetical calendar!
On the last day of spring, Buson walks in the fields to get the
pleasures of spring, and together with this, the feeling of "never
again"; this day alone remains and tomorrow is another world,
the world of summer. One more verse of Buson which belongs
to the verge of spring is this:

行く春や白き花見ゆ垣のひま

Yuku haru ya　shiroki hana miyu　kaki no hima

Departing spring:
A white flower is seen
Through a crevice in the garden fence.

天　文　SKY AND ELEMENTS

是きりと見えてどつさり春の雪　　　　　一　茶
Korekiri to　miete dossari　haru no yuki

As though this were the lot,
A great deal fell,—
Spring snow.　　　　　　　　　　　Issa

There is a sudden fall of large flakes of snow, which soon
pile up. We feel here the nature of snow in spring, as it makes
a last effort, a disparity in the snow and the season, the over-
lapping of things we think of as separate.

曙や麥の葉末の春の霜　　　　　　　鬼　貫
Akebono ya　mugi no hazue no　haru no shimo

The dawn of day;
On the tip of the barley leaf
The frost of spring.　　　　　　　Onitsura

The beginning of spring, the first rays of the sun, the tip of
the blade with its touch of frost—this has a unity of new birth
and delicacy.

すつぽんも時や作らん春の月　　　　　一　茶
Suppon mo　toki ya tsukuran　haru no tsuki

The turtle also
May tell the hour,—
This spring moon!　　　　　　　　Issa

In the West, the cock is the only creature that "tells the
hour." In China and Japan, the tortoise is believed to cry on
bright moonlight nights. But here, by the pond in spring under
the hazy moon, the turtle as it rises above the surface of the
water, or ripples it as it swims, seems for some unaccountable
yet sufficient reason about to tell the hour of night, the moon
is so occult.

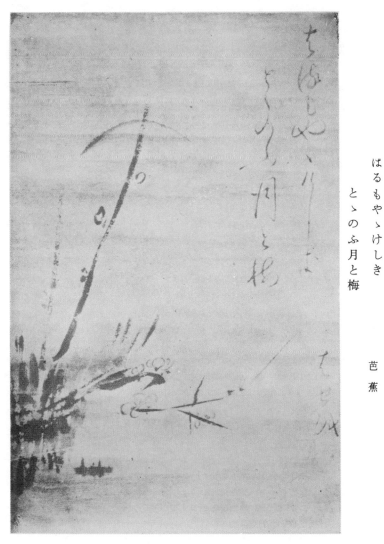

はるもやゝけしき
とゝのふ月と梅

芭蕉

Haru mo yaya   keshiki totonou   tsuki to ume

　　The spring scene
　Is well-nigh prepared:
　　The moon and the plum-blossoms.

Bashō

淺川や鍋すゝぐ手に春の月   一　茶
Asakawa ya nabe susugu te ni haru no tsuki

In the shallow river,
On hands washing the saucepans,
  The spring moon.   Issa

The water makes a rippling sound as it runs over the stones.
It never ceases all night long. At the edge of the water a young
woman is washing out her saucepans, and the spring moon
shines down on her white hands as they move above and under
the water.

月の顔年は十三そこらかな   一　茶
Tsuki no kao toshi wa jūsan sokora kana

 The face of the moon,—
 Twelve years old,—
  About that, I should say.   Issa

The first two lines might be taken as mere fancy, but in the
last line we see Issa taking it with humorous seriousness. The
sustaining of what seems a fancy gives it an imaginative value.
The reversion to so-called common-sense life is not complete.
The youthfulness of the moon is grasped poetically at this
moment, as her age is at another moment by Shelley, recorded
in a fragment:

  And like a dying lady, lean and pale
  Who totters forth, wrapped in a gauzy veil,
  Out of her chamber, led by the insane
  And feeble wanderings of her fading brain,
  The moon arose up in the murky East,
  A white and shapeless mass....

朧月蛙ににごる水や空   蕪　村
Oborozuki kawazu ni nigoru mizu ya sora

 Under the hazy moon,
Water and sky are obscured
  By the frog.   Buson

Compare this with Bashō's verse:

>   The old pond;
>   A frog jumps in,—
>   The sound of the water.

We see a great difference between the two poems. Both are haiku, but Bashō's is so intense as to approach what one might call at least "sudden (artistic) conversion." Buson's is a poem *after* conversion, when the novelty has worn off and a calmly thrilling, continuous poetic life is achieved.

Buson has his back to the moon, and is looking down into the paddy-field where the clouds are reflected. A frog suddenly swims across, and water and cloudy sky are "muddied," obscured. To see such things, and remember them

>   in vacant or in pensive mood,

is the chief of the pleasures of life.

　　牛部屋の牛のうなりや朧月　　　　　子　規
　　Ushi-beya no   ushi no unari ya   oborozuki

>   The lowing of the cow
>   In the cow-shed,
>   Under the hazy moon.   Shiki

The spring moon irradiates faintly the grasses and thickets. Everything shares in the haziness of the moon in the sky. From the stable nearby comes the mournful cry of the cow, a sound that carries with it the feeling of vast space. What the moon, the spring moon says in sight, the lowing of the cow shows in sound.

　　川下に網打つ音やおぼろ月　　　　　太・祇
　　Kawa-shimo ni   ami utsu oto ya   oborozuki

>   Down the river
>   The sound of a net thrown;
>   A hazy moon.   Taigi

Everything is quiet; there is not a sound anywhere, not a

breath of wind rustles the leaves. Suddenly, down the river,
the poet hears the sound of a net being thrown into the water.
No boat, no fisherman is to be seen, only the faint circle of the
moon shines down on the darkness. Again there is silence. It
is the perfect accompaniment of the misty moon, nature with
just a touch of man, silence with now and then that faint sound.

居酒屋 の 喧嘩 む し だ す 朧 月   子 規
Izakaya no   kenka mushidasu   oborozuki

The quarrel in the wine-shop
Breaks out again,
　　Under the hazy moon.   Shiki

There is here a *significant* relation between two things, one
beautiful, the other ugly, the misty moon and the drunken louts
fighting. Or to express it in another way, as the moon shines
upon the just and on the unjust, upon the drunk and upon the
sober, so the poet also takes the whole world as his country,
all are his children.

　　　Nature, with equal mind,
　　　Sees all her sons at play.

女 負 ふ て 川 わ た り け り 朧 月   子 規
Onna oute   kawa watarikeri   oborozuki

Carrying a girl
Across the river;
　　The hazy moon.   Shiki

On the one hand, men and women are Buddhas, and in the
Kingdom of Heaven there is no marrying or giving in marriage.
On the other hand, men are men and women are women, and
never the twain shall meet. Thus there is a special and charming
appropriateness in the misty moonlight and the fact that it is
a woman he is carrying on his back as he fords the river. To
take pleasure in it while doing so, to catch the winged pleasure
as it flies, but not to put more into it, not to go on carrying
the woman long after parting from her,—this is the art of living.

梅 が 香 の 立 の ぼ り て や 月 の 暈   蕪 村
Ume ga ka no   tachinoborite ya   tsuki no kasa

The halo of the moon,—
Is it not the scent of plum-blossoms
Rising up to heaven?   Buson

The moon is hazy, and the faint sweet scent of the plum blossoms rises up towards it. The halo of the moon is to the eye what the scent of the blossoms is to the sense of smell; the whiteness of the flowers and that of the halo reflect each other, and are one in that faint sweet perfume.

陽 炎 や 梅 散 り か ゝ る 石 の 上   子 規
Kagerō ya   ume chirikakaru   ishi no ue

Heat-waves;
Petals of the plum flutter down
Onto the stones.   Shiki

The weather is warm; the plum trees have bloomed, and here over the stones the distant scene wavers in the heat. Petals drift down, a few at a time, falling on the stones and clinging to them; the white or red petals show up against the grey green of the boulders. There is a beautiful harmony in sky and earth through the warmth of the spring sun.

Shiki has other verses which show his power of adapting old modes of feeling to modern subjects; in the following verse the brand-newness, the lack of *sabi* and poetry does not preclude nature from working in its old-accustomed way:

陽 炎 や こ の 頃 出 來 し 小 石 道
Kagerō ya   konogoro dekishi   koishi-michi

Heat-waves,
From the recently made
Gravel path.

陽炎やほろほろ落ちる岩の砂　　　　　　　土　芳
Kagerō ya　horohoro ochiru　iwa no suna

Heat-waves;
Sand of the rock
　　Falls in fits and starts.　　　　　　　Tohō

There is a close relation between the wavering lines of land-
scape above the rocks, and the sand which falls from them. In
the following verse, the relation is much less distinct:

陽炎や一鍬づゝに土くさき　　　　　　　蘭　更
Kagerō ya　hito-kuwa-zutsu ni　tsuchi kusaki

Waves of heat;
At each stroke of the hoe,—
　　How the earth smells!　　　　　　　Rankō

神田大火
陽炎や三千軒の家のあと　　　　　　　　子　規
Kagerō ya　sanzen gen no　ie no ato

The Great Fire of Kanda

Heat-waves,
From the remains
　　Of three thousand houses.　　　　　　Shiki

This is very grim indeed, but it contains within it the realiza-
tion that heat is heat from whatever source, and whatever it
does with itself. The air above quivers and has its poetical
meaning irrespective of human joy or pain. That meaning our
joy and pain intensifies, deepens, widens.

陽炎や掃捨芥の錢になる　　　　　　　　一　茶
Kagerō ya　hakisute gomi no　zeni ni naru

Heat-waves;
From cleaned-up rubbish,—
　　Money!　　　　　　　　　　　　Issa

Moralists may say what they please, there are few greater

and purer pleasures than that of getting something for nothing.
Money is the root of all evil, but it is the symbol of all material
good for body and mind. The heat-waves are the enthusiasm of
nature in the new warmth of the year, and the few pence that
Issa gets by selling some things that were intended for the
dustbin are a pleasure that he does not wish to transcend for
any fancied moral or "poetical" ecstasy.

野馬に子供あそばす狐哉   凡　兆
Kagerō ni   kodomo asobasu   kitsune kana

> The fox
> Lets her children play
> In the heat-waves.   Boncho

Foxes have for Japanese a rather creepy meaning. They are
or were thought to be able to transform themselves into other
creatures. The heat-waves ("summer colts") of a warm day of
spring give the distant scene a wavering, unreal appearance, a
background against which these rather sinister young animals
are sporting while their mother looks on. For the English
reader the verse will perhaps have a tenderer meaning; it will
be a picture of early spring without mysterious associations, but
bringing us close to the source of life.

笠でするさらばさらばや薄霞   一　茶
Kasa de suru   saraba saraba ya   usugasumi

> With their kasa,
> Good-bye, good-bye,
> In the thin haze.   Issa

A *kasa* is a kind of umbrella hat made of strips of sedge,
strips of bamboo, or the outside sheath of bamboo shoots.
This verse has the postscript "Karuizawa," showing that it
was written while on a journey. Even so, most people will not
see much in it. Just to show how one Japanese poet deals with
another, let me paraphrase what Katsumine has written about
this poem.

It is early morning, and Issa is standing on the verandah or outside the inn. Other guests have risen before Issa, and he stands watching two men saying good-bye to each other at the cross-roads. Kasa in hand, they bow repeatedly and part, their forms growing fainter and fainter until they disappear in the mist. Issa, who has unwittingly seen them off, feels some inexpressible emotion.

That is to say, *he has parted with those whom he has never met.* This is the Bodhisattva ideal, the life of those who have

entered into the essence of things, are out of the ocean of becoming, . . . dwelling in the house of nonattachment, staying in the serenity of space,

and in their compassionate interpenetration of all things, are able to remove mountains, walk on the water;

兕無所投其角、虎無所措其爪、兵無所
容其刃。　　　　　　　　　　　　　　　（老子、五十）

a buffalo cannot find a place to butt him, a tiger no place for his claws, a warrior no place for his sword to penetrate.

高麗舟のよらで過ぎゆく霞かな　　　　　蕪　村
Komabune no   yorade sugiyuku   kasumi kana

The Korean boat
Does not stop, but passes by
In the haze.　　　　　　　　　　　　　　Buson

The odd shape of the ship is the only thing present to the eye, but the far-off place of origin, the unknown destination, the strange, unseen beings are seen at a glance by the eye of the mind. All fades in the mist, but the Korean boat continues to move across the ocean of poetical feeling, long after it is seen no more.

二股になりて霞める野川かな   白　雄
Futamata ni   narite kasumeru   nokawa kana

> Forking
> Into the mist,
> The stream on the moor.   Shirao

This verse has a double quality of clarity and dreamlike vagueness. The stream divides, and just here the mist hides the farther scene from us.

ほくほくと霞んでくるはどなたたかな   一　茶
Hoku hoku to   kasunde kuru wa   donata kana

> Click, clack,
> The man coming walking in the haze,—
> Who is he?   Issa

The mist covers everything, and everything is unseen, but present there in the mist. Someone is coming, something is going to happen. Who is it? What is it? There is a whole world of mystery and suspense in the sound of the wooden *geta* on the road. And it is the spring road, spring when old meanings become new, and new things are many.

霞けり山消え失せて塔一つ   子　規
Kasumi keri   yama kie-usete   tō hitotsu

> It grows hazy,
> The mountains fade and disappear:
> A single stupa.   Shiki

This is an example of what Nature is constantly doing for us, picking out one of a multitude of things and presenting it in a new and special light. Often it is the nature within us, but in Shiki's verse it is the nature without that veils all things but this one.

浪 の 寄 る 小 嶋 も 見 え て 霞 か な   召 波
Nami no yoru   kojima mo miete   kasumi kana

Small islands are seen,
With the surf breaking round them,
In the haze.   Shōha

This verse gives a vivid impression of the white breakers round the tiny isles. The haze has the effect of poetically intensifying by pictorially blurring.

指 南 車 を 胡 地 に 引 去 霞 か な   蕪 村
Shinansha wo   kochi ni hikisaru   kasumi kana

The compass-vehicle departs
Towards the barbarians' land ˋ
Through the haze.   Buson

The compass-vehicle, as used by Chinese armies, was a cart upon which a wooden doll was set up. The base moved freely, the right arm pointing forwards, in which a compass was set, so that it always pointed south.

The army winds away over the desert through the dust and haze, the compass-vehicle first, appearing larger than the rest. This kind of historical imagination and power of ideal beauty, Buson possessed above almost any poet in the world. Another example:

易 水 に ね ぶ か 流 る ゝ 寒 か な
Ekisui ni   nebuka nagaruru   samusa kana

Down the River Ekisui
Floats a leek,—
The cold!

The Ekisui is a famous Chinese river.

春 な れ や 名 も な き 山 の 朝 霞   芭 蕉
Haru nare ya   na mo naki yama no   asagasumi

Yes, spring has come;
This morning a nameless hill
Is shrouded in mist.   Bashō

Nature can and does bring out the value of the most insignificant thing, and this value has a heightened meaning in proportion to its everyday insignificance. The important word in the poem is of course "nameless." The hill is too ordinary, too low to be noticed at other times, but when clouds of mist linger over it, it has the same beauty as the most famous peaks. This is not because the mist beautifies it or veils its insignificance. This would be to make the same mistake as Wordsworth in his Prefaces, or Hazlitt in,

> The poet spreads the colours of fancy, the illusions of his own mind, round every object, *ad libitum*.[1]

There is a waka in the *Manyōshū* in which the author has attempted in a different way, what Bashō has succeeded in doing:

> ひさかたの天の香具山このゆうべ
> 　　　霞たなびく春たつらしも　　　　　　人麻呂
> In the eternal sky,
> Mount Kagu,
> And round it,
> Lines of mist this evening:
> Spring has come, it seems.　　　　　　Hitomaro

There is also a haiku by Koshun, 湖春, which resembles that of Bashō:

> 名の付かぬ所かわゆし山ざくら
> *Na no tsukanu　tokoro kawayushi　yamazakura*
> In places without names,
> Gladsome and lovely
> Wild cherry-blossoms.

Koshun died in 1697, three years after Bashō. It may be difficult to determine which verse was written first,—not that it matters much, because as Emerson says, in *Representative Men*,

> The greatest genius is the most indebted man,

and it is not *what* is borrowed that matters.

---

[1] *On the Prose Style of Poets.*

草霞み水に聲なき日暮かな　　　　　蕪 村
Kusa kasumi　mizu ni koe naki　higure kana

> The grasses are misty,
> The waters now silent;
> It is evening.　　　　　Buson

It grows dark. Mist creeps low over the grass. The stream that rippled with cheerful voice all day now flows without a sound. All is hushed; life and light have ebbed from the world.

かへり見れば行きあひし人霞みけり　　　子 規
Kaerimireba　yuki-aishi hito　kasumi keri

> When I looked back,
> The man who passed
> Was lost in the mist.　　　　　Shiki

When we try to point at the soul-state of such a simple and profound experience we lose ourselves in words. This verse is neither a bare statement nor a symbolic representation of the instability, the impermanence of things. There is, in the mind of Shiki, a feeling that the man who was seen and who is now unseen, is the same thing; the moment when he was here and this moment when he is gone for ever are the same eternity. But this ineffable state must be expressed, and is so, in the most matter-of-fact way, otherwise we should find ourselves seeking in all kinds of "poetical" directions for what is really in the mind of Shiki as he looks back and sees nothing but the haze.

今日も今日もかすんで暮らす小家かな　　一 茶
Kyō mo kyō mo　kasunde kurasu　koie kana

> Today also, today also,
> Living in the haze,—
> A small house.　　　　　Issa

This "Today also, today also," Issa used in seven or eight haiku; in one, it is repeated three times:

今日も今日も今日も竹みる火桶かな
Kyō mo kyō mo kyō mo take miru hioke kana

Today also, today also,
Today also looking at the bamboos,—
This brazier!

Perhaps the best of them is this:

今日も今日も凧ひつかゝる榎かな
Kyō mo kyō mo tako hikkakaru enoki kana

Today also,
Today also, a kite
Caught on the enoki-tree.

It might be best to arrange the original verse like this:

Today also,
A small house, living in the haze,
Today also.

This haze is only the spring haze of Japan, yet it interpenetrates
the life of men of all times and all places, like the mist of notes
in the music of Chopin.

Issa has used this repetition, not altogether unsuccessfully, in
the following verse:

疾く霞め疾く疾く霞め離ち鳥
Toku kasume toku toku kasume hanachi-dori

Quickly become hazy,
Quick, quick, become hazy,--
Releasing a bird.

The repetition is used to indicate the urgency of the feeling of
danger to the bird unless helped by the mistiness and obscurity
of the weather.

賣牛の村を離るる霞かな   百池
Uri-ushi no mura wo hanaruru kasumi kana

The cow I sold,
Leaving the village
In the haze.   Hyakuchi

There is something mildly melancholy about the haze this evening, but still more, something inevitable, softly inexorable about it. The cow is a soft, mild creature, like the mist.

There is the same feeling expressed by Ōemaru, a contemporary of Hyakuchi, but through the autumn wind.

去年賣りし牛にあひけり秋の風
Kozo urishi   ushi ni aikeri   aki no kaze

I met the cow
I sold last year:
The autumn wind.

It shows how "symbolic" the seasons and elements are, and yet they are the real subjects of the verses, not the cow or the emotions of the owner-poets.

大舟の小舟曳きゆく霞かな   子 規
Ōbune no   kobune hikiyuku   kasumi kana

A great ship
Towing a small boat behind it
Into the haze.   Shiki

In the mist, the great ship and the little boat pulled along behind it are reduced to their most elemental difference, that of mere size. The small boat is like a faint echo, a diminished repetition of the larger one.

かの桃が流れくるかよ春霞   一 茶
Kano momo ga   nagarekuru ka yo   harugasumi

Will that peach
Come floating down?
The spring haze.   Issa

This refers to the universally known story of Momotarō, the peach-boy. One day, an old woman was washing clothes by a stream, when a huge peach (*momo*) came floating down. She took it home, and when she and her husband cut it open, they found a little boy, Momotarō, inside.

Issa fancies (the postscript says that it was on looking at a *picture* of an old woman washing) that this is the old woman of the story, and that the peach may soon come floating down the stream. There is something akin to the genius of Walt Disney here, making out of drawings something more real than human beings.

> But from these create he can
> Forms more real than living man,
> Nurslings of immortality.[1]

Issa's consummate art is manifested in the line, "The spring haze," which gives the fairy-tale scenery and atmosphere.

背 の 低 き 馬 に 乗 る 日 の 霞 か な   蕪 村
Se no hikuki   uma ni noru hi no   kasumi kana

> Riding
> A short-legged horse;
> A day of haze.   Buson

There are times when things seem to harmonize themselves without any effort on our own part, and this unwonted appropriateness of things soothes us in a certain poetical way, not intense, but profound. The horse Buson is riding on is short in the legs, a cobby sort of horse, and is in accord with the humorous tranquillity of hazy spring.

ふ り む け ば 灯 と も す 關 や 夕 が す み   太 祇
Furimukeba   hi tomosu seki ya   yūgasumi

> Looking back,
> They are lighting the barrier lanterns,
> In the evening haze.   Taigi

The barrier was a place between two provinces where travellers' passports were examined. This examination was usually strict, and travellers were often compelled to wait there the whole day. Such was the case with Bashō at the Barrier of

---

[1] *Prometheus Unbound.*

Shitomae.[1] It seems that the same thing happened to the poet Taigi. After sitting there all day, he was at length allowed to pass through. As he hurries off with a feeling of relief, he looks back through the mist that evening has brought, and sees points of yellow light in the gloom. The guards are lighting the lanterns at the great gate, which is about to be shut. He has passed the barrier, but it is still there, waiting for him. Though distant and vague, there remains something faintly sinister about it.

霞む日やさぞ天人のお退屈 　　　　　　一 茶
Kasumu hi ya   sazo tennin no   otaikutsu

A day of mist and haze:
The Dwellers of Heaven
May well feel bored and listless. 　　Issa

Compare this to Ritaihaku's poem, 題峰頂寺, written at the Temple of Hōchōji:

夜宿峰頂寺、舉手捫星辰。
不敢高聲語、恐驚天上人。

Tonight I am staying at Hōchōji.
If I raise my hand, I can touch the stars.
I do not dare speak loudly,
Lest I disturb the Dwellers of Heaven.

Issa himself did not, I am sure, disbelieve in the existence of angels and spirits, and attributed to them all our human emotions. That is to say, we are to enter into and share the life of such creatures as heavenly beings, just as much as that of flowers and frogs, slugs and flies.

遠う來る鐘のあゆみや春霞 　　　　　　鬼 貫
Tōkitaru   kane no ayumi ya   haru kasumi

The bell from far away,—
How it moves along in its coming
Through the spring haze! 　　Onitsura

[1] *Oku no Hosomichi.*

The poet is trying to express the feeling he has of the bell coming through the spring mists, the feeling of not merely there and here, far away and close to, but of actual movement through space. The mist of spring helps this feeling and its expression, for in weakening the sense of sight, the imagination is thereby strengthened, and the bell moves from there to here walking over the waves of sound. One is reminded of Cowper's

The sound of the church-going bell.[1]

霞む日や森閑として大座敷 　　　　　　　　一 茶
Kasumu hi ya   shinkan to shite   ōzashiki

A day of haze;
The great room
Is deserted and still. 　　　　　　　　　Issa

This room may be of a temple or mansion. It is silent and empty, and out of the great windows extends the fields and hills, hazy, and more imagined than seen. In this verse Issa shows the power of his maturity. From two things alone the universe is created in all its infinite extent and range, yet with a single ineffable meaning to which these two things, in combination, point.

夕霞おもへばへだつ昔かな 　　　　　　　　几 董
Yūgasumi   omoeba hedatsu   mukashi kana

The evening haze;
Thinking of past things,—
How far off they are! 　　　　　　　　　Kitō

The things of only yesterday are as past as those of centuries ago. Only a few years pass by, and everything is changed; only a dimming recollection, that in its weakness and impermanence disappoints and discourages, remains with us. A little haze and almost everything disappears; a short time, and it seems like the dream of a world unborn.

---

[1] *Alexander Selkirk.*

春風や麥の中行く水の音   木 導
Harukaze ya   mugi no naka yuku   mizu no oto

> The spring breeze;
> Through the barley,
> The sound of waters.   Mokudō

"The less Zen the better," is a good rule for life and for poetry. The breeze of spring, the green barley waving, the sound of the water trickling among the stalks after the rain,— this and no more, no less; no looking before or after, no wishing things were different from what they are.

春風に尻を吹かるゝ家根屋哉   一 茶
Harukaze ni   shiri wo fukaruru   yaneya kana

> The spring wind!
> The skirts of the thatcher
> Are blown about.   Issa

The thatcher is busy on the roof, bending over at his work. He wears a short *happi* coat, and the spring wind blows up the tail of the coat without ceremony, as cheerfully and as poetically as it does everything else. The man's hindquarters only are visible, and most poets would look elsewhere, but not Issa.

春風や牛にひかれて善光寺   一 茶
Harukaze ya   ushi ni hikarete   Zenkōji

> A spring breeze!
> Led by a cow
> To Zenkōji.   Issa

There is a beautiful and truly Buddhist story behind the second and third lines of this verse. Zenkōji, in Nagano Prefecture, is one of the most famous temples in Japan, and everyone is supposed to visit it at least once in his life-time. In a certain village, not far from Zenkōji, there lived an old woman who had no belief in religion, had never been to Zenkōji and could not be persuaded to go there. One day, a piece of white cloth

which she had hung out to dry on the fence of the back garden,
caught on the horn of a passing ox, and when she ran after it
the animal made off. However far she followed it, she could
not catch it, and at length they got to Zenkōji. The ox seemed
to disappear, and when she looked around in surprise, she saw
that she was standing before the image of Nyorai. At this, she
felt for the first time that spirit of veneration which is the
beginning and foundation of all faith, and became a firm believer.

Issa has taken this saying, merely adding "the spring breeze,"
giving the episode the season most suitable, when everything
in nature suffers some change and renewal of youth.

春 の 風 お ま ん が 布 の 形 り に 吹 　　　　一 茶
Haru no kaze oman ga nuno no nari ni fuki

> As the cloth of O-Man
> Flutters and flaps,
> So the spring breeze blows.   Issa

This is like Lyly's skylark:

> Now at heaven's gates she claps her wings,
> The morn not waking till she sings,

and a verse from the *Zenrinkushū:*

庭 前 有 月 松 無 影、欄 外 無 風 竹 有 聲。

> In the garden shines the moon,
> But there is no shadow beneath the pine-tree;
> Outside the balustrade, no wind,
> But the bamboos are rustling.

These are not mere perversions of thought; they are not an
intellectual trick of putting the cart before the horse. Thinking
will never solve the problem of which is moving, the wind or
the flag. The answer is, "Your minds are moving!" When
the mind is still and the eye is quiet, the wind blows because
the cloth of O-Man flaps, the cloth of O-Man flaps because the
wind blows.

The name of O-Man is taken from a song of Kashiwazaki,
柏崎:

高い山から谷見ればおまん

おまんが可愛いや染分は襷で布晒す

From the high hill,
Looking down upon
O-Man in the valley,

O-Man so charming
Bleaching cloth in the sun,
With the double-dyed sash for her sleeves.

東風ふくと語りもぞゆく主と従者   太 祇
Kochi fuku to   katari mozo yuku   shū to zusa

"This is the spring wind,"
Say master and servant,
As they walk along together.   Taigi

The serving-man walks a little behind his master; there is a
difference of rank between them. But the spring wind is blowing,
they tell each other, and one touch of nature makes them akin.

途に逢うて手紙ひらけば春の風   几 董
Michi ni ōte   tegami hirakeba   haru no kaze

Meeting the messenger on the road,
And opening the letter,—
The spring breeze!   Kitō

This is the long, rolled and folded Jápanese letter. As he
stands reading the letter, unrolling it, the breeze begins to flutter
and tug at the letter in an impatient, almost human way. This
kind of thing is usually irritating, but on this occasion the poet
felt something delightful in it; the letter is a living thing
struggling in his hands. While his mind is busy with the
contents of the epistle, his hands have grasped the spring
breeze; he perceives its essential nature.

朝 東 風 に 凧 賣 る 店 を 開 き け り   召 波
Asa-kochi ni   tako uru mise wo   hiraki keri

A spring breeze this morning:
Λ shop that sells kites
Has opened.   Shōha

The lively hopes, the gaiety, the boundless energy of spring
are here seized and portrayed in the mere opening of a small
shop. If we think of this as a small wayside stall or booth,
the picture has a poetical delight in it; we can see the curtains
flapping in the breeze, the kites in piles fluttering as if them-
selves anxious to be off in the hands of some eager little boy.
There is a deep meaning also in the fact that some human
beings are making a living, are existing and propagating their
species by this very breeze. This poem is an answer to Tolstoy's
question,

> "What do men live by?"

繪 草 紙 に 鎮 置 く 店 や 春 の 風   儿 董
Ezōshi ni   shizu oku mise ya   haru no kaze

The paper-weights
On the picture-books in the shop:
The spring wind!   Kitō

It is a sunny morning in spring and the shop-keeper has set
out his stock of story-books, with brightly coloured pictures of
double suicide, the triumph of love over death, tales of revenge
and glory.

The mind is nicely balanced between the fluttering of the leaves
and the round stones (or whatever it may be) on them, between
the animation of the one and the immobility of the other. The
wind is seen in the stones.

Shiki has a verse very similar to the above, but different in
tone colour.

春 雨 や 傘 さ し て 見 る 繪 草 紙 屋
Harusame ya   kasa sashite miru   ezōshiya

Spring rain;
Holding up their umbrellas, and looking
At the picture-books in the shop.

春風や烟管くはへて船頭殿   芭 蕉
Harukaze ya   kiseru kuwaete   sendo-dono

>   Pipe in mouth,
>   Mr. Boatman:
>   The spring breeze!   Bashō

This is not a sketch for you to "fill in" the rest for yourself.
The essentials are given, not that you may clobber them up
with details out of your own confusion of mind, but that you
may seize those essentials, thus becoming yourself the Essential.

春風や堤ごしなる牛の聲   來 山
Harukaze ya   tsutsumi goshi naru   ushi no koe

>   In the spring wind,
>   The voice of the cow
>   Over the embankment.   Raizan

St. Paul promises that what we now see as in a glass darkly,
we shall one day see face to face, but people do not realize that
the attraction of this "knowing even as we are also known,"
is due to its being something that will never happen. What
is perfect is dead; what is seen is not desired. The spring
wind has a meaning because it has movement, power, because
it leads to summer. The moo of the cow has a meaning because
the eye does not perceive the form of the cow, but the long
straight endless line of the river bank. The spring is seen in
the fitful trembling of the still withered grasses.

春風におさるゝ美女のいかりかな   曉 臺
Harukaze ni   osaruru bijo no   ikari kana

>   The beautiful woman,
>   Jostled by the spring wind,—
>   Her vexation!   Gyōdai

It is spring, and perhaps to see the cherry-blossoms, the
beautiful woman is walking along the road. The spring wind,
like God, is no respecter of persons, and it blows her hair in
her eyes, her kimono from her legs, her sleeves in every

direction. She does her best to compose her mind and her garments, but the wind is too much for her. She becomes really angry with the spring wind, whose nature she thus expresses.

春風に尾をひろげたる孔雀かな   子 規
Harukaze ni o wo hirogetaru   kujaku kana

The peacock,
Spreading out his tail
In the spring breeze.   Shiki

To see the spring breeze in the outstretched fan of a peacock's tail is no easier, and no more difficult, than to see a world in a grain of sand or heaven in a wild flower, but the emphasis is to be laid, not on "breeze," but on "spring."

薫風や千山のみどり寺一つ   子 規
Kunpū ya   senzan no midori   tera hitotsu

The soft breeze,
And in the green of a thousand hills,
A single temple.   Shiki

The value of figures, one, two, three, is worth a special study, especially in relation to Buson, Shiki's master. The meaning of one flower, two houses, three fishes and so on, is most profound. There is another verse by Shiki, afterwards explained, which has this similar contrast:

三千の俳句を閲し柿二つ
Sanzen no   haiku wo kemishi   kaki futatsu

Examining
Three thousand haiku,—
Two persimmons.

春風や堤長うして家遠し   蕪 村
Harukaze ya tsutsumi nagōshite ie tōshi

The spring wind is blowing:
The embankment is long,
Houses far away.   Buson

The spring wind blows soft and warm; the faint smell of new grass and young leaves with its suggestion of the future, of distance, draws the eyes along the level, monotonous embankment that stretches away to the horizon, where there is seen the roof of some house or other.

In Buson the feeling of distance is very strong. Many of his haiku show the emotion of space that we find in his paintings, the spiritual heritage of the old Chinese painters, who give us, without perspective, the desire of infinity. Other verses by Buson with the same feeling of distance:

花にくれて我家遠き野路かな
Hana ni kurete waga ie tōki nomichi kana

Overtaken by night among the blossoms,
I walk across the moor,
Home far distant.

雨の日や都に遠き桃の宿
Ame no hi ya miyako ni tōki momo no yado

The capital far away;
A day of rain
In a house of peach-blossoms.

月に遠く覺ゆる藤の色香かな
Tsuki ni tōku oboyuru fuji no iroka kana

The scent and colour
Of the wistaria
Seem far from the moon.

浴して蚊遣に遠き主かな
Yuami shite kayari ni tōki aruji kana

After a bath,
The master, far
From the smoke-smudge.

行舟や秋の日遠くなりまさる
Yuku-fune ya   aki no hi tōku   narimasaru

> The boat departs;
> How far gone
> The autumn days!

住むかたの秋の夜遠く火影かな
Sumukata no   aki no yo tōku   hokage kana

> Distant lights;
> There they live
> This autumn night.

もの焚て花火に遠きかがり舟
Mono taite   hanabi ni tōki   kagari-bune

> Lighting a fire
> On the fishing-boat,
> The fireworks far away.

鴨遠く鍬そそぐ水のうねりかな
Kamo tōku   kuwa sosogu mizu no   uneri kana

> Washing the hoe
> Makes ripples on the water,
> Wild ducks in the distance.

柿の葉の遠くちりきぬ蕎麥畠
Kaki no ha no   tōku chirikinu   sobabatake

> Leaves of the persimmon tree
> Have fallen from afar
> On the field of buckwheat.

初霜やわづらう鶴を遠く見る
Hatsushimo ya   wazurau tsuru wo   tōku miru

> The first frost of the year;
> Looking at a sick crane
> In the distance.

裾に置て心に遠き火桶かな
Suso ni oite   kokoro ni tōki   hioke kana

> Putting the brazier
> Near my feet,
> It seems far from my heart.

水鳥や堤灯遠き西の京
Mizutori ya   chōchin tōki   nishi no kyō

The water-birds;
The lanterns in the distance,
Of the Western Capital.

春雨や美しうなる物ばかり   千代尼
Harusame ya   utsukushiu naru   mono bakari

Spring rain:
Everything just grows
More beautiful.   Chiyo-ni

Even pieces of rag and paper glisten with light, and add their
peculiar music as the rain strikes on or near them.

春雨や傘さして見る繪草紙屋   子 規
Harusame ya   kasa sashite miru   ezōshiya

Spring rain;
Holding up an umbrella, and looking
At the picture-books in the shop.   Shiki

The simple patterns of the paper umbrellas, the rain falling,
the piles of story-books in the booths,—we have the circular,
the triangular and the square with none of these shapes
mentioned.

春雨や木の間に見ゆる海の道   乙 二
Harusame ya   ko no ma ni miyuru   umi no michi

The spring rain:
Between the trees is seen
A path to the sea.   Otsuji

There is something pleasant and lasting about poems that do
not try the reader, that do not pander to popular taste.

屋根に寝る主なし猫や春の雨   太 祇
Yane ni neru   nushi nashi neko ya   haru no ame

A stray cat
Asleep on the roof
In the spring rain.   Taigi

The homeless cat is sleeping on a roof under the eaves of
another. When the poet sees the cat,

a poor fellow that would live,

he feels the pathetic dignity of living creatures, the inevitability
of it all, and of the spring rain.

春雨や柳の雫梅の塵   召 波
Harusame ya   yanagi no shizuku   ume no chiri

Spring rain;
Rain-drops from the willow,
Petals from the plum-tree.   Shōha

Chiri, translated "petals," is literally "dust," what has fallen
from the plum-tree into the mud below. The big drops that
fall from the hanging branches of the weeping willow, and the
petals that lie scattered and bespattered on the ground are an
epitome of spring.

春雨やぬけ出たままの夜着の穴   丈 草
Harusame ya   nukedeta mama no   yogi no ana

Spring rain;
A hole in the bed-clothes
Where he crept out.   Jōsō

There is a deep and humorous relation between the dark,
warm spring rain and the hole in the *futon*, the heavy quilts
still retaining the shape of something human that is no longer
there.

春雨にぬれつゝ屋根の手鞠かな   蕪　村
Harusame ni   nuretsutsu yane no   temari kana

> A hand-ball,
> Wet with the spring rain falling
> On the roof.   Buson

All day the rain has continued. It seems that it has never begun and will never stop. The poet goes to the verandah and stands looking out at the melancholy scene. Caught in the gutter of the roof opposite is a ball made of cloth that children were playing with and that lodged there by accident. The rain pours down relentlessly upon it as upon everything else, soaking its pretty design and colours. The rain continues meaninglessly, uselessly to beat down on the ball. The ball continues meaninglessly, uselessly to be beaten on by the rain. The poet suddenly sees, almost without knowing it, a "meaningless" meaning in this ball, in this rain, in all things. The ball grows sodden, and still the rain falls upon it, as though it were a thing that the rain could make blossom. This is the poetical life of the verse, the sheer lack of relation between the rain and the ball and the roof,—other than that of proximity.

物種の袋ぬらしつ春の雨   蕪　村
Mono-tane no   fukuro nurashitsu   haru no ame

> Bags of seeds
> Being wetted
> By the spring rain.   Buson

There is an exquisite pleasure in perceiving some poetic meaning in yet more and more trivial things. As the poet sits looking out at the rain that comes slanting down, he notices bags of seeds that are gradually being wetted and discoloured by the rain that drives in under the eaves. There is a faint feeling of inappropriateness and the "indifference" of nature, the relation of man and the seeds in their bag and the spring rain, and an equally mild feeling of peace and warmth from them to him and him to them.

小芝居の幟ぬれけり春の雨   子　規
Koshibai no   nobori nurekeri   haru no ame

A travelling show;
The banner is wet
In the spring rain.   Shiki

In the outskirts of a town a small travelling theatre has set
up its colourful self-advertisements, and a banner floats above.
In the spring rain it hangs wet and limp. The whole of life is
seen in this small theatre, and all its hopes and ambitions and
violent passions are seen in the banner that now hangs lifeless
there. But all this, important though it seems, is not the real
aim of the verse, which is to express the mild loneliness of the
spring rain that accompanies, perhaps by reverse, the hope of
full and luxuriant life.

春雨の木下につたふ雫かな   芭　蕉
Harusame no   koshita ni tsutau   shizuku kana

Spring rain
Conveyed under the trees
In drops.   Bashō

Bashō stands looking at the large dark drops falling from the
lower boughs. The steady lines of rain in the unseen sky above
are changed into the irregular fall of drops here and there below.

春雨や人住みて烟壁をもる   蕪　村
Harusame ya   hito sumite kemuri   kabe wo moru

Someone is living there;
Smoke leaks through the wall,
In the spring rain.   Buson

This is not syllogistic or inferential, though it may appear so.
In the original the last line comes second—but the order of the
three sections is in this particular poem negligible. It is true
that there is actually a cause and effect relation among the three
elements. The smoke lingering in the rain comes from the

miserable hut which protects the occupant from rain. But in another sense, the rain, the smoke, the hut, the occupant, are all entirely independent, unrelated entities. The poem is in the region where there both is and is not a relation between these things. In other words, there is life, there is existence here, not a part of it but the whole. Smoke oozing through the wall in the misty rain; mind falling in the rain, writhing in the smoke, standing broken and helpless in the wall, still and invisible in a human being.

The prescript to this verse makes it much less realistic, more romantic than the interpretation above.

> 西の京にばけもの栖て、久しく荒れはてたる家
> ありけり。今はそのさたなくて

In the Western Capital there was a haunted house, for long left untenanted. Now this has changed.

There is a verse by Shiki similar to that of Buson, but lacking the eerie, ghostly element; the season also is appropriately different:

> 五月雨に人いて舟のけむり哉
> *Samidare ni   hito ite fune no   kemuri kana*

> Someone is there;
> Smoke from a boat,
> In the summer rain.

> 春雨やゆるい下駄借す奈良の宿   蕪 村
> *Harusame ya   yurui geta kasu   nara no yado*

> Spring rain;
> An inn of Nara
> Lends some loose geta.   Buson

There is an interesting connection between these three apparently unrelated things. The spring rain is a kind of loosening of the bonds of the skies. Nara is the old capital of Japan, the most old-fashioned and Buddhist of Japanese towns, the most Japanese. It was not and is not like active Tōkyō. The wooden clogs which Buson has borrowed from the inn have thongs that are too loose, and the place and the weather are in quiet and relaxed harmony with them.

春雨や藪に吹かるゝ捨手紙　　　　　　一　茶
Harusame ya　yabu ni fukaruru　sute-tegami

> Spring rain:
> A letter thrown away,
> Blown along in the grove.　　　　　Issa

In the windy rain of spring there is something white fluttering in the air, writhing along the ground under the bamboos. It is a long letter, thrown away, now as free to be blown along by every gust of wind and rain, as it was once to be a cause of joy or anguish, of depression or elation.

春雨や暮れなんとしてけふもあり　　　蕪　村
Harusame ya　kurenan to shite　kyō mo ari

> Spring rain;
> It begins to grow dark;
> Today also is over.　　　　　　　Buson

As the rain falls, and night comes on, time is felt to be passing; and yet in another way, time seems to be standing still, to be no more, eternity at last begun. The day is over, today is over, but there is no feeling that any other day will ever begin, or even that it will not. The verse has the sublimity that only the simple, elemental things can give. The passage of time, perhaps the deepest feeling of man, far deeper than that of space, is felt as such, through the medium only of the dusk and the falling rain.

鳩いけんして曰く
梟よ面癖なほせはるの雨　　　　　　　一　茶
Fukurō yo　tsurakuse naose　haru no ame

> The Pigeon Gives his Advice:
>
> O owl!
> Change your expression,
> In the spring rain!　　　　　　　Issa

This haiku is the words of the pigeon to the owl, and brings

out, in a most odd fashion, the characteristics of both, and of
the spring rain. The pigeon is gentle and pacific in appearance,
but the owl looks fierce and irritable. The spring rain falls
quietly and the pigeon advises the owl to make her face more
in harmony with the season.

瀧口に灯を呼聲や春の雨   蕪 村
Takiguchi ni hi wo yobu koe ya   haru no ame

At Takiguchi,
Voices calling for a light,
In the spring rain.   Buson

This kind of verse Buson no doubt got the hint of from
reading such books as the *Genji Monogatari*. Takiguchi was
the name of a place for warriors within the palace grounds, so
named probably, because there was a water-fall near by. It is
a night of spring, and suddenly there are voices heard shouting
for a light. Rain is falling, and this increases the feelings of
confusion, fear and excitement. The point of this verse is in
its very vagueness. We fear what we do not properly under-
stand, and Buson has induced this state in the reader by not
telling him what has happened. Like those who are woken by
the cries, we wonder if someone has been taken ill,—or is it a
robber, a ghost or demon?

春雨や猫に踊を教へる子   一 茶
Harusame ya   neko ni odori wo   oshieru ko

The spring rain;
A little girl teaches
The cat to dance.   Issa

The child cannot go out and play, and she has no brothers
and sisters to pass the time with, so she picks up the sleeping
kitten and begins to dance it up and down, very little to the
kitten's own pleasure. This is a charming scene, but the art
of Issa, that is, the poetic point, the living region, the Zen, is
in the relation between these things and the spring and the
spring rain. It falls in the gusts round the verandah, as thought-

lessly, as heartlessly as the child and the kitten. Somehow or other, the more we read this verse, the more the nature of the spring rain falls into our hearts, the louder and more insistently it sounds. The child and the kitten are swallowed up in the inevitability of nature. This feeling is attained to in quite a different way by the following, also by Issa:

春雨や鼠のなめる隅田川
Harusame ya nezumi no nameru sumida-gawa

> The spring rain;
> A mouse is lapping
> The River Sumida.

春雨や蓑吹きかへす川柳 芭 蕉
Harusame ya mino fuki-kaesu kawayanagi

> Spring rain;
> The river willows blow back
> The straw-coats. Bashō

The straw-coats of the villagers and the hanging branches of the willow-trees are both blown by the rain and wind; this is the so-called common-sense fact perceived by the ordinary, sophisticated, civilized man. Bashō sees and says something different,—not quite so different, however, from the Japanese as from the English. In Japanese, for example, we can say,

赤い火がさつと風を起して一尺あまり、

literally, "The glowing fire suddenly blew up the wind and shot out more than a foot." There is an interrelation of cause and effect, the wind and the fire, the fire and the wind; in the verse above, we have the relation of wind to willow, willow to wind, and of wind to straw-coat, straw-coat to wind. The relation between these pairs of relations is abbreviated in the mind, that is, in the experience, and therefore in the expression of it, to:

> The river willows blow back
> The straw coats.

There is something similar in Issa's verse:

秋 の 夜 や 障 子 の 穴 の 笛 を 吹 く
Aki no yo ya   shōji no ana no   fue wo fuku

An autumn evening;
The hole in the paper sliding-door
Is playing the flute.

春 雨 に 大 欠 び す る 美 人 か な   一 茶
Harusame ni   ōakubi suru   bijin kana

In the spring rain,
A beautiful maiden
Gives a great yawn.   Issa

Issa is not trying to make fun of the girl. He is expressing
the contradictory nature of things, it is true, but the beauty of
the maiden and her huge yawn are both necessary for the
portrayal of the rain in spring, its charm yet its monotony, and
the contrast is both in the spring and in the maiden, the paradox
which life cannot dispense with.

春 雨 や 傘 高 低 に 渡 し 舟   子 規
Harusame ya   kasa takahiku ni   watashibune

The spring rain;
In the ferry-boat,
Umbrellas high, umbrellas low.   Shiki

There is a double meaning here, that of the human picture
as represented in the umbrellas held by those standing and those
sitting in the crowded ferry-boat; and that of pure form, the
shapes and positions of the umbrellas suspended in the vertical
lines of rain above the horizontal line of the boat. The human
and the artistic-significant merge into and reinforce each other.
In *this* relation is the unplumbed, of its nature unfathomable
depth of this poem. The same is true of the work of Buson,
Shiki's master. The *purely* pictorial has no existence, even in
the wildest of cubist extravagances. How much more so with
such a poem as the present one, or Buson's verse:

春雨や綱が袂に小でうちん
Harusame ya   tsuna ga tamoto ni   kojōchin

> In the spring rain,
> Miss Tsuna holding her sleeve
> Over the small lantern.

春雨や鼠のなめる隅田川   一 茶
Harusame ya   nezumi no nameru   sumida-gawa

> The spring rain;
> A mouse is lapping
> The River Sumida.   Issa

This verse brings out Issa's love of contrast, the obvious contrast of the mouse and the river, and the more subtle contrast between the ordinary and the poetic idea of each. But we have left out the spring rain, which joins the rat and the river in a very physical way. This verse originally was:

春風や鼠のなめる隅田川
Harukaze ya   nezumi no nameru   sumida-gawa

> In the spring wind,
> A mouse is lapping
> The River Sumida.

It is easy to see the reason for the change.

狀見れば江戸も降りけり春の雨   鬼 貫
Fumi mireba   edo mo furikeri   haru no ame

> Reading the letter—
> It has been raining also in Edo,—
> The spring rain!   Onitsura

The power to see and the will to express the poetry in such a commonplace incident has been given to few if any other nations than the Japanese.

It is raining. A letter comes from the capital, brought by a messenger. Unfolding the missive, the poet reads it on the verandah. Outside, the sky is grey, the sound of the rain all around. In the letter the writer tells that the spring rain has begun in Edo too. The poet is united to his friend by the sound, the touch, the smell, the sight of the rain. There is no talk of the infinite or the eternal, but distance is annihilated, time is no more. The poet is in that Nirvana state in which the individual includes the universe.

春雨やものがたり行く蓑と傘   蕪 村
Harusame ya   monogatari yuku   mino to kasa

> Spring rain:
> An umbrella and a straw-coat
> Go chatting together.   Buson

To the artist, people are only *personae*, masks, umbrellas and straw-coats. Though in a sense this a specialist attitude, from another point of view it has something universal, something divine in it, for it means seeing without judging, without prejudice, with neither love nor hate, and yet without indifference. Shiki has a similar verse to this:

舟と岸と話してゐる日永かな
Fune to kishi to   hanashi shite iru   hinaga kana

> The long day!
> The boat is talking
> With the shore.

But more than half a century before Buson, Kikaku had written:

畑から頭巾よぶなりわかなつみ
Hatake kara   zukin yobu nari   wakana tsumi

> Gathering young greens
> In the garden, they called out
> To a kerchief.

The "kerchief" is an old man who has tied something round his head to avoid catching cold.

春雨や食はれ残りの鴨が啼く　　　　　　一　茶
Harusame ya　kuware-nokori no　kamo ga naku

> Spring rain;
> The still remaining, uneaten ducks
> Are quacking.   Issa

Christ is called "The Good Shepherd." But what are sheep kept for? As Stevenson says in *Will o' the Mill,*

> the shepherd who makes so pretty a picture carrying home the lamb, is only carrying it home for dinner.

We must say of God what we must aspire to say of ourselves,

面上夾竹桃花、

肚裏參天荊棘。　　　　　　（禪林句集）

> In face, the bamboos of Chia, peach-blossoms;
> At heart, thorns and briars of Ts'antien.

地 理 **FIELDS AND MOUNTAINS**

雪 殘 る 頂 一 つ 國 ざ か ひ   子 規
Yuki nokoru   itadaki hitotsu   kunizakai

On one of the peaks
Of the frontier,
Snow remains.   Shiki

This has nothing profound in it, but if you relax yourself and
allow your spirit to pass over the fields and plains, it goes
towards the distant mountains, towards the highest of them, on
which the retreating snow still covers the utmost summit. No
wordy description of distance can make us have that peculiar
empty feeling when the soul is drawn out of the body.

雪 解 や 深 山 曇 り を 啼 く 鴉   曉 臺
Yukidoke ya   miyama-gumori wo   naku karasu

Snow is melting,
But the remote mountain is cloudy;
A crow caws!   Gyōdai[1]

There is a feeling towards spring in the air, but in the deep
mountains it is winter still. The hoarse cry of a crow some-
where echoes up at (を) the gloomy sky.

家 遠 き 大 竹 原 や 殘 る 雪   太 祇
Ie tōki   ōtakehara ya   nokoru yuki

The dwellings of men far-off;
A grove of great bamboos,
Snow remaining under them.   Taigi

This verse is only a picture, in two contrasting colours, but
it has also the feeling of distance, and of loneliness in it.

[1] Read also Kyōtai, Gyōtai, Kyōdai.

庵 の 雪 下 手 な 消 様 し た り け り　　　　　一　茶
Io no yuki   heta na keshiyō   shitari keri

> The snow on my hut
> Melted away
> In a clumsy manner.　　　　　　　Issa

One piece slides, and catches on another, yet another piece
seems about to fall, but does not. On the thatched roof, the
snow makes a meaningless, irregular pattern. There seems
something bungling, something awkward about many things in
nature, simply because her purposes are not ours.

大 佛 の 片 肌 の 雪 解 け に け り　　　　　子　規
Daibutsu no   katahada no yuki   toke ni keri

> The snow has melted
> On one shoulder
> Of the Great Buddha.　　　　　　　Shiki

One of the most extraordinary things about Nature, from the
scientific and intellectual point of view, is its asymmetry. Life
is asymmetrical in its essential character, and it is natural for
us to rejoice in it, for it is the guarantee of our spiritual freedom.
Even on the Great Buddha, for all the Law of Karma and the
inviolable Wheel of the Law, the snow melts irregularly. On
the sunny side, the snow is gone; on the other, there still
remains a white mantle. To our human eye at least, it is a
secretly felt confirmation of our inner conviction that

> with God all things are possible.

門 前 や 杖 で つ く り し 雪 解 川　　　　　一　茶
Monzen ya   tsue de tsukurishi   yukige-gawa

> The snow beginning to melt,
> With my stick I made a Great River
> At the front gate.　　　　　　　Issa

It was a warm day in early spring. Issa went out, and at
the front gate the snow was melting, the water collecting in

pools along the alley. With his stick, an awkward implement for the purpose, he scratches away, with an energy and concentration worthy, *one might mistakenly think*, of a better cause. Gradually the water begins to run into the gutter down the channel he has made. Proudly he surveys his handiwork, which he vaingloriously names, "Snow-melting River."

雪とけて村一ぱいの子ども哉　　　　　　一　茶
Yuki tokete   mura ippai no   kodomo kana

The snow having melted,
The village
　　Is full of children.　　　　　　　　　　Issa

In three lines, Issa has expressed the life of man and of nature, seen most vividly in spring, when the returning warmth reanimates all the things in the world. The warmth and the snow and the children,—what a deep relation there is between them! Shiki has a verse that may be a distant reminiscence of Issa's:

雪解に馬放ちたる部落哉
Yukidoke ni   uma hanachitaru   buraku kana

With the melting of the snow,
The village
　　Frees the ponies.

鍋の尻干しならべたる雪解かな　　　　　一　茶
Nabe no shiri   hoshinarabetaru   yukige kana

The bottoms of the saucepans
Drying in a row:
　　The melting of the snow.　　　　　　　Issa

The snow is melting and the river is full of water again. This river is near the house, and all the saucepans that have been allowed to get black with soot, are taken to the river, scrubbed and scoured there and left on the bank to dry. Thus in this verse, the spirit of spring and spring-cleaning, the increase of water and the scene at the bank of the river are expressed in these scanty words better than pages of description could accomplish.

打解けて氷と水の仲なほり　　　　　　　貞室

Uchitokete   kōri to mizu no   nakanaori

Ice and water,
Their difference resolved,
Are friends again. Teishitsu

In spring, the ice melts, and throwing off its formal differences, is once more reconciled to the water. What is interesting here is the personification at such a low level of existence as ice and water. Personification is not a so-called "figure of speech," but a realization that all things are personal, are mind, that mind is material. When we understand this, material and spiritual, their differences resolved, are friends again.

さゞ波にとけたる池の氷かな　　　　　　子規

Sazanami ni   toketaru ike no   kōri kana

The ripples
Are melting
The ice of the lake. Shiki

Under the leafless branches of the trees, all round the edge of the pond, ice remains, of a transparent whiteness. The ripples on the water wash onto this ice, which grows thinner and thinner, less and less. We feel the warmish wind of spring on our faces.

雪解に馬放ちたる部落哉　　　　　　　　子規

Yukidoke ni   uma hanachitaru   buraku kana

With the melting of the snow,
The village
Frees the ponies. Shiki

The horses, young and old, run along, tossing their heads and swishing their tails, looking for the new grass of spring. In their pleasure and freedom we feel the pleasure and freedom of spring. This verse, like so many of Shiki's, is not deep, but it makes us feel happy, and pleased with the world. It does not stir our emotion nor provoke to thought. It makes us see the world and feel its new-born joy and energy.

春の水山なき國を流れけり　　　蕪村
Haru no mizu　yama naki kuni wo　nagare keri

 The water of spring
Flows through
  A mountainless country. Buson

The water flows almost imperceptibly, as it moves into the distance over the great plain. There is grasped here the vaster aspect of nature, and the unhurrying character of spring.

春の水ところどころに見ゆるかな　　　鬼貫
Haru no mizu　tokorodokoro ni　miyuru kana

 Here water,
And there water,
  The waters of spring. Onitsura

A runlet here, a trickle of bright water among the grasses there, a brimming stream in the distance—all are the water of promise, the water of life, the water of spring.

In *Hitorigoto*, describing the special poetical quality of the four seasons, Onitsura says,

春の雨は物ごもりて淋し。夕立は氣晴れて涼し、
五月雨は鬱々としてさびし、秋の雨は底より淋し、
冬の夜はするどにさびし。　　　　　（獨言）

 Spring rains are lonely, heavy-hearted. Showers are clear-spirited, cool. Summer rains are lonely, melancholy; autumn rains are lonely, unfathomable. Winter evenings are lonely, piercing.

Very few English poets have attained to the simplicity of Oni-
tsura in this verse. The sight and sound of water always affected
Hakurakuten deeply. The following is a poem written in his
old age.

六 十 六

病知心力減。　老覺光陰速。
五十八歸來。　今年六十六。
鬢絲千黄白。　池草八九緑。
童稚靈成人。　園林半喬木。
看山倚高石。　引水穿深竹。
雖有潺湲聲。　至今聽未足。

Sixty Years Old

Ill, I know my weakening mental powers;
Old, I feel the swiftness of time.
I retired here at fifty-eight;
I am sixty-six this year.
All the strands of my hair are white.
Eight or nine times have the grasses round the pond turned
　　green.
My children are all grown up;
Many of the trees in the garden are high.
Leaning on a tall rock, I gaze at the hills.
A stream has been made through the bamboo grove;
It is only the sound of running water,
But I never grow weary of listening to it.

橋なくて日暮せんとする春の水　　　　　　蕉　村
Hashi nakute　hi bossen to suru　haru no mizu

There is no bridge,
And setting is the sun,—
Ah, the spring water! Buson]

If we say "there is a whole philosophy of life contained in
this verse," we are not wrong, but this philosophy of life has
no relation to the poetry, can be comprehended without any
understanding of the poem as a poem, and may be called, as

abstract principle, the enemy of the poetry, as the axe is the enemy of the tree. The sun of our life is setting, we are all on our last cruise. There is no bridge to another world, there is no faith or principle of life which will meet all our difficulties or solve all our problems. Let us then take each moment as it comes, giving it the value it possesses in its own nature. This is what Buson did when he found no bridge across the darkening waters. The swelling stream had a meaning that only a failing sunlight and a no-bridge could give it, but this meaning is not a philosophy, a way of life, a plan of action. It has, quite scientifically speaking, no connection with it. Because of the darkening sky and the lonely prospect, the poet perceives the beautiful "hopelessness," the "hopeless" beauty of the spring water. He perceives that he was made for the water and the water for him.

足弱のわたりて濁るはるの水　　　　　　　蕪　村
Ashiyowa no   watarite nigoru   haru no mizu

Wading through it,
Her feet muddied
The spring water.　　　　　　　Buson

This is possibly one of those verses which Buson composed through his imagination, not as the result of an experience. Buson is thinking of the water running over a ford. He sees clearly the whorl of fine sand and muddy water that rises and swirls away where something has disturbed the bed of the stream. What *should have* disturbed it that is in harmony with the water of spring? He thinks of the soft and weary feet, 足弱, of a woman traveller who is fording the stream. These are in deep accord with the spring, its gentle warmth and unintellectual activity; with the water, the female element of nature, with the turbidity of it.

Another such verse by Buson is the following:

春雨やもの書ぬ身のあはれなる
Harusame ya   mono kakanu mi no   aware naru

Spring rain;
How pitiful,
One who cannot write.

Here also Buson seems to want us to think of some young woman, in love, but with no education and unable to write or read a love-letter. This again brings out the meaning of spring, and the falling drops of water.

行く舟に岸根をうつや春の水   太　祇
Yuku fune ni   kishine wo utsu ya   haru no mizu

> At the passing of the boat,
> Beating on the shore,
> The waters of spring.   Taigi

It is the last line which gives this verse its poetical life. When the boat has passed by, the waves beat on the shore. There is a sudden animation of the scene in motion and sound, and this is seen as expressive of the nature of spring. Boats pass in every season, and the same waves are raised in the same water, but in the spring they attain the meaning for which they come into existence.

橋踏めば魚沈みけり春の水   子　規
Hashi fumeba   uo shizumikeri   haru no mizu

> Treading on the bridge,
> The fishes sink out of sight:
> The spring water.   Shiki

This is a simple, pictorial verse, not concerned with the fishes' instinctive fear of mankind, nor with the prosaic cause and effect of the logical connection. The repetition of the *m* sound and the gentle rhythm of the verse lead us from ourselves on the bridge down through the vanishing fishes into the water that has no form or persistence, the water that is nevertheless the water of spring, different from that of any other season.

日 は 落 ち て 増 す か と 見 ゆ る 春 の 水　　　　几　董

Hi wa ochite　masu ka to miyuru　haru no mizu

> The sun has set;
> And the spring water,—
> Has it increased in volume?　　　　Kitō

This is partly an optical, partly an emotional illusion. But it is also neither, it is poetry. When the water is full of light, it seems "lighter," of less volume, than when it is dark. And when it is sombre with evening shadows, the forbidding aspect that it takes on, causes the mind to see it as greater in quantity. The true spirit of wonder is always aroused, not by the pyramids or the Great Wall of China, but by the very slightest of things, a stick or stone that

the best of us excels.

一 桶 の 藍 な が し け り 春 の 川　　　　子　規

Hitooke no　ai nagashikeri　haru no kawa

> A barrel of indigo,
> Poured out and flowing:
> The spring river.　　　　Shiki

The dark turbid waters of the spring river are seen as indigo in colour by all of us but felt so only by the artist and the poet. To most of us, the outside world is practically uncoloured, and this is partly why black and white pictures are satisfying.[1] Another point of great interest is the barrel. There is a certain fairy-tale element in it, something of the ponderous humour of the Norse mythology, or the verisimilitude of earlier Greek myths. Nevertheless, it is simply an overturned barrel of indigo seen large, the spring river seen small.

---

[1] There is, of course, a much profounder reason.

草籠を置いて人なし春の山   子 規
Kusakago wo   oite hitonashi   haru no yama

> A basket of grass,
> And no one there,—
> Mountains of spring.   Shiki

How wonderful the world is, that a basket of grass, by itself, should be able to give us the meaning of the spring mountains. The mere fact that there is no one with the basket is enough to throw us back into the arms of nature. When we are entirely alone with nature, and conscious of it, we feel an emotion that can be explained only by a contradiction, yet it is a single, elemental feeling. On the one hand it is a feeling of loneliness; on the other, it is one of fullness. It is like breathing in and breathing out at one and the same time. The spring mountains are so far off and yet so near; infinite, yet in one's breast; eternal, but of this present moment.

廻廊や手すりに並ぶ春の山   子 規
Kairō ya   tesuri ni narabu   haru no yama

> Ranged along
> The hand-rail around the corridor,
> The mountains of spring.   Shiki

There is an illusion of nearness here which hints at the real subject of the poem, the spiritual nearness, so close that it is an identity. But Shiki does not take us into this painful and dangerous region. He leaves us with the merely physical sensation of nearness, without which all the rest is nonsense. The same applies to the following verse, also by Shiki:

春の山重なり合ふて皆丸し
Haru no yama   kasanari ōte   mina marushi

> Mountains of spring
> All rising so round,
> One above another.

Another verse by Shiki, more like the original poem, is the following; the season alone is different, but the continuity of the verandah and the mountains, the unity of the works of man and nature is more explicit, more personal:

夏山を廊下づたひの温泉哉
Natsuyama wo　rōka-zutai no　ideyu kana

> At the hot-spring,
> Along the corridor,
> The summer mountains.

春の野や何に人ゆき人かへる　　　　　　　子　規
Haru no no ya　nani ni hito yuki　hito kaeru

> People coming, people going
> Over the spring moor,—
> For what, I wonder?　　　　　　　Shiki

This is not a question; it requires no answer. Indeed, when we realize that this kind of thing, and all kinds of things are questions that need no answer, are answers that correspond to no questions whatever, then we are enlightened, then ours is the real poetic life; all things have a meaning, but a meaning that is neither a question nor an answer, yet deeper and more poignant than either. These people, of all ages, occupations, costumes, some walking swiftly, others dawdling, others plodding,—we have the whole of the Canterbury Tales, the Divine Comedy, the Plays of Shakespeare on a single road across the moor in spring.

Yet again this is a poem of spring. All these people, unknown to the poet and unknown to one another, are an expression of an aspect of spring, its mysterious, upspringing vitality.

振上ぐる鍬の光や春の野良　　　　　　　杉　風
Furiaguru　kuwa no hikari ya　haru no nora

> The light
> On the hoe as it swings up,—
> The spring moor.　　　　　　Sampū

Whenever a hoe is swung up in the air, it flashes in the sunlight, but in spring that light is brighter, more living, more

expressive than at any other time of the year. This is a
subjective matter, no doubt, but this does not alter the fact that
spring is the season of light and liveliness.

春 の 海 終 日 の た り の た り 哉　　　　　蕪 村
Haru no umi   hinemosu notari   notari kana

The sea of spring,
Rising and falling,
All the day long.　　　　　　　　　　Buson

All agree in praising this verse as one of Buson's best haiku,
expressing our feelings by the spring sea and the nature of the
spring sea without leaning either to the subjective, or to the
objective. But there is a surprising disagreement as to what
the verse particularly refers to. Shiki says that *notari notari*
describes the light waves that fall on the sand of the shore.
Kyoshi says it refers to the heaving waves of the deep water
far away from the shore. Hekigodō says that it expresses the
whole scene of the spring sea. If we compare the last two
lines of Byron's *Stanzas for Music*, we get some idea of the
onomatopoeic power of Buson's verse:

With a full but soft emotion,
Like the swell of Summer's ocean.

島 々 に 灯 を と も し け り 春 の 海　　　　　子 規
Shimajima ni   hi wo tomoshikeri   haru no umi

The lights are lit
On the islands far and near:
The spring sea.　　　　　　　　　　Shiki

This verse is Shiki at his best, the objectivity of Buson, but
with no feeling of art or artificiality. It is not profound or
mystical, not lyrical or subjective, but we feel with quiet clarity
the nature of the sea in spring, and its relation to the lights
glimmering through the dusk. The sea is calm, and the islands
are visible; the lights give some feeling of humanity, the warmth
of the season.

神 佛 GODS AND BUDDHAS

何の木の花とはしらず匂ひ哉   芭 蕉
Nan no ki no hana towa shirazu nioi kana

From what flowering tree
I know not,—
But ah, the fragrance!   Bashō

Emphasizing, perhaps over-emphasizing the subjective aspect of this verse, it was translated in *Zen in English Literature* as follows:

The fragrance
Of some unknown blossoming tree
Filled all my soul.

The intellect does not know, can by its nature never know *a thing*. The mind as a whole knows it, in an eternal moment of time, at an infinite point of space. The only way the meaning of the thing can be expressed is by "Ah!" This verse was composed at the Great Shrine of Ise. The unnameable fragrance that filled his nostrils may also have been that of an actual flowering tree, but the fragrance he speaks of is one of the mind rather than of the body. He no doubt recollected Saigyō's waka:

何事のおはしますかは知らねども
忝なさに涙こぼるゝ。
What it might be
I know not,
But from awe and gratitude
My tears are falling.

This was composed at the same place, and in the same spirit. Shiki has a verse which is almost a parody in its colloquial tone:

何といふ鳥か知らねど梅の枝
Nan to iu tori ka shiranedo ume no eda
I do not know
What bird it was,—
But the spray of plum-blossom!

おのづから頭が下るなり神路山   一 茶
Onozukara   kōbe ga sagaru nari   kamiji yama

> Kamiji Yama;
> My head bent
> Of itself.   Issa

Mount Kamiji is the hill consecrated in the Inner Precincts
of Ise Shrine.

Issa's poem is far simpler than Saigyō's, far less "poetic," yet
has more Zen in it, for it is quite devoid of sentimentality, and
also of rational explanation.

山寺や誰もまゐらぬ涅槃像   樗 良
Yamadera ya   tare mo mairanu   nehanzō

> A mountain temple;
> No one comes to pray
> At the Nirvana Picture.   Chora

This temple is not far from a small village in the mountains.
It is the 15th of the Second Month of the Lunar Calendar, and
the picture portraying Buddha's Entrance into Nirvana is hung
up in the temple. This picture shows Buddha on his death-bed
surrounded by Buddhas, monks, the laity, and even animals, all
bewailing his death except the Buddhas, whose serene counte-
nances show their realization that death, like all things, is but
an appearance, not the reality.

The sun is warm, the peasants are busy in the fields. No one
comes to pray before the picture. There is a feeling of the gap
between the ordinary world and the world of devotion. Yet this
very gap is the place where the picture in the shadowy temple
and the peasants in the sunshine are not divided from each other.

小うるさい花が咲くとて寝釈迦哉   一 茶
Kourusai   hana ga saku tote   neshaka kana

> A little bit of a nuisance,
> These flowers blooming,—
> The sleeping Buddha.   Issa

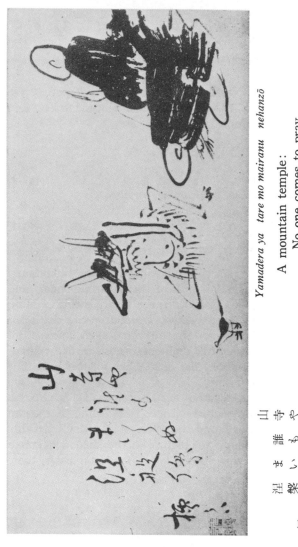

Yamadera ya tare mo mairanu nehanzō

A mountain temple:
　　No one comes to pray
　　At the Nirvana Picture.

Chora

The two monks, the ogre weeping, the pheasant (?) all express
different aspects of the serenity of Buddha and the deserted temple.

This is difficult and ambiguous in the original as well as in
the translation. Issa has the courage of a child, a child that
may be a coward, but says what he thinks without regard for
the (unknown and unconsidered) consequences. Buddha lying
there in the picture does not look as if he is sleeping an eternal,
timeless sleep in Nirvana. He looks rather, (so Issa perceives),
as if he were a little weary of the flowers blooming outside and
all that goes with them, and had lain down for a nap. Only
a child or Issa can see the picture as it really is; only these
know the Buddha and his real mind. Another verse by Issa
with the opposite meaning:

寝ておはしても佛ぞよ花の降る
Nete owashitemo   hotoke zoyo   hana no furu

E'en though he lie there,
Yet is he Buddha!
Flowers descending.

In *Ora ga Haru*, he has a yet another aspect of the same subject:

み佛や寝ておはしても花と錢
Mihotoke ya   nete owashitemo   hana to zeni

The Lord Buddha,
Though he be sleeping,—
Flowers and offerings!

Issa then quotes a haiku of Ōemaru that has more of a senryu
quality, but shows Ōemaru feeling in his own person the posture
of Buddha:

彼岸の蚊釋迦のまねして喰れけり
Higan no ka   shaka no maneshite   kuwarekeri

Lying like Shakamuni,
I was bitten by the mosquitoes
Of Nirvana week.

繪踏して念佛申す嫗かな   秋　竹
Efumi shite   nembutsu mōsu   omina kana

An old woman
Trampling on a picture of Christ,
Repeating the Nembutsu.   Shūchiku

This concerns the practice of treading on a picture of Christ to show that one was not a Christian. This law was enacted by the Government in the year 1716 to make certain of the extinction of Christianity. From the 16th of the First Month to the Third Month (Lunar Calendar) this rite was performed at Nagasaki, Ōmura, and other places.

The poet has brought out the tragedy of it all by making the person concerned a woman, and by reminding us, through the word Nembutsu, of the fact that the teaching of Christ and that of Buddha are in no way opposed, at least as far as the inculcation of gentleness, meekness and selflessness is concerned.

人　事　HUMAN AFFAIRS

藪入や墓の松風うしろふく　　　　　　一　茶
Yabuiri ya　haka no matsukaze ushiro fuku

The Apprentices' Holiday;
The wind blows behind,
In the pine-trees of the grave.　　　Issa

On the sixteenth of January in Old Japan, apprentices were
given a holiday and they returned to their homes.

Issa is perhaps speaking of himself under the guise of an
apprentice. Issa lost his mother at the early age of three, and
whenever he went back to his native place, he first visited the
graves of his parents. Seven years before the composition of
the above verse, he had written:

やぶ入や先づつつがなき墓の松
Yabuiri ya　mazu tsutsuganaki　haka no matsu

The Apprentices' Holiday:
First, safe and sound,—
The pine-trees of the grave.

The sound of the wind in the pine-trees round the graves
where his father and mother are sleeping their last sleep, the
same sound as always, the unchanged and the changing, the
timeless in time,—nothing but that wind can express what it
expresses.

やぶ入の跨で過ぬ凧の糸　　　　　　蕪　村
Yabuiri no　mataide suginu　tako no ito

The apprentice at liberty
Steps over the string of the kite,
And hastens on.　　　Buson

On his way home, the house not far distant, there stretch
across the narrow path the strings of the kites the village
children are flying. As he steps over this slightest of all ob-
stacles, he has that peculiar feeling, that presentiment which
is the infallible mark of a poetic experience. The less the

obstacle, the greater its significance, and thus, when he has
stepped over the string of the kite, the feeling of elation is
purer, because hardly entangled with the preceding events.

や ぶ 入 の 夢 や 小 豆 の 煮 る う ち   蕪 村
Yabuiri no   yume ya azuki no   nieru uchi

The apprentice on holiday
Is dreaming,
While the red beans are cooking.   Buson

This verse looks very thin and unlikely, but if we are patient
with it, a whole world of human relations and feelings is revealed.
The boy has come home, and after telling his mother all about
it, he goes to sleep while she cooks the red beans that Japanese
people seem to think are so delicious. (In Kyōto there was a
custom of giving apprentices returning home *botamochi*, rice-
cakes covered with bean-paste.) After he has finished all he
wanted to say, it is enough merely to be with his family, in a
physical rather than a mental way. His mother too likes to
watch him sleeping there while she keeps an eye on the beans.
But as he sleeps, time is passing by, and he must soon get
ready to go back to the shop or wherever it is that he works.
No educated Japanese can read this verse without thinking of
the well-known Chinese story, "The Dream while Kaoliang
Cooked," 黄梁一炊の夢.

A young man called Rosei, 盧生, intending to achieve his
ambitions, set off to the capital to take the official examination.
On the way, he entered an inn, and borrowing a pillow, slept
for a short time while the millet cooked, and in his dream passed
through all the vicissitudes of glory and ruin. There is some
resemblance to Hawthorne's *David Swan*.

Thinking of the verse as typical of Buson's treatment of his
subject, we may compare it with one on the same subject by
Taigi, 太祇, 1706-72, a contemporary of Buson:

藪 入 の 寝 る や ひ と り の 親 の 側
Yabuiri no   neru ya hitori no   oya no soba

The apprentice on holiday,
Sleeping
By one parent.

The boy is sleeping by the side of his mother, a widow. Buson avoids so much human feeling; he keeps a little further away than Taigi.

雛見世の灯を引ころや春の雨　　　　蕪村
Hina-mise no　hi wo hiku koro ya　haru no ame

As they were putting out
The lights of the doll shops,
The spring rain.　　　　Buson

The Doll Festival of Japan illustrates what Anatole France says in *Children's Playthings:*

Doubtless there is nothing human, according to the flesh, in those little personages of wood or cardboard, but there is in them something divine, however little it may be. They do not live as we do, but still they live. They live the life of the immortal gods.

There is a verse by Rogetsu (1873–1927, pupil of Shiki), which may have derived from Buson's:

雛市の灯ともし頃を雨が降る
Hina-ichi no　hitomoshi-goro wo　ame ga furu

As they were lighting up
In the Doll Market,
It was raining.

When we compare these verses, we feel two different kinds of loneliness, both hard to name or describe. That of Rogetsu is human; that of Buson is of nature, of spring, of night.

手にとればはやにこにこと賣雛　　　　梅室
Te ni toreba　haya niko-niko to　uri-hiina

Picking it up,
Soon I was smiling;
Dolls for sale.　　　　Baishitsu

The poet picked up a doll from a stall selling dolls for the Girls' Festival. The sweet little face and charming clothes, the life and humanity of this lifeless mannequin, the memories of childhood, the softening of the heart calloused by time,—these are suddenly felt when the poet realizes that he is smiling at the doll. One almost feels that men were made for dolls, not dolls for men.

石女の雛かしづくぞ哀れなる   嵐 雪
Umazume no   hina kashizuku zo   aware naru

The childless woman,
How tender she is
To the dolls!   Ransetsu

There is a distant resemblance (which is of course, the Zen that is in common) between this woman and Mr. Bodd in *The Wrecker*,[1]

who laid out, upon some deal in wheat or corner in aluminium, the essence of which was little better than highway robbery, treasures of conscientiousness and self-denial.

Life has a certain direction about it which, among many other names, we call morality. Love, duty, tenderness, self-renunciation *must* manifest themselves in some shape or other, and the more divergent or distorted the form, the more the power and the nature of instinctive life is perceived.

Another thing worth noting is how much more powerful and moving a no-thing is than the thing itself. To the poet, the childless woman is more affecting than the sight of a family, just as the death of Christ has more value than the life of Buddha.

箱を出る貌わすれめや雛二對   蕪 村
Hako wo deru   kao wasureme ya   hina nitsui

Coming out of the box,
This pair of dolls,—
I have not forgotten their faces.   Buson

[1] Stevenson.

As the young girl opens the box and the pair of dolls appear, one male, the other female, she has a rush of feeling, a combination of novelty with recognition. Only once a year is the box opened, but the well-beloved faces have the same sweet dignity as ever.

Issa has a verse whose tenderness of feeling is similar to this of Buson, but expressed with a poignant depth, a humanity which Buson did not attain, or wish to attain.

片隅に煤けし雛も夫婦哉
Katasumi ni   susukeshi hina mo   fūfu kana

> The two grimy dolls
> In the corner also,
> Are man and wife.

Others of Issa with a lighter humour:

浦風にお色の黒い雛かな
Urakaze ni   oiro no kuroi   hiina kana

> The dolls
> Are dark-complexioned
> From the wind of the beach.

居並んで達磨も雛の仲間哉
Inarande   daruma mo hina no   nakama kana

> Daruma also
> Is ranged there,
> One of the other dolls.

灯せば雛に影あり一つづつ   子 規
Hitomoseba   hina ni kage ari   hitotsuzutsu

> Lighting the light,—
> The shadows of the dolls,
> One for each.   Shiki

This is my idea of what a haiku should be,—something that catches the eye of the mind, a mere nothing, but unforgettably significant, indeed, with this significance in inverse proportion to its practical importance, its size and longevity. Each doll has a shadow, its own, its very own shadow; and having it, there is a bond between the dolls, between them and all other things.   The poet surveys God's work and sees it as good.

雛 の 顔 我 是 非 な く も 老 い に け り   星 布
Hina no kao   ware zehi naku mo   oi ni keri

The faces of the dolls!
Though I never intended to,
I have grown old.   Seifu

This is a verse by a woman,[1] but she has done what so few
woman can do, she has risen above her womanhood, and by so
doing, has expressed it. Nearly all women, but especially those
of Japan, look back on their life up to the age of sixteen or
seventeen as the happiest period. Death is the problem for men,
and growing old the problem for women.   Few there are who
solve it; it solves them.

た ら ち ね の つ ま ま ず あ り や 雛 の 鼻   蕪 村
Tarachine no   tsumamazu ari ya   hina no hana

Didn't your mother
Pinch it,
Snub-nosed doll?   Buson

One of the dolls has a very flat nose. Japanese people think,
half-seriously, that if a baby's nose is pinched and pulled often,
it will develop a prominent and aristocratic nose. Buson's verse
is humorous and light, but just because of this, shows an affec-
tion for the doll that a more beautiful doll would never evoke.

雨 漏 を 何 と お ぼ す ぞ 雛 達   一 茶
Amamori wo   nanto obosu zo   hiinatachi

Rain is leaking in:
What do you think of it,
Assembled dolls?   Issa

If the dolls could answer, they would say, "We think that

[1] A disciple of Shirao.   Died 1814.

the rain leaks in, and that we are dolls." This is the answer Issa dreads to hear as he glances from the wet patches on the floor to the mute row of dolls in the alcove. Things are as they are, and will be what they will be, and to ask even the dolls for a reason why, for a means of escape, is useless,

> Perocchè sì s'inoltra nell' abisso
> Dell' eterno statuto quel che chiedi,
> Che da ogni creata vista è scisso.[1]

> Because so far within the abyss
> Of the eternal statute lies what you ask,
> It is cut off from all created sight.

But in the humour of the verse lies the answer to all things. There and there alone, not even in the inevitability, moves the life of the universe which man has endowed it with. In the very uselessness of asking the lifeless marionettes, is revealed the *Use* of everything.

雛 の 間 に と ら れ て 暗 き ほ と け か な　　　曉　臺
Hina no ma ni　torarete kuraki　hotoke kana

Darkened is the altar of Buddha;
The room has been taken
By the dolls.　　　　　　　　　　Gyōdai

In the ordinary way, the Buddhist family altar in the corner of the room, though not over-bright and cheerful, was at least in harmony with the rest of the room, but now the dolls have been set out on their scarlet dais, the altar seems shorn of its light. Even its spiritual meaning seems dimmed by the life and joy that fills the room.

山 路 來 て 向 ふ 城 下 や 凧 の 數　　　　　太　祇
Yamaji kite　mukō jōka ya　tako no kazu

Coming along the mountain path,—
Down there a castle-town,
Many kites a-flying.　　　　　　Taigi

[1] *Paradiso*, xxi, 94–6.

The poet has been struggling up the precipitous mountain
path. At last he reaches the top of the pass with a sigh of
relief. His eyes that have been bent on the ground so long,
now gaze over the varied scene before him. But somehow or
other what affects him most, what draws the heart out of him,
what he becomes at this breathless moment, is the kites that are
being flown over the town, some high, some low, some large,
some tiny, but all alive with meaning.

地に下りて凧に魂なかりけり   九品太
Chi ni orite   tako ni tamashii   nakarikeri

> Falling to earth,
> The kite had
> No soul.

Kubonta

What the poet perceived was not the negative quality which
he states of the kite's being an inanimate, non-living thing,
but its life, its existence, its essence as an inconscient being.
When it flops down on the ground there is something ludicrous
about its inertia, its spiritlessness, its supineness, and the kite's
real nature is perceived in the form of humour.

朔日や一文凧も江戸の空   一 茶
Tsuitachi ya   ichi-mon-dako mo   edo no sora

> The first day of the month;
> The halfpenny kite also
> In the sky of Edo.

Issa

"He maketh his sun to shine upon the just and upon the
unjust," upon the rich merchant's kite and upon Issa's. The
wind blows the halfpenny kite as freely, as gladly, as unwillingly,
as any other. Matthew Arnold has expressed this thought in
his own rather pontifical way in a line of *Empedocles on Etna:*

> Nor is that wind less rough which blows a good man's
> barge.

But this is not haiku, which puts all its emotion and intellection
into the sky, into the kite.

美しき凧あがりけり乞食小屋   一 茶
Utsukushiki   tako agari keri   kojiki-goya

A beautiful kite
Rose from
The beggar's hovel.   Issa

For the moralist, the social worker, the artist, the scientist,
these things have different meanings. The poet alone combines
them all; the contrast of beauty and squalor is not purely one
of colour and line; human feeling enters into it.

凧きのふの空のありどころ   蕪 村
Ikanobori   kinō no sora no   aridokoro

A kite,—
In the same place
In yesterday's sky!   Buson

Buson suddenly notices a single kite in the sky, of the same
shape, in the same place as the day before. He feels that time
has been eternalized. The sense of time and timelessness, es-
pecially embodied in *yesterday*, Buson expresses in many other
verses:

柿の花昨日散しは黄ばみ見ゆ
Kaki no hana   kinō chirishi wa   kibami miyu

The flowers of the persimmon;
Those which fell yesterday
Look yellowish.

秋の空昨日や鶴を放ちたる
Aki no sora   kinō ya tsuru wo   hanachitaru

The autumn sky;
Yesterday
The stork was freed.

彼處にて昨日も聞きぬ閑古鳥
Kashiko nite   kinō mo kikinu   kankodori

That is the place
Where yesterday also I heard
The *kankodori*.

この蘭や五助が庭に昨日まで
Kono ran ya   gosuke ga niwa ni   kinō made

> This orchid,
> Only yesterday
> It was in Gosuke's garden.

冬の梅昨日やちりぬ石の上
Fuyu no ume   kinō ya chirinu   ishi no ue

> The winter plum
> Scattered its blossoms yesterday
> On this stone.

All these derive historically, perhaps, from Kyorai's verse:

一昨日はあの山越えて花ざかり
Ototoi wa   ano yama koete   hanazakari

> The day before yesterday,
> I crossed that mountain,
> The cherry-blossoms at their best.

拾ふものみな動くなり汐干潟   千代尼
Hirou mono   mina ugoku nari   shiohigata

> On the low-tide beach,
> Everything we pick up
> Moves.   Chiyo-ni

The verse well expresses the nature of all those living creatures left stranded at low tide. The English word animal comes from "anima," but the Japanese word for animal is *dōbutsu*, which means "moving thing," "something that moves." Also, this verse is by the most famous poetess of Japan, born seven years after the death of Bashō, in 1701, and dying in 1775. When we think of these moving, squirming things in the hands of women and children, we get a still stronger impression of their wriggly nature.

足跡を蟹のあやしむ汐干かな   盧　風
Ashiato wo   kani no ayashimu   shiohi kana

Ebb-tide;
The crab is suspicious
Of the footprint.   Rofu

As it runs across the wet sand the crab comes to a footprint,
and stops suddenly, hesitates, waving its feelers, and walks
gingerly round it. Its trepidation is that of Robinson Crusoe
at the footprint and has the same origin, the mystery of it.

The humour lies partly in the discrepancy of cause and effect,
the footprint and the crab's consternation; partly in the fact
that to our eyes a crab is a most suspicious-looking affair, much
more so than the footprint. But besides this humour, or rather,
within it, there is the life of the creature itself expressed, the
humour of all life, the life of humour.

青柳の泥にしたゝる汐干かな   芭　蕉
Aoyagi no   doro ni shitataru   shiohi kana

A green willow,
Dripping down into the mud,
At low tide.   Bashō

This is one of those melancholy scenes that Dickens and
Crabbe enjoyed more than bright, sun-lit landscapes and sub-
urban prospects. Life is a damp, green thing that needs the
darkness as well as the light, filth as well as beauty, and Bashō,
looking upon the old tree, loved it.

大船の尻のぞきたる汐干哉   子　規
Ōbune no   shiri nozokitaru   shiohi kana

Gazing up
At the end of a great ship,
At low tide.   Shiki

(*Nozokitaru* is taken transitively.) Strange scenes like this,
or rather, strange aspects of familiar things, are always impres-
sive, especially in childhood. When we are shell-gathering at

ebb-tide, concerned with the superficial remnant of the life of
the sea, and we look up at the vessel as it lies in the mud, the
propeller with its tangle of sea-weeds, the stern covered with
barnacles, we feel a sense of awe, both with regard to the great
ship that lies there,

> Like a sea-beast crawled forth, that on a shelf
> Of rock or sand reposeth, there to sun itself,[1]

and for the sea, which comes and goes, is calm and rages, floats
great ships, and leave them stranded among crabs and mussels.

人まねに鳩も雀も汐干かな   一 茶
Hitomane ni   hato mo suzume mo   shiohi kana

Imitating the human beings,
Pigeons and sparrows
At the ebb-tide.   Issa

Some animals and birds are fond of human company, and in
our loneliness we are glad to have them with us. Issa rejoices
in the presence of the sparrows and pigeons; for once, their
interests not conflicting, all are searching for treasures among
the mud and sand. There is a peculiar pleasure in the way
Issa views it, the birds imitating the humans, rather than our
imitating them.

夜に入れば直したくなるつぎほかな   一 茶
Yo ni ireba   naoshitaku naru   tsugiho kana

After it was dark,
I began to want to change
The way I grafted it.   Issa

Issa spent a long time that spring afternoon grafting a fruit-
tree, or perhaps a peony or camellia, and all was finished to
his satisfaction, so he thought. In the evening, however, some
idea which had been at the bottom of his mind came to the
surface, and he began to think he should have done it in a

---

[1] *Resolution and Independence.*

different way; not tongue-grafting but crown-grafting would
have been better. He then dismisses the subject from his mind
but it keeps coming back with a curious insistence that ultimately
is felt as significant.

There is a haiku of Shiki that seems like a continuation of
Issa's:

燭をとつて雨の接木を見る夜かな
Hi wo totte   ame no tsugiki wo   miru yo kana

> Taking a lamp,
> And looking at the grafted tree,
> In the evening rain.

Here, however, what worries Shiki is not the method of
grafting, but the clayey earth which is put round the junction
of the graft; the rain may wash it off.

畑打や木の間の寺の鐘供養   無 村
Hata utsu ya   konoma no tera no   kane-kuyō

> Tilling the field;
> From the temple among the trees,
> The funeral bell tolls.   Buson

In its picturesqueness, its subdued melancholy tones, it re-
minds us of *L'Angelus*, and of

> The curfew tolls the knell of parting day.

The tilling of the field and the tolling of the bell as a mass for
the repose of some departed soul, have some deep, inexplicable
connection. Every stroke of the hoe, every stroke of the bell
has some unfathomable meaning that is the same, though they
are different.

名所とも知らで畑うつ男かな   子 規
Meisho to mo   shirade hata utsu   otoko kana

> Not knowing
> It is a famous place,
> A man hoeing the field.   Shiki

The poetical point here is the overlapping of two worlds, that of innocence and that of knowledge. The man hoeing the field does not know, or does not remember that a great battle was fought here, the course of history changed, his own life made possible. The poet hoes the field too, in his own way, but it is a larger, fuller, older field than that of the peasant.

畑 打 や 峯 の 御 坊 の 鶏 の 聲 　　　　蕪 村
Hata utsu ya　mine no obō no　tori no koe

Tilling the field;
From the temple on the peak
　　The cry of the cock.　　　　Buson

All day the labourer has been working in the field, thought-less, mindless. Now it is late afternoon and the sun sinks towards the far-away hills behind him. Suddenly, from the small temple that lies hidden on the upper slopes of the peak that towers before him, a cock crows. Its empty, melancholy note sounds as if close at hand. The way it trails down at the end sounds like the voice of departing day.

畑 う ち や 法 三 章 の 札 の も と 　　　蕪 村
Hatauchi ya　hōsanshō no　fuda no moto

A man tilling the field,
At the foot of the notice-board
　　Of the Three Article Code.　　Buson

The founder of the Han Dynasty promulgated an edict making the killing, wounding, or robbing of a father capital crimes. This took place at the beginning of his reign, after crushing the Shin, 秦, when peace was restored to the country. Buson imagines a notice erected by the roadside, and nearby a labourer wielding his hoe with the feeling that the fruit of his labours will fall to him and his children. Buson here goes right back to the earliest ages of Chinese history, two thousand years before his own times.

畑をうつ翁が頭巾ゆがみけり　　　　　几　董

Hata wo utsu　okina ga zukin　yugamikeri

> The old man
> Hoeing the field,
> Has his head-gear on crooked.　　　Kitō

The aim of a great many haiku may seem to be to let some trivial thing or incident stand as a symbol of the greater aspects of nature or man. This cannot be so, since this symbol and that which is symbolised would be separate from each other; there would be a disunity. In the above verse, the crookedness of what the old man is wearing on his head is due to his age. He is indifferent to what he looks like, as are all other people except the poet. What does the poet *see?* He sees the old man's head-apparel worn crookedly; he sees that particular old man wearing it on one side. That is all, and that seeing is the poetry. When Keats says,

> He has his winter too of pale misfeature,
> Or else he would forgo his mortal nature,[1]

the poetry is already stiffening into prose. The life is almost gone, the particular disciplined into a generalization. The great thing is to

> keep the eye *steadily* on the object.

The golden rule for poets is,

> Let thine eye be single.

畑打や我が家も見えて暮かゝる　　　　蕉　村

Hatautsu ya　wagaya mo miete　kure-kakaru

> Tilling the field;
> My house also is seen
> As evening falls.　　　Buson

Working in the rice field all day long, with the other men and women merged into humanity, the poet has lost the feeling of his own identity. The sun falls behind the green mountains,

---

[1] *The Human Seasons.*

tiredness and hunger increase, and as he looks down the valley, lights are seen glimmering; smoke rises up into the still air, and he feels the yearning of the animal for its den. Poetry, like charity, begins at home. It is wrong to resist the feeling of the sacredness of certain days, the yearning for the presence of particular people, the desire for a house of one's own, love of one's own children. Let them be as they are, roots of our daily life, while at the same time we realize that

> Every day is a good day,

that we are strangers and pilgrims here, of no abiding place. Indeed, it is these two sets of contradictory truth in one that makes the meaning of life at all. This is what lives and moves and has its being in the poet's heart as he stands looking towards his home. It comes in the first few lines of *Rugby Chapel*, but more painfully.

> Coldly, sadly descends
> The autumn evening. The field
> Strewn with its dank yellow drifts
> Of wither'd leaves, and the elms,
> Fade into dimness apace,
> Silent;—hardly a shout
> From a few boys late at their play!
> The lights come out in the street,
> In the school-room windows.

畑 う つ や 道 問 ふ 人 の 見 え ず な り ぬ　　　　蕪 村
Hata utsu ya   michi tou hito no   miezu narinu

Tilling the field:
The man who asked the way
Has disappeared.　　　　　　　　　　　Buson

All alone under the spring sky, a man is hoeing the field. A stranger, for a wonder, passes by and asks the way to a neighbouring village. The labourer directs him and resumes his work. A moment or two afterwards (or so it seems), he straightens his back and looks along the winding road; the stranger has disappeared. Again he is alone between sky and earth.

動くとも見えで畑打つ男かな   去　來
Ugoku tomo   miede hata utsu   otoko kana

The man
Hoeing in the field,
Seems motionless.   Kyorai

The perception of the relativity of movement and repose
(caused here by the distance between the poet and the labourer)
is expressed also in Sōshi's first chapter, and in many verses
from the *Zenrinkushū*, for example:

黄昏鶏報暁　半夜日頭明。

The cock announces the dawn in the evening;
The sun is bright at midnight.

What is expressed here in a paradoxical and indigestible form,
is diluted in the poem, for common consumption, by the use
of *miede*, "seems not to." In this respect, Shiki's verse is far
better:

日一日同じところに畑うつ
Hi ichi-nichi   onaji tokoro ni   hatake utsu

One whole day
Tilling the field
In the same place.

There are some lines by Wordsworth in *Address* to *Kilchurn
Castle* which remind us of Kyorai's verse:

Yon foaming flood seems motionless as ice,
Its dizzying turbulence eludes the eye,
Frozen by distance.

The explanation kills the poetry. Kyorai's verse is simple but
profound. However, the poem in no way suggests that move-
ment is a no-movement. There is not the slightest trace of any
Mahayana philosophy in it. Nevertheless this truth is the life
and soul of the poem. There is the same thing in the following
verse by Buson, equally unexpressed. From time to time, as
we gaze at the flowering tree, there is a change. Every time
we look at the flowing water there is no change, it is ever
the same.

水に散て花なくなりぬ岸の梅
Mizu ni chitte   hana nakunarinu   kishi no ume

A plum-tree on the bank:
Falling onto the water,
Its blossoms disappear.

畑うつや動かぬ雲もなくなりぬ   蕪 村
Hata utsu ya   ugokanu kumomo   nakunarinu

Tilling the field:
The cloud that never moved
Is gone.   Buson

The original has a melodious form, *u, mo na, nu* and *ku*
being echoed:

Hata utsu ya,   ugokanu kumo mo,   nakunarinu

This expresses the passage of time in its monotony of repetition
of moment after moment. The cloud on the brow of the hill
remains there hour after hour; the man tills the field with equal
composure and persistence. Suddenly, the cloud is gone, only
the sky remains and the man under it, working on endlessly.
Spengler says of the peasant:

> He is the eternal man, independent of every culture that
> ensconces itself in the cities. He precedes it, he outlives
> it, a dumb creature propagating himself from generation to
> generation, limited to soil-bound callings and aptitudes, a
> mystical soul, a dry, shrewd understanding that sticks to
> practical matters, the origin and the ever-flowing source of
> the blood that makes history in the cities.[1]

雲無心南山の下畠打つ   子 規
Kumo mushin   nanzan no shita   hatake utsu

The clouds aloof,
He tills the field
Under the Southern Mountains.   Shiki

[1] The Soul of the City, IV.

This seems to be a picture of China, where nature is so vast that man is submerged in it. The man is tilling the field under the Southern Mountains. Above them the clouds roll by, not kindly, not relentlessly, not even irrevocably, but just so, the man and the clouds and the mountains not apart, and yet not together.

苗代や仁王のような足の跡   野坡
Nawashiro ya   niō no yōna   ashi no ato

As though the Deva Kings
Had been walking the rice-seedling field,—
These footprints!   Yaha

Those who weed the rice-seedlings tread as little as possible in the beds, and take very long steps. These footprints in the mud gradually fill with water and become double the size, or larger. They look like the footprints of the huge Niō, the demon-like Deva Kings that guard the entrance of temples.

This only, does not rise above fancy; but beyond this there is a feeling of the incommensurateness of things and their relations. A thousand men are born and nothing happens. A man is born, and the world is changed. Men creep in palaces and mansions; Deva Kings stride through the rice-fields.

苗代や短冊形と色紙形   子規
Nawashiro ya   tanzakugata to   shikishigata

The rice-seedling beds;
The rectangle of a tanzaku,
The square of a shikishi.   Shiki

A *tanzaku* is a strip of stiff paper used for writing poems on. A *shikishi* is a square of thick paper for painting pictures. The seeds of rice are planted in square and rectangular-shaped beds which resemble the tanzaku and shikishi. The poetry lies in the fact that the things compared are remote materially but identical in form.

苗 代 や 小 蛇 の わ た る 夕 日 影   大江丸
Nawashiro ya   kohebi no wataru   yūhikage

The rice-seedling bed;
A small snake crosses
In the evening sunshine.   Ōemaru

Perhaps the most interesting point of this excellent verse is
the smallness of the snake; it hardly disturbs the water as it
sways across among the young rice-plants.

櫻 散 る 苗 代 水 や 星 月 夜   蕪 村
Sakura chiru   nawashiro-mizu ya   hoshizukiyo

A night of stars;
The cherry-blossoms are falling
On the water of the rice-seedlings.   Buson

In the purple sky of the night of spring the stars are bright
points of white light. In the indigo of the water between the
deep green of the rice plants, float pale blossoms of the cherry-
trees.

苗 代 を 見 て 居 る 森 の 烏 か な   支 考
Nawashiro wo   mite iru mori no   karasu kana

The crows of the wood
Are gazing down
At the rice-seedling field.   Shikō

The peasants are working, knee-deep in the muddy water.
The crows at the edge of the grove nearby are looking down
at them from their points of vantage. There seems to be nothing
in this; but as we sink deeper into the poem we feel

the calm oblivious tendencies of nature.

In the planters' unawareness of the birds, in the birds' half-
comprehending gaze at the farmers, we see life working, as it
always does, in deadly secret, towards unknown destinies, most
potent when most unperceived, most mysterious where no ex-
planation seems required.

庭に出て物種蒔くや病み上り   子　規
Niwa ni dete   monotane maku ya   yamiagari

Going out into the garden,
I sowed a few seeds,
Convalescent.   Shiki

With feeble fingers, bending unsteadily over the ground, the
poet puts the seeds in, happy in the latent life in himself and
in what he is planting. Compare the treatment of the same
subject by Gray in his *Ode on the Pleasure arising from
Vicissitude*:

> See the wretch that long has tost,
>   On the thorny bed of pain,
> At length repair his vigour lost
>   And breathe and walk again.
> The meanest floweret of the vale,
> The simplest note that swells the gale,
> The common sun, the air, the skies,
> To him are opening Paradise.

さまづけに育てられたる蚕哉   一　茶
Samazuke ni   sodateraretaru   kaiko kana

Bringing them up,
They call the silkworms
"Mister."   Issa

Sama has a more gentle, intimate, respectful meaning than
"Mister."

All over Japan, silkworms are referred to as "O Kaiko sama"
or "O Ko sama." There is an element of gratitude in this,
since they form the entire livelihood of thousands of families.
In a humorous way, they are taken into the family itself, yet
respectfully set apart. Issa notes this "natural piety" of the
peasant, the national poetic feeling.

神棚の灯は怠らじかいこ時   蕪　村
Kamidana no   hi wa okotaraji   kaiko-doki

    Even in silk-worm time
They do not neglect
    The light of the household shrine.   Buson

    We do not live by silk-worms alone, but by our spiritual needs. Even when the young silk-worms must be fed continuously, so that everyone in the house is busy from morning to night, the candle is lit in front of the shrine, and the ancestors remembered and worshipped. The poet looks into the empty house and sees the candle burning there, a solitary flame in the dim interior, the people of the house working in the fields. Prayers are prayed though the one who prays be far away. Indeed, in its earnestness and sincerity, in its faithfulness and single-hearted zeal, the candle exceeds in its righteousness us Scribes and Pharisees.

山門を出れば日本ぞ茶摘唄   菊　舎
Sanmon wo   dereba nihon zo   chatsumi-uta

    Coming out of the temple gate,
The song of the tea-pickers:
    It is Japan!   Kikusha

    In this verse, the whole value and unique quality of Japan is contained. The poet has visited a temple of the Ōbaku branch of the Zen sect at Uji, 宇治. In the plain and slightly gloomy hall, he has heard the head priest expound the wordless doctrine. All is as it is, and it is good that it is so. Religion is not of another world, but of this eating, working, singing world,—yet we are to attain and retain a state of mind in which all these things are done without hesitation, without regret or conflict of thought and feeling. Rising at last, he passes out of the great gate of the temple and sees the fields and mountains extending before him. The voices of the women picking tea are heard, an ancient song that expresses the secret flower of the nation. Japan in its religion and poetry, its intensity and sweetness, its past living into the present,—a feeling overwhelms the poet that is love of country and something more and something deeper, for it touches the springs of human nature, and the verse is one that any man of any nation may read with unrestrained pleasure.

菅笠を着て鏡見る茶摘かな   文 考
Suge-gasa wo kite kagami miru   chatsumi kana

Tea-leaf picking:
Trying on her reed kasa,
She gazes in the mirror.   Shikō

We are reminded that women, human beings, are the same everywhere, in town or country, that picturesqueness is as much appreciated, perhaps more so, by the country people themselves. We are given, in this verse, a charming and graceful picture of a young girl before the mirror. But the touch of poetry is in the making a virtue of necessity, the desire to do everything, the commonest, most prosaic things in a beautiful way.

爐ふさぎや床は維摩に掛替る   蕪 村
Rofusagi ya toko wa yuima ni kakekaeru

Closing the fire-place,
I replace the picture in the alcove
With one of Yuima.   Buson

When the fire-place is closed over in spring, the picture in the tokonoma, the alcove, is changed. Spring has come with all its joy and activity, but we say good-bye to the fire-place, an old friend, and a slight feeling of loneliness invades our breast. For this reason he chooses a picture of Yuima, who was sick because the whole world was sick, who when he was asked concerning the meaning of things answered with silence. Buson here uses a remarkable way of conveying to us one of the many aspects of the season of spring.

動 物 BIRDS AND BEASTS

鶯や梅にとまるは昔から   鬼 貫
Uguisu ya   ume ni tomaru wa   mukashi kara

The uguisu
Has perched on the plum-tree
From ancient times.   Onitsura

In art and poetry, the uguisu and the plum-tree have always
been associated. Onitsura tries here to give us the feeling of
Keats' "immortal" bird by a plain, unornamented, "unpoetical"
statement of fact. We get a vista of birds and trees, in which
this plum-tree is all plum-trees, this uguisu all uguisu.
Onitsura's verses are often of a remarkable simplicity:

庭前に白く咲きたる椿かな
Teizen ni   shiroku sakitaru   tsubaki kana

In the garden,
The camellia blooms
Whitely.

If, however, as in the original verse, Onitsura tries to be deep
or subtle, he falls into intellectuality. Compare also:

山吹は咲かで蛙は水の底
Yamabuki wa   sakade kaeru wa   mizu no soko

The yellow-rose not blooming,
The frogs are at the bootom
Of the water.

我むかし踏みつぶしたる蝸牛かな
Ware mukashi   fumi-tsubushi-taru   kagyū kana

Long ago,
I used to tread on
These snails.

盗人の塚もむさるる夏の草
Nusubito no   tsuka mo musaruru   natsu no kusa

On the robber's grave too,
Grow rank
The grasses of summer.

白魚や目まで白魚目は黒魚
Shirauo ya   me made shirauo   me wa kurouo

> The whitefish!
> All but its eyes the whitefish,
> But those,—the "blackfish"!

盛りなる化にも絶えぬ念佛かな
Sakari naru   hana nimo taenu   nembutsu kana

> The cherry blossoms at their height,
> But the *nembutsu*[1]
> Continues unabated.

鶯のなくや小さき口あいて   蕪 村
Uguisu no   naku ya chiisaki   kuchi aite

> The uguisu is singing,
> Its small mouth
> Open.   Buson

This verse required genius to compose it; it requires genius to appreciate it for what it is, a masterpiece, but most men have this necessary genius, which is, in other words, their Buddha nature, their bird-nature.

The folllowing description of the uguisu is taken from *Japanese Birds* by Nobusuke Takatsukasa.

> This bird (the Japanese Bush-Warbler) is about the size of a sparrow, but more slim and sprightly. Its upper parts are olive brown, the brow, throat and the central part of the abdomen all dusty white. In early winter it is seen to flit from branch to branch, rather close to the ground, in a leafy hedge or in a garden shrubbery, calling, "chut, chut," as if impatient of the tardy approach of spring. When spring comes, it will bust into its melodious "ho-hoh, hokekyo..." In Japan, the bush-warbler is always associated with the plum-blossom, just as the sparrow is with the bamboo.

---

[1] Reciting the name of Buddha.

鶯 の 身 を さ か さ ま に 初 音 か な   其 角

Uguisu no   mi wo sakasama ni   hatsune kana

> Its first note;
> The uguisu
> Is upside-down.   Kikaku

Kikaku must have surveyed this verse with satisfaction, and laughed as he thought how troubled commentators would be by it. It may refer to the way the uguisu often perches, with its eager little head far below its body and tail. In any case, Kikaku wished to surprise his readers. There is a verse by Buson which may well be an imitation of this:

鶯 の 枝 ふ み は づ す 初 音 か な

Uguisu no   eda fumi hazusu   hatsune kana

> The first note of the uguisu,
> As it slipped
> Off the bough.

Kikaku's verse, however, is far superior to this, for it shows us the uguisu in a characteristic attitude. Just like Davies' description of the robin,

> That little hunchback in the snow,

we feel that we have really seen the bird for the first time. As the Impressionists painted what they actually saw, mentally undigested, not the Platonic ideas of things, so Kikaku shows us the uguisu upside-down.

鶯 の 目 利 し て な く 我 家 か な   一 茶

Uguisu no   mekikishite naku   wagaya kana

> The uguisu sings,
> Eyeing critically
> My house.   Issa

"Not much of a house, this. No one of importance lives here, to all appearances." Such is the judgement of the uguisu, who makes his appraisal of the house while he sings. This verse sounds like the pathetic fallacy; actually, however, while Issa seems to be speaking about himself, he is eyeing the bird critically, and giving us his own opinion of its nature.

There is another verse of Issa's which seems almost a continuation of the above:

時鳥俗な庵とさみするな
Hototogisu   zoku na iori to   sami suruna

Hototogisu!
Hold not in contempt
This dwelling mean and lowly.

鶯の鳴くや昨日の今時分　　　　　　　樗　良
Uguisu no   naku ya kinō no   ima-jibun

The uguisu is singing;
It was yesterday,
At this same hour.　　　　　　　Chora

Chora is perhaps the simplest of the haiku poets, corresponding to Gluck in music. The same voice, at the same time,—it gives one a feeling that not all is transitory; some things remain unchanged. Chora's verse is the pianissimo equivalent of Keats' lines:

And, happy melodist, unwearied,
For ever piping songs for ever new.

Chora is living by a stream rather away from the haunts of men, and in a bamboo thicket nearby lives an uguisu that comes at about the same hour into the garden and sings the same song.

何處やらで鶯鳴きぬ書の月　　　　　　　士　朗
Dokoyara de   uguisu nakinu   hiru no tsuki

Somewhere or other,
An uguisu sang:
The midday moon.　　　　　　　Shirō

An uguisu sings, and then is silent. Gazing vaguely round, the spring moon is seen faintly, almost transparently, in the blue sky of noon. It is mid-spring, mid-day. The voice of the uguisu comes from nowhere, from everywhere.

鶯にあてがつておく垣根かな   一 茶
Uguisu ni   ategatte oku   kakine kana

> The fence
> Shall be assigned
> To the uguisu.   Issa

Bestowing what we do not possess, commanding where we have no power, this is of the essence of poetry and of Zen.

> Think you I bear the shears of destiny?
> Have I commandment on the pulse of life?[1]

We must answer, yes, this is what manhood, Buddhahood means.

There is a similar but more intimate verse, also by Issa:

鶯の馳走に掃しかきねかな
Uguisu no   chisō ni hakishi   kakine kana

> The fence,
> Swept as a treat
> For the uguisu.

鶯にふまれて浮くや竹柄杓   鳳 朗
Uguisu ni   fumarete uku ya   take-bishaku

> Perched on by the uguisu,
> The bamboo dipper
> Still floats.   Hōrō

The drinking-water is conveyed through hollow bamboos from a spring in the hill behind the house. It falls into a tub in which a small wooden ladle stands. An uguisu perches for a moment on the handle of the ladle, which remains on the surface of the water. This is a picture for an artist rather than a poem for a poet. There is something accidental and unusual about this verse that makes the poetic feeling too diffuse. The same might be said of the verse by Kakei, given afterwards:

---

[1] *King John*, iv, 2.

暁のつるべに上る椿かな
Akatsuki no   tsurube ni agaru   tsubaki kana

> At dawn,
> Coming up in the well-bucket,
> A camellia flower.

鶯や餅に糞する椽のさき　　　　　　芭 蕉
Uguisu ya   mochi ni fun suru   en no saki

> Ah! the uguisu
> Pooped on the rice-cakes
> On the verandah.　　　　Bashō

There is a similar, and rather more "poetic" verse by Bashō's contemporary Onitsura:

鶯が梅の小枝に糞をして
Uguisu ga   ume no koeda ni   fun wo shite

> The uguisu
> Poops
> On the slender plum branch.

Things are dirty, things are clean, but it is thinking that makes it so.

> There is nothing great or small
> But the soul that maketh all.[1]

One man's meat is another man's poison. From the gardener's standpoint, dung is more precious than diamonds. There is the point of view of the man who wants to eat the rice-cakes, bt there is also the point of view of the uguisu.

Seeing sparrows make droppings on the head of a statue of Buddha, a monk, Saishō, 崔相, asked Nyoe,[2] 如會:

"Have sparrows and crows the Buddha nature?"
"They have." "Then why do they make droppings on the head of Buddha?"
"Because they can't do it on the head of the sparrow-hawk."
(鷂).

---

[1] Emerson.
[2] d. 823. A Chinese Zen monk, pupil of Baso.

Issa has a verse in which we see again how the ideas of clean-
liness and dirtiness are non-fundamental, arbitrary, dispensable:

黄鳥や泥あしぬぐふ梅の花
Uguisu ya   doroashi nuguu   ume no hana

> The uguisu
> Cleans its muddy feet
> Among the plum-blossoms.

鶯の遠音につるゝ日の出かな   楢 良
Uguisu no   tōne ni tsururu   hinode kana

> Enticed by the distant voice
> Of the uguisu,
> The sun rises.

Chora

There is the world of cause and effect, constructed by the
intellect, and there is the world as seen by the poetic mind,
given by the imagination. To the intellect, what is seen by
the poetic faculty must seem nonsensical, at best fanciful. And
even to the poet himself, what he wrote in the fire, the élan
of personal experience must appear, at times of low vitality,
doubtful, hyperbolic, self-deceiving. When Chora heard and
saw what he expresses in the above verse, when Lyly wrote of
the skylark,

> The sun not rising till she sings,

they had no doubt that this was so. What they say is not a
denial, a contradiction of what science or common-sense tells
us. They are speaking of their life in what seems another
world, because it is this world with that dimension restored to
it which the intellect must of its nature always ignore and omit.

木の股の辨當箱よ鶯よ   一 茶
Ki no mata no   bentō-bako yo   uguisu yo

> Ah! my lunch-box
> In the crotch of the tree!
> Ah! the uguisu!

Issa

This has a resemblance to *Don Juan:*

They grieved for those who perished with the cutter,
And also for the biscuit-casks and butter.

But this similarity is on the surface only. Byron takes eating
as an unpoetic thing, something to be ashamed of, whereas Issa
thinks it to be a delight of the mind-body, as interesting, as
significant as the song of the bird. There is the same feeling
in the following:

財布から焼飯出して櫻かな
Saifu kara   yakimeshi dashite   sakura kana

> Taking out from my wallet
> The toasted rice-balls,—
> The cherry-blossoms!

Another, more vague and "poetical":

飯けぶり聳る里やほとゝぎす
Meshi keburi   sobiyuru sato ya   hototogisu

> Smoke from cooking rice
> Towers above the hamlet:
> The voice of the hototogisu!

The following, by Buson, is of a different nature:

うぐひすや家内揃ふて飯時分
Uguisu ya   kanai soroute   meshi-jibun

> The uguisu is singing,
> All the family assembled
> At the meal-time.

They are all sitting decorously partaking of their food in silence,
when suddenly outside the uguisu begins to sing, and brings
something that was missing from the perfect pleasure of family
harmony in the religious atmosphere of the common meal.

鶯の鳴くやあち向きこちら向き   蕪 村
Uguisu no   nakuya achimuki   kochira muki

> An uguisu is singing,
> Turning this way,
> Turning that way.   Buson

This verse expresses the overpowering desire of the bird to sing. It turns this way and that, as if singing in one direction will not suffice, as though it wished to sing in all directions at once. No one knows what it is that makes birds sing so ceaselessly. Sexual selection and other laws are insufficient to explain this overwhelming instinct, yet we human beings who chatter night and day and in look and gesture never cease to communicate with one another, know profoundly, where we cannot explain, this mysterious urge in the uguisu. Buson has here grasped something in the bird deeper than the nature of the creature itself, for it is our own nature, not our human nature, but that nature which the uguisu shares with us, the Buddha nature.

There is another verse by Buson, with the same animation:

うぐひすのあちこちとするや小家がち
Uguisu no   achi kochi to suru ya   koie gachi

> The uguisu,
> > Flying here and there
> > > Among some small houses.

鶯や柳の後藪の前   芭 蕉
Uguisu ya   yanagi no ushiro   yabu no mae

> The uguisu!
> Behind the willow,
> Before the grove.   Bashō

The grove is still blue-green, dark with its bamboos, but the willow hangs down its long slender branches, now yellowish-green. The voice of the uguisu, a timeless, spaceless thing, hovers between the grove and the willow. The willow-tree and the bamboos give a local habitation and a name to that which is but "a wandering voice." The song of the bird gives to those that are without language (the willow and the grove) a place in the realm of sound.

This verse does not say that the uguisu is singing, but it is to be so understood. The poetical appeal of animals and birds, from earliest times, was not so much in form and colour as in sound. The insect or bird and its cry are hardly separated.

無人境うぐひす庭を歩きけり　　　　　召 波
Mujinkyō uguisu niwa wo aruki keri

> The uguisu walked
> In the garden,
> A realm uninhabited by man.　　　Shōha

The garden is deserted, the uguisu alone in it, as if in the grove. We are alternately astounded at the separateness of things, and their unity. Here it is their independent existence that is perceived,

> For each enclosed spirit is a star,
> Enlightening its own proper sphere.

Though it is but one world in which we live, each animal, each inanimate thing subsists in complete isolation.

> And once when she saw him pick up a bird that had stunned itself against a wire, she had realized another world, silent, where each creature is alone in its own aura of silence, the mystery of power.[1]

In the following waka by the Emperor Meiji, there is something of the same feeling:

春雨のふる日しづけき庭の面に
ひとりみだれてちる櫻かな

> Today spring rain is falling;
> Out in the quiet garden,
> Petals of the cherry-blossoms
> Fall and scatter by themselves.

家にあらで鶯聞かぬひと日かな　　　蕪 村
Ie ni arade uguisu kikanu hitohi kana

> Not being at home,
> The uguisu unheard
> One whole day.　　　Buson

Out of the house all day long, Buson has not heard the voice of the uguisu once. He feels as if something were lacking, as

---

[1] Lawrence, *St. Mawr.*

though insufficiently clothed, or having missed a meal, or having
been rude to someone. It is the same frame of mind which
gave birth to the following, also by Buson:

吾宿の鶯聞かん野に出でて
Waga yado no   uguisu kikan   no ni idete

>   Going out on the moor,
> I will listen
>   To our uguisu.

"Our uguisu" is "the uguisu of our house." Issa also expresses
this proprietary feeling in his own way :

來るも來るも下手鶯ぞおれが垣
Kuru mo kuru mo   heta uguisu zo   ore ga kaki

>   They come and come,
> But they are all poor singers,
>   The uguisu of my fence!

鍬の柄に鶯なくや小梅村   一 茶
Kuwa no e ni   uguisu naku ya   koume-mura

> Little-Plum-Tree Village:
> An uguisu sings,
>   Perched on the handle of the hoe.   Issa

This might well be by Buson. It is a picture of peace and
sunshine, a mid-morning scene of tranquillity in spring.

うぐいすに終日遠し畑の人   蕪 村
Uguisu ni   hinemosu tōshi   hata no hito

>   The man in the field;
> All day long
>   The uguisu were far away.   Buson

It is interesting to compare this to the following verse by
Ryōta:

鶯 の 人 な き 畑 に 遠 音 か な
Uguisu no   hito naki hata ni   tōne kana

> An empty field;
> The distant voice
> Of the uguisu.

鶯 や 茶 の 木 畑 の 朝 月 夜   丈　草
Uguisu ya   cha-no-ki-batake no   asa-zuki-yo

> The tea-plantation
> Under the moon of early dawn;
> An uguisu is singing.   Jōsō

The moon, the round, dark-green bushes of tea, the dusky stillness of dawn, and the flute-like voice of the uguisu.

鶯 に 手 も と 休 め む な が し も と   智　月
Uguisu ni   temoto yasumen   nagashimoto

> Stopping what I am doing
> At the sink:
> The voice of the uguisu!   Chigetsu

Chigetsu, who died in 1705, was the best of the poetesses of the Bashō school. In the cessation of what she is doing, peeling potatoes or washing dishes, all the energy of mind and body is poured into the voice of the bird. What the value of women is in this world I find hard to explain, but we see it in this verse, expressed so clearly, yet without any words that one could repeat.

鶯 の 鳴 け ば 何 や ら な つ か し う   鬼　貫
Uguisu no   nakeba naniyara   natsukashiu

> The uguisu sings,
> And my heart is filled
> With vague yearning.   Onitsura

The voice of the uguisu is one of those

airs and floating echoes that convey
A melancholy into all our day.

うぐひすの曲たる枝を削りけん   其 角
Uguisu no   magetaru eda wo   kezuriken

He must have whittled down
The branch
Bent by the uguisu.   Kikaku

This verse was written on a picture of an uguisu perched on
the handle of a tea-ladle. This was almost certainly bamboo,
and Kikaku means that when the maker saw the piece of
bamboo on which an uguisu was perched, bending it, he cut it
off and whittled it down for the handle of the tea-ladle.

鶯の兄弟づれや同じ聲   一 茶
Uguisu no   kyōdai zure ya   onaji koe

The uguisu,—
Are they brothers?
The same voice!   Issa

Difference and sameness, different yet the same, the same yet
different,—the whole of nature, the whole of life is contained
in these two aspects. When we cease to oppose one to the
other but simply marvel at both, then we are living our true
human, poetic, divine life.

鶯の聲遠き日も暮れにけり   無 村
Uguisu no   koe tōki hi mo   kure ni keri

All day long, the voices of the uguisu
Were far off; this day too,
Has drawn to its close.   Buson

Spengler says,

The distance-impressions made by deep landscapes, clouds,

horizon and setting sun attach themselves without an effort
to the sense of a future.

Space and time are here at one. The world stretches out and
above into the infinite distance. The moments as they pass are
of almost eternal duration; even when they are gone by, they
seem to linger still in the mountains to which the uguisu have
flown to rest.

鶯 や 御 前 へ 出 て も 同 じ 聲　　　　　一 茶
Uguisu ya　gozen e detemo　onaji koe

The uguisu!
Even before His Lordship,
That same voice!　　　　　Issa

With this may be compared Andersen's fairy-tale of *The
Nightingale* where the real bird sings to the Chinese Emperor
after the artificial bird has broken down. Keats in one of his
least inspired lines says,

The voice I hear this passing night was heard
In ancient days by emperor and clown.

Issa's verse has not the scope of the *Ode to a Nightingale;* he
is not even thinking of the eternal nightingale. His is the real,
flesh and blood creature that "mocks comparison" with lords
and ladies. Indeed, as far as it is a comparison, it is not poetry
at all. All the poetry of this verse lies in the word "same."
The difference of peers and ploughmen is not a subject for
poetry but for sociology, but the "sameness" of the voice of
the nightingale is not a logical thing; it is poetry alive in the
mind of the poet.

朝 ご と に 同 じ 雲 雀 か 屋 根 の 空　　　　丈 草
Asagoto ni　onaji hibari ka　yane no sora

Every morning
In the sky above my roof,—
Is it the same skylark?　　　　　Jōsō

The poet wishes that the bird which sings above his house

at day-break every day should somehow or other belong to him,
be his special skylark. There is something pathetic in this
weakness of mind, but also something deeply human which Jōsō
recognizes as poetic. It is for this reason that he records this
apparently trivial and superficial thought.

朝 風 や た ゞ 一 筋 に 揚 雲 雀   蓼 太
Asakaze ya   tada hito-suji ni   age-hibari

> In the morning breeze
> Rise skylarks,
>   Single-heartedly.   Ryōta

Hito-suji ni has two meanings; in a straight line, undeviat-
ingly; and earnestly, with all one's heart, intently, as if pos-
sessed. The first meaning shows the peculiar, fluttering, almost
vertical rising of the skylarks up to the clouds. The second
gives us the feeling of intensity, vehemence, whole-heartedness,
that the incessant singing of the skylark reinforces.

永 き 日 を 囀 り 足 ら ぬ 雲 雀 哉   芭 蕉
Nagaki hi wo   saezuri taranu   hibari kana

> All the long day—
> Yet not long enough for the skylark,
>   Singing, singing.   Bashō

The skylark does not sing by Trade Union rules. This is
the Zen of the skylark, seen by the child in the cow:

> The friendly cow, all red and white,
>   I love with all my heart;
> She gives me cream with all her might,
>   To eat with apple-tart.

From the white dawn that hides the stars until the purple
evening that reveals them again, the skylark is singing, singing.
Its eagerness to begin singing is expressed in Issa's verse:

藪 尻 は ま だ 闇 い ぞ よ 鳴 く 雲 雀
Yabujiri wa   mada kurai zoyo   naku hibari

> Ah, singing skylark!
> The tail-end of the grove
> Is still in darkness.

Another of Issa's with a similar meaning:

有明や雨の中より鳴く雲雀
Ariake ya ame no naku yori nuku hibari

> Day-break:
> The skylark is singing
> From the midst of the rain.

Compare *Paradiso*, xx, 73-75, to Bashō's verse:

> l'odoletta che in aere si spazia
> Prima cantando, e poi tace, contenta
> Dell' ultima dolcezza che la sazia.

> the lark that soars in air,
> First singing, then silent, content
> With the last sweetness that sates her.

子や待たんあまり雲雀の高あがり　　　杉風
Ko ya matan amari hibari no taka-agari

> Your children will be waiting,
> Skylark,
> So high in the sky!　　　Sampū

From one point of view this is a verse expressing the feelings of the young birds as they await their parent's return in the barley field. From another, the more poetic, the anxiety and danger increase the feeling of height. The skylark rises higher and higher, until its voice is alone heard, and in the thought of the young ones we feel the distance of the parent bird.

白雲の上に聲ある雲雀かな　　　許六
Shirakumo no ue ni koe aru hibari kana

> Voices
> Above the white clouds:
> Skylarks.　　　Kyoroku

This has a mysteriousness which even Shelley's *Skylark* has not attained to, a mysteriousness which the length itself of his poem forbids. It is the pure, simple mystery of space and invisibility.

隈 も な き 空 に か く る ゝ 雲 雀 か な   六　度
Kuma mo naki   sora ni kakururu   hibari kana

>   The skylark
> Hides itself
>   In the expanse of blue sky.   Rikuto

This is Wordsworth's

> Leave to the nightingale her shady wood;
> A privacy of glorious light is thine,

but without the comparison, (which is always intellectual and odious) and without the unpoetical associations of "privacy." There is the skylark, there is the blue sky, and now there is only the blue sky. Tennyson, in *In Memoriam*, cxv, 2, has two lines that are worthy of Ella Wheeler Wilcox:

> And drowned in yonder living blue,
> The lark becomes a sightless song.

原 中 や 物 に も つ か ず 鳴 く 雲 雀   芭　蕉
Haranaka ya   mono nimo tsukazu   naku hibari

>   In the midst of the plain
> Sings the skylark,
>   Free of all things.   Bashō

Bashō would never have felt the doubt that Spengler expresses:

> It is perhaps too fantastic to argue something of religious world-feeling in the song of the mounting lark.[1]

Bashō's poetic experiences were deep enough to make any doubt of their validity impossible. "I feel it to be so, therefore it is so." This argument, dangerous as it is, is the only one that

---

[1] Peoples, Races, Tongues, 1.

poets and artists can use to justify their assertions. They can
be tested and attested only by those with the same experiences.
So all poetical people know that the lark is free of all things
and expresses this world-feeling in its song.

小島にも畠打つなり鳴雲雀　　　　　一　茶
Kojima nimo　hatake utsunari　naku hibari

Even on a small island,
A man tilling the field,
　A lark singing above it.　　　　　Issa

This is also a picture of sky and sea, though they are not
mentioned in the verse. All three things are small, swallowed
up in the vast ocean of water and air.

青麥や雲雀があがるあれ下る　　　　鬼　貫
Aomugi ya　hibari ga agaru　are sagaru

The skylark rises,
The skylark falls,—
　How green the barley!　　　　Onitsura

Objectivity, when it fails, becomes only dry and lifeless;
subjectivity, when it does not attain its true condition, stinks.
Thus it is that with objective art we feel a kind of relief, a
lack of anxiety, and when it succeeds, as in the above poem,
we feel perfectly at ease, all our self resolved into the object
contemplated.

川船や雲雀啼き立つ右左　　　　　　闌　更
Kawabune ya　hibari nakitatsu　migi hidari

The river-boat;
Skylarks rising, singing,
　On the right side, on the left side.　Rankō

This has something of the simplicity and comprehensiveness
of Rupert Brooke's

Men coming and going on the earth.

What is unexplainable, what is inexpressible is the meaning of the infinitely simple fact of the skylarks' rising and falling as they sing, on this side of the boat and on that side of the boat. Not on both sides, indiscriminately and promiscuously, but on the left side *and* on the right side.

雲に波たてゝ囀る雲雀かな   晴　燕
Kumo ni nami   tatete saezuru   hibari kana

    The skylark singing
Ripples
      The clouds.   Seien

This may be compared with Shelley's

    All the earth and air
    With thy voice is loud,

where the skylark is the voice of nature, the voice of mountain, tain, river, tree and sky. In Seien's verse, the form of the bird's song is the form of the cloud. The waves of the lines of cloud are the trilling of the skylark.

耕作の野はしづまりぬ夕雲雀   希　因
Kōsaku no   no wa shizumarinu   yūhibari

    In the fields of labour,
All is still;
      Skylarks in the evening.   Kiin

The quietness and lack of movement in the fields is in wonderful harmony with the skylarks that sink lower and lower towards the darkening earth through the last rays of light. It reminds one of the hymn the children sing before they return home from school:

    Now the day is over,
    Night is drawing nigh;
    Shadows of the evening
    Steal across the sky.

聲ばかり落て跡なき雲雀かな   鞍　風
Koe bakari ochite ato naki hibari kana

The skylark:
Its voice alone fell,
Itself invisible.   Ampū

The poet has said here poetically what Shelley says prosaically,

Bird thou never wert.

The voice is bodiless. It has no source of origin. It merely
exists, sounding throughout all space.

くさめして見失ひたる雲雀かな   也　有
Kusame shite miushinaitaru hibari kana

Sneezing,
I lost sight
Of the skylark.   Yayu

Where is the poetry here? It is in the unexpressed perception
in this simple experience of how tender are the flowers of our
life. The slightest thing and our souls are delighted; the slightest
thing and we are in the depths of despair. A sneeze and the
skylark is gone for ever. There is also an expression of the
height and smallness of the skylark by the fact of its being lost
to sight so easily. And last, there is a feeling of the weakness
and pathos of man that Pascal knew.

春風にちからくらぶる雲雀かな   野　水
Harukaze ni chikara kuraburu hibari kana

The skylark
Struggles
With the spring winds.   Yasui

This describes not only the flight of the skylark, its fluttering,
"struggling" way of flying even on windless days, but indirectly,
its singing, which also has this persistently victorious sound.
Its flying and singing are so continuous that we feel it almost
as a kind of task, and in this sense understand Issa's verse:

畫めしをたべにおりたる雲雀かな
Hiru-meshi wo   tabe ni oritaru   hibari kana

The skylark
Has dropped down
For its midday meal.

雲を蹈み霞を吸ふや揚雲雀   子 規
Kumo wo fumi   kasumi wo suuya   age-hibari

Skylarks are soaring,
Treading the clouds,
Breathing the haze.   Shiki

The very language Shiki uses shows that it is the poet, not
the skylark, that is mounting on the clouds, inhaling the mist,
rising ever higher and higher. Sōshi says:

孰能相與於無相與、相爲於無相爲。孰能登天遊霧、

撓挑無極、相忘以生、無所終窮。   （莊子、六）

Who can live in the world, yet not live in it, act without
acting? Who can mount up to heaven, and sport upon the
fleecy clouds, soaring endlessly, living unconscious of self,
throughout all eternity?

There is only one answer to this,—the poet.

橫乘の馬のつゞくや夕雲雀   一 茶
Yokonori no   uma no tsuzuku ya   yū-hibari

Their riders sitting sideways,
One horse after another,—
Skylarks in the evening.   Issa

One of the marks of a poet is the seizing, by intuition (or
rather, by following the intuition which all have, but only a
poet follows) the connection between apparently unrelated things,
—here, the connection between the skylarks, and sitting side-
ways on the horses, and evening.

Three or four horses walk slowly homeward, one behind the
other, their drivers sitting sideways on them. In the level rays

of the evening sun, the skylarks are falling towards the earth, their song taking on a more plaintive sound.

雲雀 な く 中 の 拍子 や 雉子 の 聲   芭 蕉
Hibari naku   naka no hyōshi ya   kiji no koe

Through the skylark's singing
Comes the beat
Of pheasants' cries.   Bashō

This natural orchestra reminds us of Beethoven's Sixth Symphony, but there is something deeper in it. The skylark and the pheasant are

Bound each to each
In natural piety,

and Wordsworth has a line in *Resolution and Independence* which resembles Bashō's verse:

Over his own sweet voice the Stock-dove broods;
The Jay makes answer as the Magpie chatters;
And all the air is filled with pleasant noise of waters.

Issa has a similar verse, but the season is autumn, and it is with a sound of human origin that the notes of the bird are blended:

梟 が 拍子 と る な り 小夜 き ぬ た
Fukurō ga   hyōshi toru nari   sayo kinuta

The owl beats time
For the fulling-block,
At midnight.

The same applies to the following verse by Shiki, in which a certain comical element is blended.

蟬 な く や 行水 時 の 豆腐 賣
Semi naku ya   gyōzui-doki no   tōfu-uri

A cicada is crying;
While having an open-air bath,
The call of the bean-curd vendor.

Again in the following, also by Shiki:

山寺や畫寝のいびき時鳥
Yamadera ya   hirune no ibiki   hototogisu

A mountain temple;
Snores from mid-day naps,
The voice of the hototogisu.

父母のしきりに戀し雉子の聲   芭 蕉
Chichi-haha no   shikiri ni koishi   kiji no koe

The voice of the pheasant;
How I longed
For my dead parents!   Bashō

Modern Christianity is not entirely without blame in the
matter of the decrease of respect and affection for parents. The
words of Christ are certainly strong,

If any man come to me and hate not his father and
mother . . .

but it is equally to be remembered that he who loves not his
parents whom he has seen, how shall he love God whom he
has not seen! The same is true of parents to children, and
Bashō rightly says,

子に飽くと申す人には花もなし
Ko ni aku to   mōsu hito ni wa   hana mo nashi

The man who says,
"My children are a burden,"—
There are no flowers for him.

Bashō's verse has the prescript "At Takano." In this place
also, the poet Gyōgi Bosatsu[1] wrote the following:

山鳥のほろほろとなく聲きけば
父かとぞ思ふ母かとぞ思ふ

When I hear
The copper pheasant
Crying *horo horo*,—
"Is it my father?" I wonder,
"Is it my mother?"

[1] 670–749. A Korean priest who came to Japan and taught that the
Shintō gods were manifestations of Buddha.

美しき顔掻く雉子の距哉　　　　　　其　角
Utsukushiki   kao kaku kiji no   kezume kana

> The pheasant scratches
> Its beautiful face
> With its spurs.　　　　　　Kikaku

This verse is a picture, but not a mere still-life. The spurs
bring something dynamic, something of dramatic contrast and
affinity with the serpent-like head.

山里や屋根へ來て啼く雉子の聲　　　　樗　良
Yamazato ya   yane e kite naku   kiji no koe

> A mountain village;
> Alighting on the roof,
> A pheasant screeches.　　　　　　Chora

The line between poetry and ordinariness is a fine but distinct
one. In the above verse, as a mere picture, there is little to
arrest our attention. The point of the poem is in the sensation
of being in

> a quiet place
> That's green, away from all mankind,[1]

aroused by the strange, unmelodious call of the pheasant on the
roof above. Just in that cry, at that time, in that place, lies
the poetry, and only another poet can bear witness to its poetry.

日くるゝに雉子うつ春の山邊かな　　　蕪　村
Hikururu ni   kiji utsu haru no   yamabe kana

> As day darkens,
> The shooting of a pheasant,
> Near the spring mountain.　　　　　　Buson

Buson had a remarkable interest in the pheasant, and wrote
a large number of verses on it. Here, Buson felt at the sound
of the shot some peculiarly deep harmony between the spring

[1] Davies, *The Kingfisher*.

evening, the slopes of the mountain, and the pheasant. No
doubt other pheasants had been shot during the day, but it is
only now, in this particular place, at this time, that the full
meaning which is non-moral and non-humanitarian, comes out.
Another, more difficult verse on the pheasant:

龜 山 へ 通 ふ 大 工 や 雉 子 の 聲
Kameyama e   kayou daiku ya   kiji no koe

A carpenter
Going to Kameyama;
The cry of the pheasant.

"Kayou" implies going and coming several times. Kameyama
is a castle-town in Tamba near Kyōto, to which the carpenter
is going. What is the connection between this and the cry of
the pheasant? Was there something in the harsh clearness of
the pheasant's voice which seemed akin to the active walk and
preciseness of the carpenter? Is there a similar relation in the
following?

む く と 起 て 雉 子 追 ふ 犬 や 宝 寺
Muku to okite   kiji ou inu ya   takaradera

A dog suddenly sprang up,
And chased away a pheasant,
At Takaradera.

Takaradera is the name of a temple in Yamazaki, near Kyōto.
It was founded in 728 A.D., and is a temple of the Shingon Sect.
    The dog and the pheasant are in perfect "harmony"; but
what of the temple? This was one built on the hill-side, and
was a likely place for pheasants to come down.

雉 子 打 つ て 歸 る 家 路 の 日 は 高 し   蕪 村
Kiji utte   kaeru ieji no   hi wa takashi

On the way back home
After shooting a pheasant,—
The sun still high.   Buson

Buddhism can find no pleasure in this verse, though there is
poetry in it. The poet has gone out killing things and manages,
to his great joy, to shoot a pheasant. He slings it over his

shoulder and walks proudly home. It is early afternoon and
the sun is still high in the sky. He has not taken all day to
secure his booty but is back long before nightfall. The pride
of the successful hunter is augmented by this fact, and some-
where in this elation moves that secret life which is the soul
of poetry. It is nothing, it is only an accident, it is even an
unnecessary taking of life and the destruction of beauty, but *all
the same*, (in this "all the same," is the secret of the mystery)
there is an invincible joy and glow of life which is unmistakable.

美しき男もちたる雉子かな　　　　　　太　祇
Utsukushiki   otoko mochitaru   kigisu kana

The pheasant,—
She has indeed
A handsome lover!　　　　　　　　Taigi

The male pheasant, even more than in the case of other birds,
is a beautiful creature. This verse has a light and bantering
tone, characteristic of Taigi and Kikaku, which is refreshing.
Haiku might well endeavour to absorb into itself the virtues and
courage of senryu.

廣き野をたゞ一のみや雉子の聲　　　　野　明
Hiroki no wo   tada hito-nomi ya   kiji no koe

In one single cry,
The pheasant has swallowed
The broad field.　　　　　　　　Yamei

For a moment, in the shrill cry of the pheasant, Yamei *hears*
the fields. The stream, the distant hills, the sky are all swal-
lowed up in the bird's harsh voice. We can find parallel experi-
ences recorded in the Old Testament, or in music, for example,
the final 'hallelujah' of the *Messiah*, in the final syllable of
which the whole universe is engulfed.

Translating literally, we get:

Broad fields,
Only one gulp,
Pheasant's voice.

雉子なくや見かけた山のあるやうに　　一　茶
Kiji naku ya　mikaketa yama no　aru yō ni

> A pheasant cries,
> As if it had noticed
> A mountain.　　　　　　　　Issa

This verse is difficult because of its simplicity and subtlety.
A pheasant suddenly cries out, in such a "tone of voice" that
it seems to Issa to denote recognition, satisfaction, a kind of
"Well, here we are at last!" Issa is struggling to express his
most remote impression of the nature of the pheasant and
its voice.

古き戸に影うつり行く燕かな　　　　召　波
Furuki to ni　kage utsuriyuku　tsubame kana

> As the swallow flies to and fro,
> Its shadow is cast
> Upon the old door.　　　　　Shōha

The most important thing here is not the swallow, but the
door. What is perceived is the sublime indifference of the door,
intensified by its age; but when this is *said*, not only this fact
disappears but the swallow and its shadow and the old door too.
What is seen with the eye is seen; what is seen with the
poetical eye is "overseen," all the life which springs from the
dead material of bird and door.

大津繪に糞落しゆく燕かな　　　　蕪　村
Ōtsu-e ni　fun otoshi-yuku　tsubame kana

> The swallow makes a dropping
> On the Ōtsu picture,
> And flies off.　　　　　　Buson

This kind of picture,[1] at first of Buddha, was a crude sketch,
cheap enough to be bought by poor people, but having some
rustic flavour pleasing to eyes jaded with over-refinement and

---

[1] Originating in the 17th century.

sophistication. Some were of dancing-girls, some of demons with glowing eyes intoning the *nenbutsu*, some of the catfish and gourd. These were spread out by the roadside in the outskirts of the town to catch the eye of the country people going back to their villages. Upon such daubs, the droppings of the swallow are a matter of small concern. There is a somewhat similar verse, also by Buson:

かきつばたべたりと鳶のたれてける
Kakitsubata   betari to tobi no   taretekeru

> The kite's droppings
> Stuck
> On the irises

But this is purely a coloured picture of green, purple and white, all things being used impartially and without prejudice, as colours of his palette.

簾に入つて美人に馴るゝ燕かな   嵐 雪
Ren ni itte   bijin ni naruru   tsubame kana

> Flying in by the bamboo-blind,
> The swallow is tame
> With the beautiful girl.   Ransetsu

One beautiful thing is enough, but here there are two. This reminds us of Davies:

> A rainbow and a cuckoo's song
> May never come together again;
> May never come
> This side the tomb.

But in the Japanese poem there is still another beautiful thing, the idyllic, fairy-tale relation between the girl and the bird.

ふためいて金の間を出る燕かな   蕪 村
Futameite   kin no ma wo deru   tsubame kana

> Agitatedly,
> The swallow flies out
> Of the chamber of gold.   Buson

Somehow or other the swallow makes a mistake and enters the room. Fluttering about for a moment, it darts out of the room and resumes its former course. Against the glowing gold sliding-screens, the black and white of the clear-cut figure of the swallow stands out boldly.

Such moments are moments of life for the poet who can snatch them from time; when the swallow disappears there is no sense of loss, no wish for it back again, only the afterglow of the life that was lived between poet and bird, a life that is one of colour and form as well as animate existence.

藏並ぶ裏は燕のかよひ道   凡 兆
Kura narabu   ura wa tsubame no   kayoi michi

Behind a line of warehouses,
Where the swallows
          Fly up and down.   Bonchō

There is a contrast here of movement and motionlessness, lightness and weight, openness and secrecy, nature and man. In the level rays of the late afternoon sun the swallows slant and fleet in the same yet different flight behind the black and white, solid warehouses that stand in line along the road. The poetic point lies in the word "behind." Their life, like our own lives, is lived in a realm that is known, yet unknown; it is in the shade, in the dark, though it may be daylight; it is "behind" us.

燕や何を忘れて中がへり   乙 由
Tsubakuro ya   nani wo wasurete   chūgaeri

The swallow
Turns a somersault;
          What has it forgotten?   Otsuyū

This describes the flight of the swallow, its peculiar manner of suddenly turning round and returning. The humour and fancifulness aptly express that of its movements. There is a similar verse of the dragon-fly by Akinobō:

遠山やとんぼついゆきついかへる
Tō-yama ya   tombo tsui yuki   tsui kaeru

The dragon-fly,
Swift to the distant mountain,
Swift to return.

This also uses humour through which to express the nature of
the creature. Or is it rather that the essential nature of these
things, and all things, is humorous?

大佛の鼻から出たる乙鳥かな   一 茶
Daibutsu no   hana kara detaru   tsubame kana

A swallow
Flew out of the nose
Of the Great Buddha.   Issa

This great statue of Buddha will be the one at Nara, or at
Kamakura.

From the ordinary, relative point of view, we have a contrast
between the sacred and the profane in the swallow's flying out
of the nose of the Buddhist image. From the absolute point of
view, it is all the same whether the swallow flies out from the
Holy Nose of Buddha or from the eaves of a public house.
But the region of this poem is in neither the relative nor the
absolute. It is in life itself, life which is neither law nor destiny
but both. If, leaving this meaningless abstract talk, we recon-
struct the poetical experience of Issa, we get the same thing,
only expressed in more understandable terms. Issa felt the
rightness of the swallow's flying wherever its wings would carry
it, yet recognized that the image was more than a mere mass
of metal. Above all, he felt there was a significance in this
clash between law and freedom, a significance which dries up
into words when it is explained.

Another verse by Issa, belonging to the winter season, which
also illustrates his fusion of contraries, is the following:

野佛の鼻の先から氷柱かな
Nobotoke no   hana no saki kara   tsurara kana

From the end of the nose
Of the Buddha on the moor,
Hang icicles.

燕啼いて蛇をうつ小家かな   蕪 村
Tsubakurame   naite ja wo utsu   koie kana

>   The swallows twitter at night;
> People of the cottage
>   Are striking at the snake.   Buson

A snake has crawled near the nest of the swallows, in which there are eggs or young ones. The parent birds fly out with a loud twittering, and flutter agitatedly round the eaves. The people of the house come out with a lantern and staves, and are striking at the snake as it writhes along the eaves trying to escape.

夕燕我には翌日のあてもなし   一 茶
Yūtsubame   ware ni wa asu no   ate mo nashi

>   Ah, evening swallow!
> My heart is full of fears
>   For the morrow.   Issa

This has in it perhaps something of Burns'

>   How can ye chant, ye little birds,
>   And I so fu' o' care?

It is Keats'

>   'Tis not through envy of thy happy lot,
>   But being too happy in thine happiness.

夜通しに何を歸雁のいそぎかな   浪 化
Yodōshi ni   nani wo kigan no   isogi kana

>   Why should the returning
> Wild geese hasten,
>   All through the night?   Rōka

This expresses the mystery of the will to live, to exist, that all animate and inanimate things have, and which they can never lose. There is no answer to the question, which is not a question, but a kind of yearning of the mind with the geese

as with outstretched neck and eager wings they pass invisible
through the sky of night.   The form of this verse has a deep
meaning; as Spengler says,

Infinitely more important than the answers are the *ques-
tions*, the choice of them, the inner form of them.[1]

順禮にうちまじり行く歸雁かな   嵐　雪
Junroi ni   uchima,iri-yuku   kigan kana

The returning wild geese
Mingle
With the pilgrims.   Ransetsu

The deep pathos of the pilgrims is perceived when the wild
geese fly above them and their lines seem to blend and join with
those of the pilgrims as they wend their way over the moor.
It may be that even the discordant cries of the wild geese are
blended with the inharmonious chanting of the pilgrims.   Life
is a journey for all creatures, and there is an unspoken because
unspeakable realization of the fact, a fact that lies so deep in
the nature of things that the geese and the pilgrims are uncon-
scious of it, and of each other.   Only the poet, momentarily,
sees them as God always sees them, travelling onward together to

That one far-off divine event
To which the whole creation moves.

歸る雁田毎の月の曇る夜に   蕪　村
Kaeru kari   tagoto no tsuki no   kumoru yo ni

Wild geese returning,
On a night when in every rice-field
The moon is clouding.   Buson

The poetry of this verse, in the sound and rhythm of the
original, and its meaning, is that of waka rather than haiku.
The poetic point is less intense, more diffuse.   It is a verse of
particular things,—this night, the forms of the geese in the

[1] Buddhism, Stoicism, Socialism, VI.

heavens and their cries, the moon and the bright clouds in the
rice-fields on the slopes of Ubasute Yama in Shinshu,—yet the
feeling is of the vaster movements of nature, above all joy and
sadness, beyond all thought and intellection.

雁行きて門田の遠く思はるゝ　　　　　蕪　村
Kari yukite　kadota no tōku　omowaruru

The wild geese having gone,
The rice-field before the house
Seems far away.　　　　　　　Buson

This haiku is difficult from the delicacy and faintness of the
feeling described. The wild geese have left the field before the
gate and flown away to northern climes, and in some way or
other, the fields in which they lived have also changed their
character. Something, some virtue seems to have gone out of
them, and not only so, but the poet himself in some sense has
flown away with the geese.

今日からは日本の雁ぞ樂に寢　　　　　一　茶
Kyō kara wa　nihon no kari zo　raku ni ine

From today onwards
You are geese of Japan;
Sleép in peace.　　　　　　　Issa

Issa loves his country because he loves it, the blind prejudice
for the place one is born in, but in addition he loves it because
it loves the wild geese and will not harm them. We love God,

We love him because he first loved us.

Or as Dante says,

Amor, che a nullo amato amar perdona;[1]

this is the love which Issa feels for that which loves, for to
love is everything, to be loved is nothing.

[1] *Inferno*, V, 105.

きのふ去にけふ去に雁のなき夜哉　　蕪 村
Kinō ini   kyō ini kari no   naki yo kana

Last night departing,
Today also, wild geese departing,—
None tonight.　　　Buson

The grief we feel at such things is faint, but deep. It is a melancholy that cannot be expressed in words. We hear in the voices and the silence of the wild geese those thoughts which the ancients had and never recorded, the feelings which generations of men that come after us will realize that we too shared.

山鳥の尾を踏む春の入日かな　　蕪 村
Yamadori no   o wo fumu haru no   irihi kana

The setting sun
Treads on the tail
Of the copper pheasant.　　　Buson

Such a word as "tread" is usually called a figure of speech, as though it were a different way of saying the same thing. Actually it is a way of saying a different thing. We say that "treads" means "shines," but it does not; no word means what another means. "Treads" means "treads," and just as in the tea-ceremony the tea-master *walks as if he were not walking*, in and out of the room, so the sun treads as if it were not treading, on the tail of the pheasant.

There are two forms of the function of the imagination, which we may call, with no invidious distinction, the passive and the active. The passive form, most common in haiku, is that in which the nature of a thing is perceived by removing all obstacles in oneself to its perception. All prejudices, all relations of profit and loss, good and bad, beautiful and ugly, are discarded, and the thing lives and moves and has its being in us. In its active form, that of Keats and Shakespeare, for example, and of the present verse, the poet enters into the object and reinforces its life with his own. This is more difficult, but also more dangerous, because it may lead to falsity, to unnaturalness, to the "literary" poem, to mere playing with words devoid of real connotation.

The expression "treading on the tail of the copper pheasant" is to some extent a literary convention, but through it Buson is trying to express his peculiar feeling of what the setting sun meant to him. Other verses of his on the same subject are the following:

海越えて霞の網へ入る日かな
Umi koete   kasumi no ami e   iru hi kana

> Crossing the sea,
> The setting sun
> In the net of the mist.

紅梅や入日の襲ふ松かしは
Kōbai ya   irihi no osou   matsu kashiwa

> The red plum-blossoms;
> The setting sun reddens[1]
> Pine and oak.

麻かれと夕日此頃斜なる
Asa kare to   yūhi konogoro   naname naru

> Cut the hemp-plants!
> The setting sun
> Slants recently.[2]

若竹や夕日の嵯峨となりにけり
Waka-take ya   yūhi no saga to   nari ni keri

> Young bamboos;
> Now it is Saga,
> At sunset.[3]

---

[1] Literally "attacks." The pine-trees and oak-trees are above the plum-trees, and receive the last rays of the sun.

[2] It is drawing on towards winter, and the sun sets early recently.

[3] This is the time and place when the bamboos are seen at their most poetic. Gazing at the bamboos, we see Saga under its deepest aspect.

掃きだめへ鶴が下りけり和歌の浦   一 茶
Hakidame e tsuru ga orikeri   waka no ura

Waka-no-Ura:
The crane alighted
On a rubbish heap.   Issa

Here Issa has taken a proverbial expression, "hakidame ni
tsuru," which corresponds to "a jewel in a dunghill," and rean-
imated it by making the scene of it Waka-no-Ura, one of the
most beautiful places in Japan. It is perhaps more perverse
than profound, but illustrates Issa's *weltanschauung*, and love
of the whole truth. If he could have made us see the significance
of the rubbish heap, this would have been a great poem.

食堂に雀鳴くなり夕時雨   支 考
Shokudō ni suzume naku nari   yūshigure

At the refectory,
Sparrows are chirping
In the evening rain.   Shikō

Sparrows have an obvious but not unpoetical connection with
eating, and the evening rain of early winter somehow softens
and deepens that relation.
(It should be noted that the season for *young* sparrows is
spring. Mature sparrows have no particular season, though
autumn would be suitable. Here all the sparrow verses are put
together.)

ぬれ足で雀のありく廊下かな   子 規
Nureashi de suzume no ariku   rōka kana

The sparrow hops
Along the verandah,
With wet feet.   Shiki

This might be taken as a model for all haiku. It is poetical
and yet extremely matter-of-fact. It is like one of those perfect
jokes, so simple, so inexplicable. The delicate three-pronged

little marks on the floor of the verandah, so soon to dry up and
vanish for ever, as transitory as the pyramids or the solar
system,—what an infinity of meaning in them!

落ちてなく子に聲かはす雀かな   太 祇
Ochite naku   ko ni koe kawasu   suzume kana

The chirps of the fallen fledgeling
Mingle with the chirping
Of the mother-sparrow.   Taigi

This verse could easily fall into sentimentality. If saved from
it, it is by the "exchange" of the cries of mother and child.
The young one cannot return to the nest; the mother is afraid
to leave it. What can we do? What God does, look on or look
away in silence.

稲すゞめ茶の木畠や逃げどころ   芭 蕉
Ina-suzume   cha-no-ki-batake ya   nige-dokoro

Rice-field sparrows;
The tea-plantation
Is their haven of refuge.   Bashō

Like the churches of Europe or the temples of Japan, the
tea-plantations are places of refuge, sanctuaries which the man-
hunters and sparrow-hunters will not enter. This verse is a
simple expression of Bashō's spontaneous feelings. It does not
derive from any Buddhistic theory of life or abstract love of
animals. It illustrates Thoreau's remark;

> Very few men can speak of Nature with any truth. They
> overstep her modesty somehow or other, and confer no
> favor.

茶 の 花 に 隠 ん ぼ す る 雀 哉 　　　　　一　茶
Cha no hana ni　kakurenbo suru　suzume kana

> The sparrows
> Are playing hide-and-seek
> Among the tea-flowers. 　　　Issa

What is noteworthy here is what establishes the spontaneity and genuineness of the experience, namely, the perfect appropriateness and congruity of the parts. The sudden movements exactly resemble someone jumping into a hiding place. The tea-bushes, low, small, round, compact, impenetrable, are ideal for hide-and-seek. The yellowish white flowers against the dark green of the leaves give a sober touch of colouring that does not overwhelm the sad-suited sparrows. (The season here is really winter, that of tea-flowers).

There are two other verses by Issa which, though weaker, have the same congruity of circumstance:

猫 の 子 の か く れ ん ぼ す る 萩 の 花
Neko no ko no　kakurenbo suru　hagi no hana

> The kitten
> Is playing hide-and-seek
> Among the flowers of the lespedeza.

草 の 葉 に か く れ ん ぼ す る 蛙 哉
Kusa no ha ni　kakurenbo suru　kawazu kana

> Among the leaves of grass,
> The frogs
> Are playing hide-and-seek.

雀 子 や 明 り 障 子 の 笹 の 影 　　　　　其　角
Suzume-go ya　akari-shōji no　sasa no kage

> On the paper window,
> The shadows of the dwarf bamboos;
> Sparrows are chirping. 　　　Kikaku

If we say any more than this, if we say that the shadows of the leaves on the white paper are in sight what the chirping of the sparrows is in sound,—we have said too much.

人 に 逃 げ 人 に 馴 る ゝ や 雀 の 子　　　　鬼 貫

Hito ni nige   hito ni naruru ya   suzume no ko

> Now making friends,
> Now scared of people,—
> The baby sparrow.　　　　Onitsura

Two deep-seated instincts, fear of man and desire of his society, struggle in the young sparrow's breast. Such a dilemma requires a Buddha to solve it by years of painful meditation. In Thomson's *Winter* there is a similar picture of the robin, warmer, and more tender:

> then hopping o'er the floor,
> Eyes all the smiling family askance,
> And pecks and starts and wonders where he is.

雀 子 と 聲 な き か わ す ね づ み の 巣　　　　芭 蕉

Suzume-go to   koe nakikawasu   nezumi no su

> Mice in their nest
> Squeak in response
> To the young sparrows.　　　　Bashō

The young mice in the ceiling and the young sparrows under the eaves are both chirping. These so different forms of life have the same pathos and faint humour of all incomplete things. Bashō, like Wordsworth, is saying,

> I have heard the call
> Ye to each other make.

我 と 來 て 遊 べ や 親 の な い 雀　　　　一 茶

Ware to kite   asobe ya oya no   nai suzume

> Come and play with me,
> Fatherless, motherless
> Sparrow.　　　　Issa

Issa's mother died when he was three. Issa was an orphan; the parent sparrows had long ago flown away and left it alone in the world. But over and above this is the fact that all things animate and' inanimate are alone, are orphaned in the very fact of coming into existence, of being finite. Nevertheless, since

> Some strange comfort every state attends,

in another sense, everything is our mother and father, every-thing "loves" us. Thus it is that

> not a sparrow can fall to the ground but your Heavenly Father knoweth it.

This fact also is included in, "Come and play with me." These two opposing forces in the world, love and hate, unity and separateness, when they come together and where they come together, are the primordial stuff of existence.

雀 の 子 そ こ の け そ こ の け お 馬 が 通 る   一　茶
Suzume no ko   soko noke soko noke   o-uma ga tōru

> Little sparrow,
> Mind, mind out of the way,
> Mr. Horse is coming.   Issa

Between tenderness and sentimentality, as between heaven and hell, the gulf is narrow but unfathomable. Sentimentality means having more tenderness about a thing than God has. God has infinite tenderness for everything, but for the small and weak, a little more. Stevenson says,

> He loves to be little, he hates to be big.

With Issa also, animals and children drew out the best in him. People often got on his nerves. He looked at them as bitterly sometimes as Pope or Swift. But with animals and children, all his egoism disappears; he is materialized (to use a spiritualistic term) into the fly or louse or infant that he is beholding. A young sparrow is hopping about the road, so intent on what it is pecking that it is unaware of the great equine monster ap-proaching. Anyone would say what Issa says here. But what distinguishes Issa from us, is that in him the dull weight of personality, of self, is gone.

If a sparrow come before my window, I take part in its existence, and peck about the gravel.

This is stated unselfconsciously, with no attachment to the idea of the oneness of things:

一亦莫守。（信心銘）
Be not attached to the One, either.

大ぜいの子に疲れたる雀哉 　　　　　　一 茶
Ōzei no　ko ni tsukaretaru　suzume kana

An exhausted sparrow
In the midst
Of a crowd of children. 　　　　　　Issa

How shall we look at such a scene? With pity for the helpless bird, with loathing for the children, or with indifference to both? It must be with pain, but as at the birth pangs of a mother. Such things must be, not as exceptions that our eyes can be closed to, but as the rule of the universe where change, birth, suffering and death make possible the values that compensate for them,—compassion and courage. This scene of the intent children and the sparrow weary unto death is one that must be seen with a feeling of grief, but a grief to which the only alternative is suicide, spiritual or physical.

夕顔の花踏む盲すゞめかな 　　　　　　暁 臺
Yūgao no　hana fumu mekura　suzume kana

The blind sparrow
Hops on the flower
Of the evening-glory. 　　　　　　Gyōdai

The season of this verse is summer, that of the *yūgao*. This at first sight will appear to some as sentimental, to others as repulsive, but there is a way of understanding it which is neither of these almost identical attitudes.

In his garden, the poet has often noticed a certain sparrow different in movement and behaviour from the rest; it is blind.

This particular evening, it comes again with the rest, and as it moves here and there, hesitating, uncertain and blundering, it pops onto the just-opened flower of the evening glory. In this simple action there is a deep meaning, which is not that of pathos or aversion. In fact, the whole point lies in not allowing one's thoughts and feelings about the blind sparrow to have anything to do with it. Let it tread on the flower, tread on the flower yourself, not in spite, not in perversity, not as a sensual experience, not with pity, not in indifference. Then how are we to tread on it? As the blind sparrow treads on it.

雀子やお竹如來の流しもと　　　　　　　　一 茶
Suzumego ya   otake-nyorai no   nagashimoto

Baby sparrow,—
The servant-Buddha,
Under the sink.　　　　　　　　　　　Issa

A certain man in Edo in the Bunroku (some say Kan-ei) Era, had a model servant named O-Take. In particular, she never wasted or threw away a single grain of rice but ate it herself. It was said that an aura surrounded her, and that she was an incarnation of Dainichi Nyorai of Haguro Yama. After her death, her master had a plank of the sink she worked at consecrated at Zōjōji Temple. She became the subject of many senryu, for example:

お竹の尻をたたいたらくわんと鳴り
Otake no shiri wo   tataitara   kwan to nari

Smack O-Take's bottom,
And "Clang!"
It will sound.

That is, she was a kind of Buddhist image, which are usually made of metal.

The little sparrow pecking up the grains of rice that fall under the sink is like O-Take. She how, without any philosophising or pantheism or mysticism, Issa connects in the tender part of the mind, Dainichi Nyorai, the famous O-Take, and the baby sparrow, so lightly that we are quite unaware of it.

善光寺へ行つて來た貌や雀の子　　　　　　　一　茶
Zenkōji e itte kita kao ya suzume no ko

    The sparrows
Look as if back from a pilgrimage
    To Zenkōji.　　　　　　　　　　　Issa

Zenkōji is one of the most famous Buddhist temples in Japan.
It is at Nagano. Dedicated to Amida, Kwannon and Daiseishi,
it was founded in 670 A.D. Every good man and woman is
expected to go there once in a life-time.

The young sparrows look so cheerfully complacent, so stim-
ulated, so renewed in spirit that Issa says that look as if they
have been to Zenkōji Temple. Several other haiku of Issa repeat
this idea:

雀子も梅に口明く念佛哉
Suzumego mo ume ni kuchi aku nenbutsu kana

    The young sparrows too,
Opening their mouths at the plum-blossoms,—
    It is the Nenbutsu.

雀子も朝開帳の間にあひぬ
Suzumego mo asa kaichō no ma ni ainu

    At the morning exhibition
Of the Buddhist image,
    The sparrows also are in time.

開帳に逢ふや雀も親子連
Kaichō ni au ya suzume mo oyako-zure

    At the exhibition of the image,
Parent sparrows,
    And their children also.

Issa includes the sparrows, especially the young ones, in his
own religious life. To worship the Buddha as sincerely, as
wholeheartedly as a young sparrow, is difficult indeed.

雀子や羽ありたけのうれし貌   赤 羽
Suzumego ya   hane aritake no   ureshi-gao

The young sparrow
Manifests happiness
In all its wings.   Sekiu

There is here a simple expression of a simple thing, infant
joy, the youthful feeling of power, not tyrannical but self-guiding
and self-propelling, similar to that when we have just learnt to
swim or to ride a bicycle, or put on long trousers. The young
sparrow enjoys the wings with which it flies; every feather is
a separate pleasure.

竹にいざ梅にいざとや親すゞめ   一 茶
Take ni iza   ume ni iza to ya   oya-suzume

"Well now, let's be off to the bamboos,
To the plum-tree!"
The mother sparrow.   Issa

Issa, not knowing, but instinctively realizing the love of a
mother, bestows on small creatures that love. From one point
of view the above verse is subjective, expressing through the
mother sparrow, humanized, the love that Issa always desired
but never received. From another, it is objective, describing
the concern and solicitude of the parent bird. Which is it in
reality? Muro Kyusō, 1658–1734, says:

If our hearts are true, we can feel the spirit of the
universe.

In other words, the depth of Issa's own experience enabled him
to see with unsentimental tenderness and truth, the spirit of
the mother sparrow. The love of the mother bird is a weak
attempt, the best a sparrow can do, at the love of God, and it
finds its life and its expression in the poetical activity of Issa.
But the sparrow is necessary too; it is essential, for without it
Issa is also dumb and blank.

Buson has a similar verse:

飛かはすやたけ心や親すゞめ
Tobikawasu   yatake-gokoro ya   oyasuzume

> Hopping back and forth,
> Uneasy and fretful,
> The parent sparrows.

Shiki has several verses on this subject, for example:

垣に來て雀親呼ぶ聲せはし
Kaki ni kite   suzume oya yobu   koe sewashi

> Coming to the fence,
> The mother sparrow calls
> With insistent voice.

慈悲すれば糞をする也雀の子   一 茶
Jihi sureba   fun wo suru nari   suzume no ko

> If you are tender to them,
> The young sparrows
> Will poop on you.

         Issa

Issa's attitude is that of a mother to her baby, who finds nothing dirty or ungrateful in the urine and excretion of her child; rather, there is something mildly humorous, slightly exciting in it.

寝て起きて大欠して猫の戀   一 茶
Nete okite   ō-akubi shite   neko no koi

> Having slept, the cat gets up,
> And with great yawns,
> Goes love-making.

         Issa

Sleeping or waking or yawning or making love, the cat is in earnest, without pretence, without romance, the same in old age as in youth.

> Still is that fur as soft as when the list
> In youth thou enter'dst on glass-bottled wall.[1]

[1] Keats, *Sonnet to a Cat*.

In the strange subject of the Loves of the Cats, haiku shows
some of its non-poetical, humorous origins.

鬢につく飯さへ思へず猫の戀   太 祇
Hige ni tsuku meshi sae omoezu neko no koi

Loves of the cat;
Forgetful even of the rice
Sticking on his whiskers   Taigi

"Bin," in the original, means, not "whiskers," but the side-
locks, the hair on both sides of the head. How is poetry to deal
with life in the raw, dreadful in its blind urge towards the
unknown and unknowable? The most astounding thing about
life, the tragic movement of the blood in its cosmic beat towards
its destiny, is that it has its lighter side. God is love; but God
has bits of rice sticking on his whiskers.

おそろしや石垣崩す猫の戀   子 規
Osoroshi ya ishigaki kuzusu neko no koi

How awful!
They have broken the stone wall,—
Cats in love!   Shiki

The Zen of the cats is held up for our admiration. They can
remove mountains. They can batter down stone walls. They
are able to do such shocking things, because they are in a state
of enlightenment.

鳴猫に赤ン目をして手まり哉   一 茶
Naku neko ni akamme wo shite temari kana

The little girl playing ball,
Now makes a face
At the mewing kitten.   Issa

What is translated "makes a face" is literally "makes a red
eye," by pulling down the lower eyelid, to express derision.

The little girl has been playing with the kitten but has tired
of it and begins to play ball. The kitten, feeling neglected,
begins to mew disconsolately and tries to touch the ball as it
bounces on the ground. The little girl makes a face at the
kitten and goes on with her play. The Zen of this is in the
little girl's attitude to the kitten. She treats it entirely as
another human being, another child; it is not one of the "lower
animals." She, and Issa with her, is in that state

> where there cannot be Greek and Jew, circumcision,
> barbarian, Scythian, bondman, freeman; but Buddha is all,
> and in all.

猫 の 子 や 秤 に か ゝ り つ ゝ じ や れ る   一 茶
Neko no ko ya   hakari ni kakari   tsutsu jareru

The kitten,
Weighed on the balance,
Is still playing.   Issa

Weighing vegetables and other things, they sometimes weigh
the kitten to see how heavy she has got. After reaching a
certain age, the kitten is no longer frightened, but continues
to frolic and play about even when put on the balance. It is
dogs' delight to bark and bite, and it is cats' delight to play
and fight. Issa has taken this essential nature of the kitten
and revealed it all within the compass of a haiku. If we com-
pare this verse with its predecessor, of more than ten years
before, we cannot help being struck with Issa's tremendous
power of self-improvement:

桃 の 門 猫 を 秤 に か け る な り
Momo no kado   neko wo hakari ni   kakeru nari

The peach-blossoms at the gate:
They are putting
The cat on the scales.

The relation of cats to peach-blossoms is a "poetical" one, but
the expression of the cat's Buddha nature is poetry.

米蒔も罪ぞよ鶏が蹴合ぞよ 一 茶
Kome-maki mo tsumi zoyo tori ga keau zoyo

> Scattering rice too,
> This is a sin:
> The fowls are kicking one another. Issa

There is no such thing as goodness or badness. All things are inextricably mixed. Gandhi's non-violence was a form, a passive form, of violence. People are more or less this or that. Only in the eye, in the will, there may be purity, simplicity. Whatever we do, good *and* evil results. But this theology, however sound, is not poetry. The poetry of Issa's verse lies in the unexpressed but hinted depth of grief at the imperfection of the world, necessary for religion and poetry themselves. (For the context of this verse, see Vol. I, p. 303).

柳からももんぐわあと出る子かな 一 茶
Yanagi kara momongā to deru ko kana

> The child
> Came out of the willows,
> "A flying squirrel!" Issa

To get more of the force of the original, we should translate it in the same order, that is:

> "A flying-squirrel,"
> He came out of the willows,—
> The child!

This was composed when Issa was fifty four, that is, before he married and had children of his own.

The child, in a short kimono of some brown or speckled colour, comes running out from among the willows with arms extended, with not only the appearance but the vivacity and character of the flying squirrel. The comparison brings out the nature of both child and animal. Actually this is a kind of game, to which Issa has added the willow-trees to give it the dramatic yet natural background of the long, drooping branches. The child cries out "Momongā!" "Flying-squirrel gho-o-st!" to frighten the other children.

白 魚 や さ な が ら 動 く 水 の 色 　　　來 山
Shirauo ya　sanagara ugoku　mizu no iro

> The whitebait,—
> As though the colour of the water
> Were moving. 　　　Raizan

There is something moving in the water. Reason tells the poet that it must be a whitebait, but it is so intangible, so translucent, that it is almost inexpressible,—not even that the water is moving in the water, but that something even more materially remote, the colourless colour of the water is moving. The blurring of the line between the animate and the inanimate, between the material and the spiritual is akin to the *sfumato* of Leonardo da Vinci, by which the object is released from its corporeal bounds.

Another form of this verse is the following:

白 魚 や さ な が ら 動 く 水 の 魂
Shirauo ya　sanagara ugoku　mizu no tama

> The whitebait,—
> As though the spirit of the water
> Were moving.

Is seems as though the water itself has come to life. This version expresses the nature of water and the nature of fish, and their *inner* relation.

手 を つ い て 歌 申 上 ぐ る 蛙 か な 　　　宗 鑑
Te wo tsuite　uta mōshiaguru　kawazu kana

> Placing his hands on the ground,
> The frog respectfully recites
> His poem. 　　　Sōkan

Unless one has seen the costume of the aristocracy of Old Japan, the full aptness of the comparison is lost. He is dressed in the Japanese style with his *kamishimo*, 上下, stiffly sticking out and exaggerating the shoulders. Bowing low from the squatting posture, he begins his recitation in a strangely frog-like, sepulchral voice.

In the Introduction to the *Kokinshu*,[1] we have:

花 に な く 鶯 水 に 住 む 蛙 い づ れ か 歌 を 詠 ま ざ り け る 。

The nightingale that chants in the flowers, the frog that dwells in the water—are not both makers of poetry?

In China the croaking of the frog has not been considered a charming sound; in the *Saikontan*,[2] 275, we read:

人 情 聽 鶯 啼 則 喜 。 聞 蛙 鳴 則 厭 。

When we hear the singing of the nightingale, we feel pleasure; when we hear frogs croaking, we feel antipathy.

Sōkan's poem is a kind of joke on the frog, but in addition, and what makes it poetry, it shows us something of the real frog, something of its essential nature.

There is a similar verse by Issa:

西 行 の や う に 座 つ て 鳴 く 蛙
Saigyō no yō ni suwatte naku kawazu

> The frog,
> Sitting and singing
> Like Saigyō.

Saigyō, 1118-1190, became a monk at twenty three and travelled all over the country composing waka.

Sōkan, who is one of those who established the fundamental relation of haiku and humour, did not lose this sense of humour up to his last moments. His death verse is a waka:

> 宗 鑑 は 何 處 へ と 人 の 問 ふ な ら ば
> ち と 用 あ り て あ の 世 へ と い へ
> Should people ask
> Where Sōkan has gone,
> Then answer,
> "He has gone on some business
> To the next world."

Like Hood, Sōkan puns everywhere, and here there is a pun on *yo*, "world," and *yō*, "business."

---

[1] Completed about 922 A.D.
[2] By Hang Ming Ying, 1575-1619. See Vol. I, pp. 74-80.

春は啼く夏の蛙は吠へにけり   鬼　貫
Haru wa naku   natsu no kawazu wa   hoe ni keri

> In spring, frogs sing;
> In summer,
> They bark.   Onitsura

The point of this verse lies in the word 吠へる, "bark,"
opposed to 啼く, "sing," in the first line. This change of voice
is partly objective, partly subjective, for we gradually grow
weary of their singing as time goes on.

Some other verses that express the special characteristics of
the frog are the following:

一つ飛ぶ音に皆飛ぶ蛙かな   和　及
Hitotsu tobu   oto ni mina tobu   kawazu kana

> At the sound of one jumping in,
> All the frogs
> Jumped in.   Wakyu

橋渡る人にしづまる蛙かな   凉　菟
Hashi wataru   hito ni shizumaru   kawazu kana

> Someone passed over the bridge,
> And all the frogs
> Were quiet.   Ryōto

風落ちて山あざやかに蛙かな   大江丸
Kaze ochite   yama azayaka ni   kawazu kana

> The wind falls,
> The mountains are clear,—
> Now the frogs!   Ōemaru

日は日くれよ夜は夜明けよと啼く蛙   蕪　村
Hi wa hi kure yo   yo wa yo ake yo to   naku kawazu

> By day, "Darken day,"
> By night, "Brighten into light,"
> Chant the frogs.   Buson

This is highly successful piece of simple onomatopoeia in the
original. What is most striking however is the way in which
Buson has included in it the expression of the frogs' character

and wishes, making it a poem, and not merely a literary exercise.

我 を 見 て に が い 顔 す る 蛙 か な   一 茶
Waro wo mito   nigai hao suru   hawazu hana

> The frog
> Looks at me,—
> But with a sour face!   Issa

There is a lack of human conceit, of self-centredness, an emphasis on the frog rather than on himself, that is characteristic of Issa. Indeed, we feel that the frog is justified in looking at Issa in the same way that the caterpillar looked at Alice. How few people have been born into the world with enough sense and enough humility to look into the countenance of a frog, and feel sincerely, yet with humour, the frog's indifference, its superciliousness. Issa's love of and interest in frogs may be guaged from the fact that he wrote about three hundred haiku on them. Here are three more humorous verses:

お れ と し て に ら み く ら す る 蛙 か な
Ore to shite   niramikura suru   kawazu kana

> The frog
> Is having a staring-match
> With me.

親 分 と 見 え て 上 座 に 啼 く 蛙
Oyabun to   miete jōza ni   naku kawazu

> No doubt the boss,
> That frog croaking there,
> In the seat of honour.

産 み さ う な 腹 を か ゝ へ て 啼 く 蛙
Umisō na   hara wo kakaete   naku kawazu

> The frog is croaking,
> With a stomach
> Ready to give birth.

取り附かぬ力で浮む蛙哉 丈草
Toritsukanu　chikara de ukabu　kawazu kana

The frog rises to the surface
By the strength
Of its non-attachment. Jōsō

This Buddhist verse should be taken humorously, perhaps, though not fancifully. The frog is not attached to the water; it does not fight against it or go down deeper and deeper but rises in the same way that it plunges in. It "follows nature."

押合ふて鳴くと聞ゆる蛙かな 北枝
Oshiōte　naku to kikoyuru　kawazu kana

From their croaking,
The frogs sound as if
Elbowing one another. Hokushi

This is not a piece of logical deduction. The frogs are *heard* jostling one another. In their broken and spasmodic croaking the movements are seen-heard.

田を賣りていとど寝られぬ蛙かな 北枝
Ta wo urite　itodo nerarenu　kawazu kana

After selling the field,
All the more I could not sleep,—
The voices of the frogs. Hokushi

In order to appreciate this verse, we must first enter into the spirit of the farmer, to whom a field is not merely so much earth, representing so much money, but something to which he has been deeply attached since his birth, and even before it, which is a part of the life of his ancestors, who look down to it from their grave on the hill. It is with their sweat and blood and tears that the field came down to him; and now it is in the hands of a stranger. A second point, of less strong feeling, but more necessary for the poetry of the verse, is the relation between the frog and the field. Though usually at night they are useless, noisy creatures, after selling the land their voices have all kinds of emotional overtones, mocking, chiding, indifferent, triumphant, and his sleeplessness and misery are as if felt through his ears.

いうぜんとして山を見る蛙哉 　　　　　　　　　一　茶
Yūzen to　shite yama wo miru　kawazu kana

> Calm and serene,
> The frog gazes
> At the mountains. 　　　　　　　　　　　　　　Issa

Issa here is making fun of the frog and of the Chinese poet Tōenmei, 365–427 A.D.:

採菊東籬下、悠然見南山。

Plucking chrysanthemums along the east fence;
Gazing in calm rapture at the Southern Hills,

and of both equally and in the same spirit, not of mocking or cynicism or ennui, not Byronically instead of weeping, but because we must not take things too seriously. This is one of the most difficult and easily forgotten "principles" of art and life. Above all, we take ourselves too seriously, and this is the cause (and effect) of egotism and self-pity.

痩蛙負けるな一茶これにあり 　　　　　　　　　一　茶
Yasegaeru　makeru na issa　kore ni ari

> Thin frog,
> Don't be beat,
> Issa is here! 　　　　　　　　　　　　　　　Issa

We have an instinct against the survival of the fittest that Nietzsche could not shout away. In Heaven also there is more rejoicing over the salvation of one poor sinner than over the goodness of ninety nine just men.

What was Issa's state of mind when he composed this verse? It is not said seriously, as Ryōkan would have said it, nor with pious compassion, like Bashō, or mischievously, like Kikaku, or picturesquely, like Buson. We shall not be far wrong if we say Issa's attitude is a mingling of all these, plus a real fellow-feeling

for the physically and spiritually weak. (One can hardly imagine
Issa as anything but an emaciated man.) Also, there is that
element of childlikeness which sweetens all the other qualities,
something angelic which transfigures them.

泳ぐ時よるべなきさまの蛙かな　　　　蕪　村
Oyogu toki　yorube naki sama no　kawazu kana

> When it swims,
> The frog seems
> 　　Helpless. 　　　　　　　　Buson

It is a strange thing, and one that struck Buson, that the
frog, an aquatic animal, should be so little at ease in the water.
Awkward on land, it seems to take no pleasure in swimming
as such.

The following is another example of "looking steadily at the
object," by Rakugo :

飛び入つてしばし水ゆく蛙かな
Tobiitte　shibashi mizu yuku　kawazu kana

> Jumping in,
> The frog moves through the water
> 　　For a little.

When the frog jumps in, it does not swim, but moves along
for a little space with outstretched arms and legs. This is only
a picture of life, but there is something so charming, so
characteristic, so near to life and far from what one would
have expected, that it takes us with it into the poetical world.

其の聲でひとつ踊れよ鳴蛙　　　　　一　茶
Sono koe de　hitotsu odore yo　naku kawazu

> With that voice,
> Give us a little dance,
> 　　Croaking frog! 　　　　　Issa

There is something in the energy and timbre and rhythm of
the frog's croaking that makes Issa wish to see it put into action
and dance to its own accompaniment. There is nothing fanciful

in this, any more than there is in a child's view of the animal world. This how we feel in reading *Alice in Wonderland*, where Bill the lizard and the Dormouse are as human as the Mad Hatter. It is painfully pleasant to think how Issa would have enjoyed that book.

むきむきに蛙のいとこはとこかな　　　　　一　茶
Mukimuki ni　kawazu no itoko　hatoko kana

Frogs squatting this way,
Frogs squatting that way, but all
Cousins, or second cousins.　　　　Issa

Neither "squatting" nor "all" is the original, but that scarcely matters. What does matter is the onomatopoeia of *itoko hatoko*, which is missing in the translation. In the very similarity of the words used is expressed, by Issa's deep empathy, the family likeness of the frogs. And this sameness that Issa perceives is not the monotonous sameness that we see in a flock of sheep, but a *delightful* sameness; he gets a thrill of pleasure at it.

Dante, in a far-off country, had already marked the frogs in their semi-gregarious life; he compares the people burning in the pitch to them:

All 'orlo dell' acqua d'un fosso
Stanno i ranocchi pur col muso fuori,
Sì che celano i piedi e l'altro grosso.[1]

At the edge of the water of a ditch
Stand the frogs with only their muzzles out,
So that their feet and the rest of their bodies are hid.

萍に乗つて流るゝ蛙かな　　　　　圭　左
Ukikusa ni　notte nagaruru　kawazu kana

The frog
Riding on the duckweed,
Drifting.　　　　Keisa

[1] *Inferno*, XXII, 25-27.

The nonchalant and composed air of the frog, its adaptiveness, its opportunism, not wishing to be in some other place, at some other time,—this is the nature of the frog.

松 風 を 打 ち 越 し て 聞 く 蛙 か な   丈　草
Matsu-kaze wo   uchikoshite kiku   kawazu kana

Above the noise
Of the gale in the pine-trees,
The voices of the frogs.   Jōsō

A stormy wind is blowing through the branches of the pine-trees. But above the rushing sound comes the croaking of the frogs. Like the wood-wind and the brass alternating in the last movement of the Jupiter Symphony, above the roar of the elements sounds the voice of life, frantic to live.

The doom of death was a shadow compared to the raging destiny of life, the determined surge of life.[1]

We may contrast the following waka by Ryōkan:

里 べ に は 笛 や 太 鼓 の 音 す な り
み 山 は さ は に 松 の 音 し つ

Ah! there in the village
The sound of fife and tabor:
On this sacred mountain,
The multitudinous sounds
Of the pine-trees.

た ゝ づ め ば 遠 く も 聞 ゆ 蛙 か な   蕉　村
Tatazumeba   tōku mo kikoyu   kawazu kana

Standing still,—
The voices of frogs
Heard also in the distance.   Buson

Buson ordinarily heard the frogs close by, all round the house, but coming home through the mountains one calm night, he

[1] D. H. Lawrence, *The Man who Died.*

heard them also in the distance. Close to, things are pathetic; far distant, in time or space, they are intolerable. Wordsworth felt this deeply:

> Yes, it was the mountain echo,
> Solitary, clear, profound.

It is like the sound of the horn in the *Song of Roland*.
There is another verse by Buson:

閣 に 座 し て 遠 き 蛙 を 聞 く 夜 か な
Kaku ni zashite tōki kawazu wo kiku yo kana

> Seated in the tower,
> Listening to the distant frogs,
> At night.

我 が 庵 や 蛙 初 手 か ら 老 を 鳴 く   一 茶
Waga io ya kawazu shote kara oi wo naku

> Round my hut,
> From the first,
> The frogs sang of old age.   Issa

In spring, when the frogs begin to sing, it is a lively, cheerful note, sometimes making us smile at its pomposity and hollowness. As time goes on their voices deepen, and take on a sad, tragic tone. As Issa sits listening to the notes of the frogs in the paddy-field behind his house, they sound grim and resigned. Not only so, they were like this from very beginning. There was no levity about their croaking, no merry bandying of voices one to another. They spoke, from the first tentative sounds, of melancholy and death. Issa knows that he is attributing to the voices of the frogs what really belongs to himself, his own pessimism, and we know also that he knows it, and thus instead of a subjective poem on the frogs, we get an objective poem on the poet himself.

古池や蛙飛びこむ水の音　　　　　　芭蕉

Furuike ya　kawazu tobikomu　mizu no oto

　　The old pond:
A frog jumps in,—
　　The sound of the water.　　　　Bashō

　The pond is old, in an old garden. The trees are ages old, the trunks green with the moss that covers the stones. The very silence itself goes back beyond men and their noises. A frog jumps in. The whole garden, the whole universe contained in one single plop!—sound that is beyond sound and silence, and yet is the sound of the water of the old pond.[1]

我門へ知らなんで這入る蛙哉　　　　一茶

Waga kado e　shiranande hairu　kawazu kana

　　The frog
Enters my gate,
　　Unawares.　　　　　　　　　　Issa

This "unawares" is mutual.

　And whoever wakes in England sees, some morning, unaware,
　That the lowest boughs and the brushwood sheaf
　Round the elm-tree bole are in tiny leaf.

And Issa felt also, that

　　Some have entertained angels, unawares.

出ずとよい蜥蜴は人を驚かす　　　　來山

Dezu to yoi　tokage wa hito wo　odorokasu

　　Lizard,
If only you wouldn't come out,—
　　You frightened me.　　　　　Raizan

This is a common experience with all kinds of creatures, even

---

[1] In *Zen in English Literature* there is a laboured explanation occupying eight pages, pp. 217–224. I have changed my mind about it, as above. See another change, Vol. IV, pp. xxxv–xxxvi. (hard cover ed.)

with human beings. We do not mind such things existing, if
only they would not pop out and make us jump. In this kind
of unreasonable attitude, in the very unreasonableness of it,
there is something poetical. (Strictly speaking, this verse refers
to the "coming-out" of the lizard at the beginning of spring.)

蝶消へて魂我に返りけり　　　　　　　　和　風
Chō kiete　tamashii ware ni　kaeri keri

The butterfly having disappeared,
My spirit
Came back to me. 　　　　　　　　　　Wafū

Sōshi (Chuangtse) says:

昔者莊周夢爲胡蝶、栩々然胡蝶也、自喩適
志與、不知周也。　俄然覺、則蘧々然周也。
不知周之夢爲胡蝶與、胡蝶之夢爲周與。　（第二章）

Long ago I, Chuangtse, dreamed I was a butterfly, flitting
about lightly as if I were really one, happily following my
fancies. Suddenly awakening, again I was in the form of
Chuangtse. Was it a case of Chuangtse dreaming he was
a butterfly, or is it now that a butterfly is dreaming that
it is Chuangtse? I do not know.

Sōshi's experience of the fact that he and the butterfly were
one, has been shared by countless human beings to some degree;
for example, Kotomichi, 言道, 1798-1868:

あくがるる心はさとも山櫻
散りなむ後や身に歸るべき

My heart
That was rapt away
By the wild cherry-blossoms,—
Will it return to my body
When they scatter?

What Sōshi did was to *name* it by expressing it. Before it
was named, it was formless, like a new-born child, inchoate, a
day-dream in the mind of God. But when it had been enunci-
ated, it had a soundless tone that still echoes faintly in the

recesses of our soul, a life which still moves to be born again in the womb of our spirit. So Wafū's experience was not only of the butterfly before his eyes, but also of Sōshi's, though not of two things. The coming back to himself was a feeling of loss and discomfort, typical of what the soul suffers upon alienation from God. This coming and going of God, that is, of the butterfly, Eckhart describes as follows:

> Wüsste die Seele, wann Gott in sie einträte: sie stürbe vor Freuden. Wüsste sie auch, wann er von ihr fährt: sie stürbe vor Lied. Sie weiss nicht, wann er kommt, und wann er geht. Wann er aber bei ihr ist, das spürt sie recht wohl. Ein Meister spricht, "Sein Kommen und sein Gehen sind verborgen." Seine Gegenwart aber ist nicht verborgen. Denn er ist Licht, und Lichtes Natur ist Offenbarung.

蝶々や何を夢みて羽づかひ　　　　千代尼
Chōchō ya   nani wo yumemite   hanezukai

O butterfly,
What are you dreaming there,
Fanning your wings?　　　　Chiyo-ni

This is Sōshi's thought still thinking itself in the minds of later poets and poetesses.

The following verse of Shiki has the proscript, 荘子, Sōshi, and gives a tentative answer:

石に寝る蝶薄命の我を夢むらん
Ishi ni neru chō   hakumei no ware wo   yumemuran

Butterfly asleep on the stone,
You will be dreaming
Of the sad life of me.

花の夢聞きたき蝶に聲もなし　　　　鈴竿
Hana no yume   kikitaki chō ni   koe mo nashi

The butterfly's dream of flowers
I fain would ask,—
But it is voiceless.　　　　Reikan

Even though it had a voice and could speak with the tongues of men and of angels, there could be no answer to the question. What the butterfly feels about the flowers, what I feel or what Wordsworth felt, these are mysteries hid forever from each of us. All the more when language differs, and still more when things are bound to an eternal silence, we feel a pain of separation that is yet fainter than we pretend, for this separation is but a shallow thing that disappears whenever we roam the fields with the butterfly, lie as stones under the foot of the traveller, shine with the stars over the waves of the sea.

繰り返し麥の畝縫ふ胡蝶哉　　　　　　曾　良
Kurikaeshi mugi no une nuu kochō kana

To and fro, to and fro,
Between the lines of barley,
The butterfly.　　　　　　　　　　Sora

The straight lines of barley and the straggling irregular flight of the butterfly between them are well contrasted, bringing out something essential in grass and insect.

釣鐘に止りて眠る胡蝶かな　　　　　　蕉　村
Tsurigane ni tomarite nemuru kochō kana

The butterfly
Resting upon the temple bell,
Asleep.　　　　　　　　　　　　Buson

A great black temple bell; a white butterfly perched upon its side. For the mind in its *thoughtless*, poetic state, this is enough. There is nothing symbolised. As Goethe said, it is life that matters, that is significant, not the result of life. There is a verse by Shiki which, though not an imitation, must have been composed with Buson's poem in mind:

釣鐘にとまりて光る螢かな
Tsurigane ni tomarite hikaru hotaru kana

On the temple bell,
Glowing,
A firefly.

In Buson's verse, however objective it may be, we feel the
intensity and absorption of the poet and the butterfly as one
thing.

> O immaginativa, che ne rube
>   Tal volta sì di fuor, ch'uom non s'accorge,
>   Perchè d'intorno suonin mille tube.

> O imagination, which at times so snatches us
>   Out of ourselves, that we are conscious of nothing,
>   Even though a thousand trumpets sound about us.[1]

起きよ起きよ我が友にせん寝る胡蝶　　芭 蕉
Oki yo oki yo   waga tomo ni sen   neru kochō

> Wake up, wake up,
> Sleeping butterfly,
>   And let us be companions!   Bashō

Bashō preserved this butterfly lightness in spite of the seri-
ousness with which he followed his *Haiku no Michi*, the Way
of Poetry, and taught his disciples this ethico-poetical way
of life.

君や蝶我や荘子が夢心　　芭 蕉
Kimi ya chō   ware ya sōshi ga   yume-gokoro

> You are the butterfly,
> And I the dreaming heart
>   Of Sōshi?   Bashō

This is both playful and profound. It corresponds to Donne's
lightly-treated passion:

> Our two souls, therefore, which are one,
>   Though I must go, endure not yet
> A breach, but an expansion,
>   Like gold to airy thinness beat.[2]

[1] *Purgatorio*, XVII, 13–15.
[2] *A Valediction, Forbidding Mourning.*

It was addressed to Dosui, 怒誰, on being sent a writing-brush by him.

吹 く た び に 蝶 の 居 直 る 柳 か な　　　　芭 蕉
Fuku tabi ni　chō no inaoru　yanagi kana

With every gust of wind,
The butterfly changes its place
On the willow.　　　　　　　　　　　　　Bashō

The butterfly is quite different from the dragonfly, which comes back to the same place however many times it is disturbed. The butterfly settles on a different place each time.

小 男 鹿 や 蝶 を ふ る つ て ま た 眠 む る　　　一 茶
Koojika ya　chō wo furutte　mata nemuru

The fawn
Shakes off the butterfly,
And sleeps again.　　　　　　　　　　　Issa

There is an indescribable harmony here between two gentle, beautiful things. In the following verse by Buson we have harmony of colour alone:

伊 勢 武 者 の 錣 に と ま る 胡 蝶 か な
Ise musha no　shikoro ni tomaru　kochō kana

A butterfly perched
On the neck-plates of the helmet
Of a knight of Ise.

追 は れ て も い そ が ぬ ふ り の 胡 蝶 哉　　我 樂
Owarete mo　isoganu furi no　kochō kana

The butterfly,
Even when pursued,
Never appears in a hurry.　　　　　　　Garaku

This is a fact which every child and every entomologist has experienced with chagrin. The pursuer dances about madly

striking here and there, but the butterfly follows the uneven
tenor of its way quite oblivious of the frantic, blundering,
wingless biped who seeks his life.

地車に起き行く草の胡蝶哉　　　　　　召波

Jiguruma ni　okiyuku kusa no　kochō kana

At the wagon's approach,
Out from the grass
　　Flies the butterfly.　　　　　　　Shōha

This is harmony by contrast, the piccolo and the big drum,
where there is nevertheless some inner identity of pitch and
timbre in spite of our judgements, intellectual or sensory.
However light or heavy, weight is still weight. Movement
whether by volition or by instinct, by itself or by another force,
is still movement.　It is hard indeed to determine from which
the greater pleasure comes, from the perception of difference
or of identity, of the lumbering, purposeful wagon, and the
light fantastic butterfly.

蝶々や順禮の子おくれがち　　　　　　子規

Chōchō ya　junrei no ko　okuregachi

Butterflies;
The pilgrims' child,
　　Apt to lag behind.　　　　　　　Shiki

A few men and women are trudging along the wet road
chanting the sutras, with the future and the distant in their
hearts, but the children, truer and happier followers of Christ
and Buddha, are enjoying the present, the road itself.　The
spring butterflies, so light and wanton, so symmetrical in colour
and shape, so irregular in flight, are asking to be caught by
the children, who trail behind their parents.　Very faintly in
the mind, is the knowledge that the pilgrims are only chasing
butterflies, and the child is like Wordsworth's child by the
seashore :

If thou appear untouched by solemn thought,
Thy nature is not therefore less divine.
Thou liest, in Abraham's bosom all the year
And worship'st at the Temple's inner shrine,
God being with thee when we know it not.

畫からあんな胡蝶が生れけり   — 茶
Mugura kara anna kochō ga umarekeri

From the burweed,
Such a butterfly
      Was born!   Issa

The mugura, or kanamugura, 金畫, is a creeping weed, some-
times called the Japanese hop. It has a five-petalled flower in
autumn.

Issa did not, of course, suppose that the butterfly was actually
born from the burweed, nor is it a question whether the cater-
pillar fed on it or not. What Issa experienced at the moment
the butterfly flew out from the burweed, was the fact that the
butterfly originated from it (directly or indirectly, scientifically
or mystically is not the question) and the wonder that cause
and effect should be so disproportionate.

あたふたに蝶の出る日や金の番   — 茶
Atafuta ni chō no deru hi ya kane no ban

Helter-skelter
Comes a butterfly today,—
    Watching over the money!   Issa

The contrast here is a simple and obvious one. Outside, a
butterfly suddenly appears, dancing and sidestepping in the
spring sunshine, free and happy. In the shop, a sour-visaged,
leather-faced old man looks round the room at the assistants
over his horn-rimmed spectacles, not a thought above the money
he is in charge of. In this verse the poetry consists almost
wholly in the brevity, but there is a little something more
which is lost in the translation. The original is:

In a flurry, the day a butterfly appears, money-watching.

The word "day" takes us to something larger than the mere

contrast of the happy-go-lucky butterfly and the miserly shop-
man; it leads us to the idea of spring and warmth and joy.

夕 日 影 町 中 に 飛 ぶ こ て ふ か な   其　角
Yūhi kage   machinaka ni tobu   kochō kana

In the rays of the setting sun
There flutters along the city street,
A butterfly.   Kikaku

In the *Gogenshū*, 五元集, a complete collection of Kikaku's
poetical works, there is a proscript, "Without the noise of horses
and carts." This refers to one of twelve "drinking poems" of
Tōenmei:

結 廬 在 人 境　　而 無 車 馬 喧
問 君 何 能 爾　　心 遠 地 自 偏
採 菊 東 籬 下　　悠 然 見 南 山
山 氣 日 夕 佳　　飛 鳥 相 與 還
此 中 有 眞 意　　欲 辯 已 忘 言

I built myself a dwelling-place among the habitations of men,
But yet no sound of horse or carriage is heard.
You ask, "Sir, how can this be?"
Following its own nature, the mind is in a world afar.
I pluck chrysanthemums under the Eastern hedge;
I gaze in deep silence at the Southern Hills.
The soft air of the mountains at even,—
The birds flying back in pairs,—
In these things there is a reality, a meaning,
But when we would express it,
Already the words are forgotten.

Kikaku uses the second line of the poem simply to create the
atmosphere of solitude and silence in the city street. It would
be unfair to take these two poems and compare them as typical
of Chinese and Japanese poetry, since Tōenmei's verse is a great
poem, whereas Kikaku's is not specially noteworthy. The
Chinese poem is in the Wordsworthian sublime, passing from
particular things, through the soul of the poet to

Something evermore about to be.

The poet is present, but as vicar of mankind. Man is becoming Nature. In the Japanese poem, there is no talking of distant realms, no philosophizing, no poet to be seen; only a white butterfly flickering in the level rays of the yellow sunlight, aimless and lost in the city street. The pathos of life is seized and expressed,—so strongly, so quickly, that the intellectual and emotional factors are all subsumed into the life of the sun and the street and the wandering butterfly.

蝶 飛 ぶ や 此 世 に 望 み な い や う に　　　　一 茶
Chō tobu ya　kono yo ni nozomi　nai yō ni

The butterfly fluttered along
As if it despaired
Of this world.　　　　　　　　　Issa

The fancy of the poet, used by the imagination, has enabled him to portray the broken, hesitating flight of the butterfly. Issa does this, not through the fancy, not with the intellect, but through our religious emotions. Our souls flutter with the inadequate wings of the butterfly, pilgrims and strangers in a world that was not made for us. And in this poem, once more Sōshi's question remains unanswered.

門 の 蝶 子 が 這 へ ば と び は へ ば 飛 ぶ　　　一 茶
Kado no chō　ko ga haeba tobi　haeba tobu

Outside the gate, a butterfly:
The baby crawls, it rises,
She crawls, it rises again.　　　　　Issa

Where is the poetry in this? It is a charming picture no doubt, but a charming picture is not poetry. Or to put it another way, if this is a real poem, a man who dislikes babies and has no great love of butterflies will be able to see the poetry of it, that is, if he is a poet. It is the sphere of Keishin of Chōsa, 長沙景岑, when he was asked by a monk concerning the meaning of "Your ordinary mind, that is the Way," 平常心是道：

要 眠 即 眠、要 坐 即 坐。　　　　（傳燈録、十）

"When you feel sleepy, sleep; when you wish to sit, sit."

蝶 と ん で 我 が 身 も 塵 の た ぐ ひ 哉　　　　一 茶

Chō tonde　waga mi mo chiri no　tagui kana

The flying butterfly:
I feel myself
A creature of dust.　　　　　　　　　　　Issa

Besides and beyond the dissatisfaction of the poet with himself,
there is the light, free joyousness of the insect and that of Issa
breaking through our heavy earthiness. He who feels himself
a creature of dust has already passed beyond this state into a
region of light and air.

む つ ま し や 生 れ 替 ら ば 野 邊 の 蝶　　　　一 茶

Mutsumashi ya　umare-kawaraba　nobe no chō

How happy, how affectionate they are!
If I am reborn, may I be
A butterfly in the fields.　　　　　　　　　Issa

As Issa stands watching these bright and beautiful creatures
fluttering round the flowers and round each other, he feels like
the Ancient Mariner:

O happy living things! no tongue
Their beauty might declare:
A spring of love gushed from my heart,
And I blessed them unaware!

Instead of thanking fate that he was born a man, he hopes that
in his next reincarnation he may be a carefree butterfly, roam-
ing with his companions the flowery fields of spring.

花 に 狂 ひ 月 に 驚 く 胡 蝶 か な　　　　　樗 良

Hana ni kurui　tsuki ni odoroku　kochō kana

Distracted with the flowers,
Amazed at the moon,
　　The butterfly!　　　　　　　　　　　　Chora

This hyperbolical description of the butterfly expresses on the one hand its fluttering, as-if-panic-stricken flight that Davies has caught and fixed by a not dissimilar means:

> Butterflies will make side leaps
> As though escaped from Nature's hand
> Ere perfect quite

But in addition, it expresses the ecstacy of the poet in the flower, his quivering sense of the wonder of the moon. Thus the union of the poet and the butterfly is not even hinted at; it is taken for granted.

道づれは胡蝶をたのむ旅路かな   子 規
Michizure wa   kochō wo tanomu   tabiji kana

For a companion on this journey,
I would fain have
A butterfly.   Shiki

Shiki is on a journey, and he wishes, like all of us, to have the pleasures of companionship with none of its inevitable drawbacks. Even a dog will frighten the chickens, want to go faster or slower, make himself a nuisance in some way. Perhaps a butterfly is best. It gives us its grace and beauty, its carefree spirit, and asks for nothing in return.

氣の毒やおれをしたふて來る小蝶   一 茶
Kinodoku ya   ore wo shitōte   kuru kochō

What a pity
You should fondly follow me,
Butterfly!   Issa

Issa walks between the rice-fields gazing at the flowering grasses all around him, and notices a small butterfly at rest on a leafy plant. As he passes, it rises, flutters near him, and as he walks, follows him. Why does it not fly off, seeking after the bright golden flowers? Issa has a feeling almost of responsibility, a feeling of having deceived the little wavering thing into falling in love with him and following him wherever he goes. When we compare this with the previous verse by Shiki, we see the difference between the two men. Issa does not ask for anything. He indeed puts the butterfly above himself in importance, and wonders that such a bright creature should follow a poor thing like himself.

花桶に蝶も聞くかよ一大事   一　茶
Hanaoke ni   chō mo kiku kayo   ichidaiji

At the flower-vase,
The butterfly too seems to be listening
To the One Great Thing.   Issa

"The One Great Thing" is not Zen enlightenment, but being born in the Western Paradise of Amida, but this does not affect the poetic point, the sudden realization that the butterfly also is moving towards

That one far-off divine event
To which the whole creation moves.

Issa is listening to a sermon in one of the six temples where Gyōgi Bosatsu[1] had enshrined an image of Amida.

うつつなきつまみごゝろの胡蝶哉   蕪　村
Utsutsunaki   tsumami gokoro no   kochō kana

I would take hold of it,
It seems insubstantial,—
This butterfly!   Buson

If he were to take the butterfly gently between his fingers, he feels that he would be holding something unreal, something with form and colour, but no solidity, spirit rather than matter. This verse expresses in part the nature of the butterfly, but equally the nature of Buson, his delicacy of feeling, a sympathy with living things which is never allowed to pass beyond the bounds of accord with nature.

[1] 670–749. A Korean priest and artist.

木 の 陰 や 蝶 と や ど る も 他 生 の 縁   一 茶
Ki no kage ya   chō to yadoru mo   tashō no en

Sheltering with a butterfly
Under the shade of the trees,—
This also is the Karma of a previous life.

Issa

The verse by itself is a beautiful example of the way in which
Buddhism supports the poetic intuition we have that nothing in
our lives is insignificant or accidental, no creature is unrelated
to us, no place unvisited, no time not lived through by us in
our eternal wanderings.

But a proscript shows that this verse also has another
application:

て ふ と い ふ 娘 山 路 の 案 内 し け る に 俄 雨 は ら は ら
と ふ り け れ ば

Not knowing the path over the mountain, he was guided by
a young girl called Butterfly. It suddenly came on to rain, and
they took shelter under a large tree. Under its shade he com-
posed the above verse. Issa is always, invariably subjective;
humanity blended with nature.

それ 虻 に 世 話 を や か す な 明 り 窓   一 茶
Sore abu ni   sewa wo yakasu na   akari-mado

Hey! don't let that horse-fly
Do everything,
At the skylight.

Issa

This is a little difficult in the original and much more so in
the clumsy translation. A horse-fly comes in, and in the un-
intelligent manner of that tribe, it begins banging away at the
skylight window in an exasperated and exasperating way. Issa
bawls to someone who is not so sensitive as he is, "Why don't
you open the window for that horse-fly to get out?" The poetry
is partly in the sentiment of a common nature in all things,
which causes some of us to pick up beetles that fall on their
backs, and try to stop moths from burning themselves to death
at the lamp; and partly in the humour with which the expres-

sion is permeated, "Don't let the horse-fly open the window all
by himself!"

拾 ひ 殘 す 田 螺 に 月 の ゆ う べ 哉　　　　　　　蕪 村
Hiroinokosu   tanishi ni tsuki no   yūbe kana

Mud-snails:
A few remain uncaught
　　Under the evening moon.　　　　　　　Buson

"Tanishi" are edible snails, supposed to be a cure for beri-
beri.

The poet has been collecting, in rather a desultory way, these
snails in the rice-field. It begins to grow dark. The spring
moon rises, and from the rice-field come the voices of a few
mud-snails that have been left behind. There is something
ironical, that is, something both pathetic and comical in the
sound.

In actual fact, these snails do not, of course, make any sound
at all. Some other creatures' squeaking or crying is still mis-
taken, by ordinary Japanese, for the sound of the tanishi. This,
however, in no way affects the value, the poetry of the verse,
which is not in the region of science any more than of human-
itarianism.

ぬ り た て の 畦 を ゆ り 出 る 田 螺 哉　　　　　十 丈
Nuritate no   aze wo yurideru   tanishi kana

The mud-snail
In the newly-made rice-field bank,
　　Joggles its way out.　　　　　　　　Jūjō

The path between the rice-fields has just been remade, and
the edges are plastered with soft mud. Some tanishi have been
mixed in the mud, and now come out in an oozing, slowly-
wriggling way. The slowness of their movements is depicted
in a verse by Gomei:

二三尺這うて田螺の日暮れけり

Nisanjaku hōte tanishi no higurekeri

The mud-snail
Crawls two or three feet,—
And the day is over.

植　物　TREES AND FLOWERS

椿落ち鶏鳴き椿又落ちる　　　　　　　　　梅　室
Tsubaki ochi tori naki tsubaki mata ochiru

> A camellia flower fell;
> A cock crew;
> 　　Another fell.　　　　　　　　　Baishitsu

The best haiku on the camellia are concerned with its falling.
One kind falls suddenly, bodily,—like a head being cut off,
Japanese people think.

Is there a connection between the crowing of the cock and
the falling of the flower, or is there no connection? If there
is no connection, the poem is meaningless. If there is a con-
nection, it is a scientific one and the verse is not poetry. We
may contrast this mystical verse with a pictorial one by Shiki:

鳥啼いて赤き木の實をこぼしけり
Tori naite   akaki ko-no-mi wo   koboshikeri

> 　　Birds singing,
> And knocking down
> 　　Red berries.

一つ落ちて二つ落ちたる椿かな　　　　　　子　規
Hitotsu ochite   futatsu ochitaru   tsubaki kana

> 　　One fell,—
> Two fell,—
> 　　Camellias.　　　　　　　　　　Shiki

The simpler the verse becomes, the stronger and purer and
deeper the meaning. The one flower falling, the two flowers
falling are as significant as Lucifer falling from Heaven.

落ざまに水こぼしけり花椿　　　　　　　　芭　蕉
Ochizama ni   mizu koboshikeri   hana tsubaki

> 　　The flower of the camellia-tree
> Fell,
> 　　Spilling its water.　　　　　　Bashō

There is something extraordinarily final in this falling of the flower bodily, and the spilling of the rain or dew within its cup. Its inevitability has the cadence of

> Suffer it to be so now.

Compare the following, by Shirao:

音なして疊へ落る椿かな
Oto nashite   tatami e ochiru   tsubaki kana

> The camellia flower
> Fell on the tatami,
> Making a sound.

This is a less dramatic, more subdued and quietistic verse.

はき掃除してから椿散りにけり　　　　　野坡
Hakisōji   shite kara tsubaki   chiri ni keri

> After the garden
> Had been swept clean,
> Some camellia flowers fell down.　　　Yaha

The poet perceives with joy the divine uselessness, the useless divinity of his work. Nothing is fixed or finished, everything is moving, changing. But when we say these words, the meaning of the fallen flowers has gone.

> Gott its namenlos.[1]

落ちなんを葉にかかへたる椿かな　　　　召波
Ochinan wo   ha ni kakaetaru   tsubaki kana

> The camellia flower
> Was going to fall,
> But it caught in its leaves.　　　Shōha

Everything in nature is perfect,—yet everything is imperfect. The flowers that bloom to fall, lodge in their surrounding leaves. When the *whole truth* is told, it is not purely poetic or tragic,

[1] Eckhart.

it is invariably mixed with humorous or inharmonious or "meaningless" elements. In art, on the other hand, these elements are omitted; all things have perfection not seen in life. From this comes the antithesis of art and life, but even in art there is a meaning in imperfection and incompletion, a dumb yearning, a latent aspiration that makes perfection seem cold and insipid.

水 入 れ て 鉢 に う け た る 椿 か な 　　　　　　鬼　貫
Mizu irete　hachi ni uketaru　tsubaki kana

Putting in the water,
The vase received
The camellia.
Onitsura

This is an example of supreme objectivity, not of that dead kind in which the thing is divided from the rest of the world, (of which man is the most vital and dynamic part), but in which each thing is alive with its own life, that is, with the life of all things. The water, the flower and the vase are in perfect harmony, though it is only chance that has brought them together. This is expressed by the flower being received in the vase, for in the hands of the poet both the vase and the camellia are alive.

流 れ 得 ざ る 水 の よ ど み の 椿 か な 　　　　　子　規
Nagare ezaru　mizu no yodomi no　tsubaki kana

In the backwater,
The water that could not flow away,—
Camellias.
Shiki

The water lies stagnant, with a circular pattern of whitish scum. Floating in it, as beautiful as when they fell, are a few camellia flowers. It is a scene for a quiet eye, that gazes on it, and receives an indelible though vague impression.

白 椿 落 つ る 音 の み 月 夜 か な   蘭　更
Shirotsubaki   otsuru oto nomi   tsukiyo kana

All the evening the only sound,
The falling
Of the white camellia flowers.   Rankō

The sound of the falling of the camellia flower is faint yet unmistakable. This sound repeated again and again, irregularly, but without stop, has a cumulative effect which is heightened by the colour, the whiteness of the flowers. The sound, so soft and palpable, is white.

暁 の 釣 瓶 に あ が る つ ば き か な   荷　兮
Akatsuki no   tsurube ni agaru   tsubaki kana

Up in the well-bucket
Of the dawn of day,—
A camellia.   Kakei

There are white camellias also, but here it is the red camellia that comes up in the bucket this spring morning, when the sky is turning pink in the east. The whole world is now concentrated in this deep red flower that floats in the dark water.

柳 あ り 舟 待 つ 牛 の 二 三 び き   子　規
Yanagi ari   funematsu ushi no   nisanbiki

A willow;
And two or three cows,
Waiting for the boat.   Shiki

The scene is a river, and the cows are waiting for a ferry-boat, or one to take them down-stream. Shiki succeeds, as he so often does, in giving us a clear and vivid picture, but he cannot avoid the defects of his virtues. In a sense, the willow is not alive; it a kind of stage property, and the cows are made of cardboard. To express emotion without sentimentality, to be perfectly objective and yet not exclude human feeling, to see things as they exist for themselves, yet in their relations to other things,—these are the problems of every poet and artist, that is, of every man.

岸崩れて小魚たまりぬ川柳　　　　　　子　規
Kishi kuzurete   kouwo tamarinu   kawayanagi

> Where the ˈcliff has broken down,
> Small fish gather,
> Under the river willow.　　　　　Shiki

The water of the river is in the shade under the willow which hangs down its branches into the water. The small fish, all moving together, turn here, turn there, but remain in the deep water that lies under the high bank. It is one of the pleasures of life to stand and look down into the water at the small fish.

橋落ちてうしろさむしき柳かな　　　　子　規
Hashi ochite   ushiro samushiki   yanagi kana

> The bridge has fallen down;
> Behind the willow-tree
> It is lonely.　　　　　　　　Shiki

The willow-tree, especially the hanging variety, has an innate melancholy that nothing can assuage. Here, the bridge over the stream having broken down, the willow-tree stands out in intensified pathos that harmonizes with the desolation behind it.

町中を小川流るる柳かな　　　　　　　子　規
Machi-naka wo   ogawa nagaruru   yanagi kana

> A stream
> Flowing through the town,
> And the willows along it.　　　Shiki

Shiki excels at these pictures of the fleeting world. The combination of nature and man, town and country, houses and stream, willows and road represent a contradictory ideal world

that we all desire. Shiki was fond of willows, and wrote well
about them, feeling keenly the contrast between their wayward
freedom and beauty, and the works of man:

眞直に堀割遠き柳かな
Massugu ni   horiwari tōki   yanagi kana

> Into the distance,
> The straight line of the canal,
> And the willow-trees.

大門や柳かぶつて火をともす
Ōmon ya   yanagi kabutte   hi wo tomosu

> Lighting the lamps
> Of the Great Gate,
> With a willow over him.

四五本の柳とりまく小家かな
Shigohon no   yanagi torimaku   koie kana

> Four or five willow-trees,
> Encompassing
> A small house.

あら青の柳の糸や水の流   鬼貫
Ara ao no   yanagi no ito ya   mizu no nagare

> Oh, how green
> The threads of the willow,
> Over the sliding waters!   Onitsura

This verse has a joyous, lyrical tone that is not so common
in haiku, which incline to be subdued, to verge on silence.

人ごみの中へしたるる柳かな   浪化上人
Hito-gomi no   naka e shitaruru   yanagi kana

> Hanging down
> In the midst of the throng of people,—
> The willow-tree   Rōka-Shōnin

What is it about the willow-tree that makes it more affecting than the throngs of people around it? With its drooping branches that hang down in the sunshine, so near, yet so far from the hearts of the human beings that move beneath it, it is no more permanent than they, but fulfils the law of its being as they do not, and cannot. It is the old law. He who would be greatest among you shall be your servant. The first shall be last and the last shall be first.

若草に根を忘れたる柳かな   蕪 村
Wakakusa ni   ne wo wasuretaru   yanagi kana

The willow-tree
Has forgotten its root
In the young grasses.   Buson

This is not so much a personification of the willow, an expression of its growing upwards and outwards without giving attention to its roots, as an expression of the luxuriance and rank growths of spring. The willow-tree breaks forth uncontrollably into green leaves and branches, and the grasses below grow wildly, and all spring burns with a green flame. What was only root all the winter is now nothing but leaves. What was bare earth and dead grass is now alive with every size and shape of yellowish green undergrowth.

白猫のような柳も御花かな   一 茶
Shironeko no   yō na yanagi mo   ohana kana

This willow-tree
That looks like a white cat,[1]
Is also a votive flower.   Issa

This has the prescript, 善光寺堂前, Before the Hall of Zenkōji Temple. It it spring and the willow-tree in the temple grounds is white with blossom; the graceful curving lines of the drooping branches remind one of the sinuous shapes of the cat, awake or asleep. In its beauty of form, colour and movement, this willow-tree is fit for a flower to be offered to Buddha,—in fact,

----
[1] In *Oragaharu* this is given as 灰猫, "an ash (grey) cat."

it is such, standing there in the spring sunshine.

To the average Japanese of Issa's time, the cat was an object of superstitious fear, but Issa disregards this in his praise of beautiful things, and the willow-tree's appropriateness for worship is enhanced by the white cat from which it might well have been metamorphosed.

旅人の見て行く門の柳かな　　　　　　　　　樗良
Tabibito no　mite yuku kado no　yanagi kana

The willow-tree at the gate;
Gazing at it,
Travellers pass on.　　　　　　　　Chora

This willow is a most beautiful tree. The poet sees the travellers go by, looking at the willow-tree that stands by the gate. They both see the same tree; this is indeed a rare thing, an experience that we seldom have. Further, the travellers take the tree with them, yet leave it behind them, with the poet.

Another verse by Chora on the same subject is the following. The willow-tree is perhaps the same, but the poet speaks here of himself:

ふるさとへ戻りて見たる柳かな
Furusato e　modorite mitaru　yanagi kana

Going back to my native place,
I gazed
At the willow-tree.

What did he see? He did not say, because it cannot be said.

舟と岸柳へだつる別れ哉　　　　　　　　　子規
Fune to kishi　yanagi hedatsuru　wakare kana

In our parting,
Between boat and shore
Comes the willow-tree.　　　　　　　Shiki

The poet says a final farewell to his friend. They may never meet again and each gazes at the other, as the ferryman plies his oar, across the increasing space between them. But the current of the river is strong, and unwillingly yet swiftly the landing stage is hidden behind the willow-tree that overhangs it. Their parting is finished; all that remains is the water, the sound of the oar, and the lessening willow-tree that falls in calm and silent beauty, aloof and yet deeply related to our human life and its meetings and partings.

This willow-tree has the same meaning and value as Rossetti's woodspurge:

> From perfect grief there need not be
> Wisdom or even memory:
> One thing then learnt remains to me,—
> The woodspurge has a cup of three.

We may compare the following, less simple verse of an older poet, Kitō:

戀々として柳遠のく舟路哉
Renren to shite　yanagi tōnoku　funaji kana

> Reluctantly
> The willow leaves the boat
> Far behind.

In order to express the pain of separation, Kitō reversed the position of the boat, and the willow on the shore. *Renren to shite* is the lingering emotion expressed in his slow but irrevocable departure in the boat.

人聲にもまれて青む柳かな　　　　　　　　一　茶
Hitogoe ni　momarete aomu　yanagi kana

> Jostled by people's voices,
> The willow
> 　　Grows greener.　　　　　　　　　　　Issa

This willow is probably one in the temple grounds. Spring is here, and many people come to worship at the temple; children play, beggars make their appearance, voices of young and old pass to and fro among the hanging branches. The willow-tree shares in this new excitement of life resurgent. The same life that raises the pitch and changes the timbre of people's voices in spring greens the willow.

犬 の 子 の ふ ま え て 眠 る 柳 か な   一 茶
Inu no ko no fumaete netaru   yanagi kana

> ### The puppy asleep,
> Pushing his feet
>> Against the willow-tree.   Issa

To appreciate this verse, it is better, though not necessary,
to compare it with an earlier verse:

犬 の 子 の 咥 へ て 寝 む る 柳 か な
Inu no ko no   kuaete nemuru   yanagi kana

> The puppy asleep,
> Biting
>> The willow-tree.

The puppy has been playing with the long branches, and even
in his sleep he still bites one of them. This is a pretty, ac-
cidental picture of the fun-loving young puppy, but the later
verse brings out not only the nature of the puppy, but the
feeling of spring as well, and the two are combined in sleepy
warmth.

けろりくはんとして烏と柳哉   一 茶
Kerorikan   to shite karasu to   yanagi kana

> ### As if nothing had happened,
> The crow,
>> And the willow.   Issa

Kerorikan has the meaning of "nonchalant," "calm," and here
refers to the smugness of the crow, its perkiness, but runs over
onto the willow, which is also, in its own inimitable way, self-
possessed. We have too the contrast of the graceful stillness
of the willow, and the powerfully-controlled movement of the
crow. Katsumine compares this verse to Bashō's:

枯枝に烏のとまりけり秋の暮
Kareeda ni   karasu no tomari keri   aki no kure

> On a withered bough
> A crow is perched,
> This autumn evening.

He speaks of the pantheism of both. If we are to make comparisons we may speak rather of the mysticism of Bashō's verse and the Zen of Issa's.

The crow and the willow have no conventional association in Japanese art and literature, and from this we can see that Issa is describing something before his eyes. The crow is the crow existing for itself alone. The willow moves gently in the spring breeze. But in their very self-sufficiency there is a fundamental relationship, an identity.

捨てやらで柳さしけり雨の音   蕪 村
Suteyarade   yanagi sashikeri   ame no oto

> Unwilling to throw it away,
> I stuck the willow branch in the ground:
> The sound of the water.   Buson

On his way home, the poet had a willow wand in his hand. It was raining, and thinking that the willow would take root, he did not throw it away on reaching the house, but stuck it in the damp, sodden ground. Entering the house, he sat down, and looking out at the grey sky, listened to the sound of the falling drops of rain. The wet sound of the water had now a special meaning to him, the meaning of life and growth to the willow branch he had stuck in the ground outside. In the sound of the rain falling, he could hear the branch drawing in life and giving out its rootlets to the damp earth. His own life was continued and continuous in the cold stick that he could still feel in his hand.

This verse has another form:

捨やらで柳さしけり雨のひま
Suteyarade   yanagi sashikeri   ame no hima

> Unwilling to throw it away,
> I stuck the willow branch in the ground,
> While it was not raining.

ちよんぼりと富士の小わきの柳哉   一　茶
Chonbori to　fuji no kowaki no　yanagi kana

    Tinily,
Just at the side of Mt. Fuji,
    The willow!   Issa

This is one of Issa's many loving caricature sketches.

五六本よりてしだるる柳かな   去　來
Gorokuhon　yorite shidaruru　yanagi kana

    Five or six,
Drooping down together,
    Willow-trees.   Kyorai

    This is the simplest kind of harmony, and requires the mind
to be quite devoid of greed for beauty or gorgeousness. "But
one thing is enough."

君ゆくや柳みどりに道長し   蕪　村
Kimi yuku ya　yanagi midori ni　michi nagashi

    You going away,—
How long the road!
    How green the willows!   Buson

    When we compare this verse of Buson's with Chinese poems
of parting, we see what a great advance, or rather, what a
deepening there has been in haiku, of poetic experience. The
friend who has gone, the length of the road, the greenness of
the willow-trees are suffused with the same emotion, are mani-
festations of one spirit. It is not man with a background of
nature; it is not even an apprehension of nature through human
feeling overflowing into it. All is blent and dissolved into one
mass of colour and size and feeling, where the willow is not
green and his friend has not gone, and the road leads from
nowhere to nowhere,—and yet the friend has departed, the road
stretches out to the horizon, the willows are like green fire.

入口のあいそになびく柳かな   一 茶
Iriguchi no   aiso ni nabiku   yanagi kana

> The willow
> Waves smilingly
> At the gate.   Issa

What appears to be a subjective interpretation of the willow-
tree's waving branches turns out to be an indirect characteri-
zation of the willow, its gentle, affable appearance. In the wind
it is never irritable or menacing or sullen, but gracefully and
smoothly courteous to all comers, in all weathers lovely and
amiable. This may be the same tree that we have in another
of Issa's verses:

門柳天窓でわけて這入けり
Kado-yanagi   atama de wakete   hairi keri

> The willow at the gate:
> I entered, pushing the branches aside
> With my head.

ちる柳あるじも我も鐘をきく   芭 蕉
Chiru yanagi   aruji mo ware mo   kane wo kiku

> Leaves of the willow-tree falling,
> The master and I listen
> To the sound of the bell.   Bashō

This is like Millet's picture of the Angelus, but with a more
spiritual mellowness. These two people are poets.

もろもろの心柳にまかすべし   芭 蕉
Moromoro no   kokoro yanagi ni   makasubeshi

> Yield to the willow
> All the loathing,
> All the desire of your heart.[1]   Bashō

---

[1] This is said to be wrongly ascribed to Bashō, being in fact the
work of Bashō's pupil 涼菟, Ryōto.

Wordsworth gives the counterpart, the other half of the tally to "Yield to the willow your likes and dislikes," in *Three Years She Grew in Sun and Shower.* From Nature, the maiden shall receive law and impulse,

> And hers the silence and the calm
> Of mute insensate things.
> The floating clouds their state shall lend
> To her; for her the willow bend.

The willow bends for me, gives her pliancy to me. I give my heart to the willow, I give up my life to it. The willow and I are one. There is no giving and receiving at all. Life appears, there in the form of a willow, here in the form of a man.[1]

むつとして戻れば庭に柳かな　　　　　蓼 太
Mutto shite　modoreba niwa ni　yanagi kana

I came back,
Angry and offended:
The willow in the garden.　　　Ryōta

From the point of view of Zen, what was wrong with Ryōta was not that he was angry, but that he was not angry enough, not sufficiently angry to be oblivious of the garden and all the trees in it. The fact is however, that his anger was enough to arouse the mind so as to perceive the beauty, and still more, the harmony of the willow-tree. The poet notes his own confusion of mind, the divided interest. The subject of the verse is what Dante calls "the unloosing of the knot of anger."[2]

---

[1] *Zen in English Literature.*
[2]　　　　　　　　Tu vero apprendi,
　E d'iracondia van solvendo il nodo.
　　　　　　　　Purgatorio, XIV, 452.

柳から日のくれかかる野路かな　　　　　蕪　村
Yanagi kara　hi no kurekakaru　nomichi kana

> From the willow-tree
> On the road over the moor,
> 　　　Day begins to darken.　　　　Buson

Over the vast expanse of earth and sky, shadows are falling, but it is only when he passes beneath the shade of the willow-tree that Buson realizes that this is so. Evening begins then from the shadows there and gradually extends over all things. Compare his verse on page 583.

Buson's feeling of the meaning of the falling of night is profound, because entirely unsentimental. He has a great many verses on this subject in all seasons, for example:

春雨や暮なんとしてけふもあり
Harusame ya　kurenan to shite　kyō mo ari

> 　　Spring rain;
> It begins to darken;
> 　Today also is over.

日暮るるに雉子うつ春の山邊かな
Hi kururu ni　kiji utsu haru no　yamabe kana

> Though night draws nigh,
> Shooting pheasants
> 　In the spring hills.

花にくれて我家遠き野路かな
Hana ni kurete　waga ie tōki　nomichi kana

> Late from flower-viewing,
> The road over the moor,
> 　Home far-off.

嵯峨へ歸る人はいづこの花に暮れし
Saga e kaeru　hito wa izuko no hana ni kureshi

> People going back to Saga,—
> Where were the cherry-blossoms,
> That kept them till dusk?

菜の花や摩耶を下れば日のくるる
Na no hana ya maya wo kudareba hi no kururu

> Coming down from Mt. Maya,
> Rape-flowers,
> Shadows of night falling.

いとまなき身に暮かかる蚊遣かな
Itoma naki mi ni kurekakaru kayari kana

> Busy all day long,
> Evening begins to fall;
> The mosquito smudge.

山くれて紅葉の朱を奪ひけり
Yama kurete momiji no ake wo ubai keri

> The mountains darken,
> Taking the crimson
> From the autumn leaves.

古寺に唐黍を焚く日暮かな
Furudera ni tōkibi wo taku higure kana

> Burning millet-stalks
> In the old temple;
> Darkening day.

炭賣に日のくれかかる師走かな
Sumi-uri ni hi no kurekakaru shihasu kana

> The day darkens
> On the charcoal-seller
> At the year-end.

枇杷の花鳥もすさめず日くれたり
Biwa no hana tori mo susamezu hi kuretari

> Flowers of the loquat;
> Even the birds cannot fly hither and thither;
> The day is over.[1]

---

[1] This verse belongs to winter.

ひたすらに咲かうでもなし門の梅   一　茶
Hitasura ni   sakō de mo nashi   kado no ume

> It doesn't seem
> Very anxious to bloom,
> This plum-tree at the gate.   Issa

There is in this verse a hardly expressed union of Issa with the plum-tree. The tree has apparently no earnest desire to bloom. Warm days have come but the buds steadily refuse to open. Issa feels a kind of stolidity, a botanical obstinacy and lack of good faith in it. There is nothing remarkable about this verse but the writing of it; Issa is a poet because he writes down the things we see, and even say, but do not think worth recording.

隅々に殘る寒さや梅の花   蕪　村
Sumizumi ni   nokoru samusa ya   ume no hana

> In nooks and corners
> Cold remains:
> Flowers of the plum.   Buson

In the warmer, sunny places of the valley, the plum-trees are in full bloom, but here and there, in the shade or under the bluffs, plum-tree show only a few blossoms. Buson sees the cold in the scarcity of blossoms. He feels it with his eyes, quite irrespective of any physical sensations of warmth or coolness.

梅一輪一輪ほどの暖かさ   嵐　雪
Ume ichirin   ichirin hodo no   atatakasa

> Another blossom of the plum,
> And that amount
> More warmth.   Ransetsu

This is a justly famous verse. There is first the simple banal fact that the amount of warmth and the blooming of the plum-blossoms are vitally connected. The almost thermometric nature of the plum-tree is an interesting point.

In addition there is the inversion of cause and effect, the warmth and the blossoming, somewhat similar to Chaucer's

> the nightyngale
> That clepeth forth the grene leves newe;

but somewhere in the background of the mind there is a feeling of the mystery of the suchness of things.

Buson has a verse with a somewhat similar object, but here the relation is a rather fanciful one:

欠け欠けて月も無くなる夜寒哉
Kake kakete   tsuki mo naku naru   yosamu kana

> Waning, waning,
> The moon also is gone,—
> How cold the night!

Another, by Rotsū, has a fainter resemblance:

彼岸前寒さも一夜二夜かな
Higan-mae   samusa mo hito-yo   futa-yo kana

> Before the spring equinox;
> The cold will last
> Only a night or two more.

春もやゝけしきとゝのふ月と梅　　　　芭蕉
Haru mo yaya   keshiki totonou   tsuki to ume

> The spring scene
> Is well-nigh prepared:
> The moon and plum-blossoms.　　Bashō

To make the moon and the plum-blossoms a pleasure, an ornament of life, is not so difficult. But to make such things the chief delight of the passing days, to live for them, to see them now, remember them, in retrospect, with longing, to wait eagerly for their yearly return,—this is given to few. When we read Bashō's words, knowing them to be his, we feel that it is in his heart that the spring scene has been prepared for us.

(See p. 405.)

白梅や墨芳しき鴻鸕館　　　　　蕪　村

Shiraume ya　sumi kanbashiki　kōrokan

The white plum-blossoms;[1]
In the Kōrokan,
The Chinese ink is fragrant.　　　Buson

The Kōrokan was a Chinese Office where foreign guests, ambassadors, etc., were received. This was later, in about the 9th century, imitated in Kyōto. (Apparently 鴻臚館, with the same reading, is the proper form.) It had already fallen into disuse by the time of the Emperor Murakami, 947-967. It is not clear to which Kōrokan Buson is referring. In either case it is the historical flavour which he wishes us to appreciate in connection with the plum-blossoms. The official building of the Kōrokan, with its Chinese scribes and Japanese and Korean ambassadors, brings to the mind at once the documents and writings with Chinese ink and brush. The ink is black, the plum-blossoms are white. There is a peculiarly subtle and yet simple contrast between the white blossoms that are seen and the black ink that is imagined. To this is added the historical associations of the relations of China, Korea and Japan.

Buson does not, like many of the early haiku poets, merely use Chinese subjects in order to make haiku. He also takes haiku back into the past and shows us it from the point of view of haiku, thus making it live in the present. This is his great power. Buson put himself into the life of the T'ang Dynasty, already six or seven hundred years past when Buson was living, in much the same way that Goethe and Keats entered into the life of the ancient Greeks. Zen is said to be a thing of this place and this moment; Buson shows us how it is to be lived in a world of far away and long ago.

二もとの梅に遅速を愛す哉　　　　蕪　村

Futamoto no　ume ni chisoku wo　aisu kana

The two plum-trees:
I love their blooming,
One early, one later.　　　Buson

[1] It should perhaps be mentioned that the plum-tree was a comparatively late importation from the continent.

うたがはぬ

心に白し

梅の花

木因拝

Utagawanu   kokoro ni shiroshi   ume no hana

For the heart
That doubts not,
The white flowers of the plum.

Mokuin

This verse depends upon the following lines from the *Wakan-rōeishū*, 和漢朗詠集; they are by Yasutane, d. 997:

東岸西岸之柳遅速不同、
南枝北枝之梅開落已異。

On the eastern and western banks the willows are late and early, not the same; the southern and northern boughs are different, in the blooming and falling of the plum-blossoms.

From this we see that the two trees in his garden, (草庵), are respectively in sunny and shady places. It is not that Buson thinks of the matter as a competition between them; rather that the power of nature operates equally in both, but in one quickly, in the other slowly.

The Chinese expression "slow-fast," *chisoku*, is followed by the Chinese form to love, 愛する, instead of the Japanese form, 愛づる. In 離俗論, *Rizokuron*, Buson elaborates his ideal of a complete fusion of Japanese and Chinese art and literature together with the avoidance of the vulgar spirit, 俗氣, and the becoming imbued with the spirit of harmony. In the present verse he illustrates the former by a combination of Japanese and Chinese modes of expression. That is to say, Buson's life-long study of Chinese poetry, particularly that of the T'ang, was not only to increase his own poetical fertility, but to enable him to reproduce, as far possible, the forms and language in which the spirit of Chinese verse was contained. Sometimes, indeed, his missionary zeal made him overdo this latter, and we feel that Chinese expressions are used without sufficient justification, detrimentally both to the verse and to the cause he espoused. Zen is not the spirit of poetry as opposed to its form, but something far more subtle than this. It is the balance between content and form.

The translation given above fails to emphasize one point. Literally the verse runs:

> I love
> The early-lateness
> Of the two plum-trees.

That is to say, "I love the way in which some are slow, some fast, some short, some long; and this is exemplified in these two plum-trees." It is these small differences in things which are the delight of the poet, especially when there is the sameness of their both being plum-trees.

There is one other point to be noted, and that is that the rather hard, Chinese form of expression corresponds to the nature of the plum-tree with its straight, new branches rising from the crooked old boughs.

臭 水 の 井 戸 の 際 よ り 梅 の 花　　　　　　　一 茶
Kusa-mizu no   ido no kiwa yori   ume no hana

   Beside a well
Of foul water,
     Flowers of the plum.　　　　　　　Issa

This verse is both a pictorial verse and one of thought. The well is old and dilapidated. It stands in a deserted corner of the garden, never cleaned, never used. Children occasionally look into it for a moment and see their reflections in the bottom. Ferns and weeds grow between the stones, and the undrinkable waters harbour frogs and water-beetles. By the side stands an old plum-tree. From the black boughs are springing blossoms that glow in contrast to the desolation and disorder around.

There is, no doubt, in Issa's mind the thought of the active indifference of Nature. Not only does the lotus flower grow in the mud, but is the mud transformed. Stinking water is what the plum-tree likes, and so must the poet who admires the blossoms; love me, love my dog.

お と ろ へ や 花 を 折 に も 口 ま げ る　　　　　　一 茶
Otoroe ya   hana wo oru ni mo   kuchi mageru

   Failing strength:
Even in breaking off this flowering spray,
     A grimacing mouth.　　　　　　　Issa

There is no escape from poetry. Every moment of every part of our life, up to the death-rattle, can be, should be, shall be made into poetry, made alive. Value is received from it, value is given to it.　In strength, in weakness, in what we do, in what is not done by us; every place is everywhere, every moment is eternity.

梅が香にのつと日の出る山路かな　　　　芭　蕉
Ume ga ka ni　notto hi no deru　yamaji kana

Suddenly the sun rose,
To the scent of the plum-blossoms,
Along the mountain path.　　　Bashō

"*Notto*," "suddenly," represents the "jerk" to the mind of the poet of his impressions, rather than the suddenness of the sun rising.　The two senses of smell and hearing were so simultaneously affected that Bashō felt as if he had smelled the sun, had seen the scent of the plum-blossoms.

山の月花盗人を照らし給ふ　　　　　一　茶
Yama no tsuki　hana nusubito wo　terashi tamō

The moon over the mountains
Kindly shines
On the flower-thief!　　　Issa

The sun shines, the rain falls upon the just and upon the unjust.　The moon also shines impartially upon all.　The moon over the mountains is a common symbol of Perfect Truth, and there may be such an association here.　But taking Issa himself as the flower-thief, the feeling of guilt makes his mind receptive to the bright rays of the moon that is rising from the distant mountains.

Though the original does not say that plum-blossoms are meant here, it is perhaps better to take it as plum-blossoms, since Issa was much more affected by these than cherry-blossoms.　It is said that he wrote about three hundred and fifty haiku on plum-blossoms.

月 の 梅 の 酢 の こ ん に や く の け ふ も 過 ぬ　　　一　茶

Tsuki no ume no su no konnyaku no kyō mo suginu

The moon, the plum-blossoms,
Vinegar and konnyaku,—
And there goes today too!　　　Issa

The moon and plum-blossoms are connected in oriental art
and literature, just like the tiger and bamboo, willow and
swallow, moon and wild geese, lion and peony. *Su*, a kind of
vinegar, is sour like the plum (in Japan). *Konnyaku*, a paste
made from the starch of the fibrous root of the devil's tongue,
is used with "vinegar" in a proverbial saying.[1] Thus all these
apparently disconnected but actually connected things, go to
make up the day in the life of Issa. This reminds us of Darwin's
account, in the *Origin of Species*, of the relation between the
number of old maids and of humble bees. The point that must
not be missed is that the vinegar and the *konnyaku* and moon
and flowers are necessaries of life. There is a somewhat similar
thought at the beginning of the 87th Case of the *Hekiganroku*:

雲門示衆云、薬病相治。盡大地是薬。那箇是自己。

Unmon said to the congregation: "Sickness and medicine
cure each other. The universe is the medicine: what is
yourself?"

Buddhism is used to cure our sinful condition, but becomes
itself a poison to life. In the same way, poetry and art, used
as a cure for the ills of life, take the mind from reality, to
which we are called back by vinegar and *konnyaku*.

There is a verse by Bashō similar to this:

木 の 下 に 汁 も 膾 も 櫻 か な

Ko no shita ni shiru mo namasu mo sakura kana

Beneath the tree,
In soup, in fish-salad,—
Cherry-blossoms!

It can be said that Issa freed himself from Bashō's aestheticism,
but retained his earthiness and close touch with reality, and
gave it a more universal application.

[1] "Su no konnyaku no" means "all at sixes and sevens."

匂ひして隣の梅の見へぬかな   樗　良
Nioi shite   tonari no ume no   mienu kana

How it smells,
The plum-tree next door,—
But I cannot see it!   Chora

The world in which we live is a light-world. The senses of
hearing, smell and touch, are less subtle than those of the lower
animals.[1] There is a natural yearning to translate the sweetly-
heavy scent of the plum-flowers into terms of sight. An odour
has no form, no detail, no direction. The poet wishes to see
the boughs of the plum-tree tapering off into the sky, to see
the pale blossoms against the black branches, to *see* the still
life of it.

塊に笞うつ梅のあるじかな   蕪　村
Tsuchikure ni   muchi utsu ume no   aruji kana

The master of the plum-tree
Strikes a clod
With his stick.   Buson

The significance of this lies not in the meaninglessness of the
action of striking the dry clod of earth, but in the region of
the relation between the meaningless action of the striking and
the equal meaninglessness of the plum-blossoms that bloom
overhead. Goethe asks us not to look for anything behind
phenomena:

Sie selbst sind die Lehre.

This is what we find also in the following:

春色無高下、花枝自短長。   （禪林句集）

In the scenery of spring, nothing is better, nothing worse;
The flowering branches are of themselves, some short, some
    long.

[1] There is of course the notable exception of the world of music.

梅咲て帯買ふ室の遊女かな　　　　　　　蕪村
Ume saite　obi kau heya no　yūjo kana

Plum-trees blooming;
Courtezans in their room
Buying sashes.

Buson

The first two lines are concerned with the world of nature alone; the second two with the world of nature and the world of men, mixed and distinguishable by the uninspired mind, seen in their oneness and indivisibility by the imagination. Nevertheless, in Buson this fusion is rather external than internal, compared to that of Bashō, for example, in the following:

一家に遊女も寝たり萩と月
Hitotsuya ni　yūjo mo netari　hagi to tsuki

Sleeping under the same roof
With courtezans:
Lespedeza flowers and the moon.

The moon here represents Bashō or at least his ideals; and the lespedeza flowers are the courtezans lodging in the same inn.

鳥の音に咲うともせず藪の梅　　　　　　一茶
Tori no ne ni　sakō to mo sezu　yabu no ume

The song of the bird!
But the plum-tree in the grove
Is not yet blooming.

Issa

The bird here must be the uguisu, which is so deeply associated in poetry and art with the plum-tree, that we feel that they must be so in fact, in nature. When the uguisu sings, the plum-tree must bloom. When the plum-tree blossoms, the uguisu must sing. This truth Issa expresses in another verse, but in this case it is the hototogisu and the spring rain that have their fated connection.

此雨にのつびきならじ時鳥
Kono ame ni　noppiki naraji　hototogisu

This rain,
And its inevitable
Hototogisu.

手折らるる人に薫るや梅の花　　　　　千代尼
Taoraruru   hito ni kaoru ya   ume no hana

> The flowering branch of the plum
> Gives its scent
> 　　To him who broke it off.　　Chiyo-ni

This has the prescript, "In regard to requiting evil with good."

しら梅の枯木にもどる月夜哉　　　　　蕪　村
Shiraume no   kareki ni modoru   tsukiyo kana

> In the moonlight,
> The white plum-tree becomes again
> 　　A tree of winter.　　Buson

Shiki, who was great admirer of Buson, thought little of this verse. It is more clever than spontaneous, it is true. The moonlight makes the white flowers almost invisible, and we can see only the black branches, which look bare and barren. The original says "returns to a withered tree." Shiki approved of a similar verse, also by Buson:

手燭して色失へる黄菊かな
Teshoku shite   iro ushinaeru   kigiku kana

> Lighting the lantern,
> The yellow chrysanthemums
> Lose their colour.

Compare *Aen.* vi, 272: "Et rebus nox abstulit atra colorem," and Buson's verse at the middle of page 571.

病僧の庭掃く梅のさかり哉　　　　　曾　良
Byōsō no   niwa haku ume no   sakari kana

> The sick monk
> Is sweeping the garden,
> 　　The plum-trees in full bloom.　　Sora

The real subject of this verse is the new warmth of spring

expressed by the beauty of the plum-blossoms, but also by the pale face and feeble movements of the monk. Compare a sick-bed verse by Shiki:

一枝は薬の瓶に梅の花
Hitoeda wa   kusuri no bin ni   ume no hana

> One of the sprays
> Of plum-blossom,
> In the medicine bottle.

梅やせて麥はまばらなり籔畑   子　規
Ume yasete   mugi wa mabara nari   yabubatake

> The plum-tree straggling,
> The barley thin and sparse:
> A field in the groves.   Shiki

This field is overhung by clumps of trees so that it gets little sunshine. Even the plum-tree is impoverished and feeble-looking, with but few flowers.

白梅に明る夜ばかりとなりにけり   蕪　村
Shiraume ni   akuru yo bakari to   nari ni keri

> Every night from now
> Will dawn
> From the white plum-tree.   Buson

It has no further, no ulterior meaning beyond the simple fact that every day now, dawn comes from the direction of the white plum-blossoms. But the emphasis on the night brings out the power of the glimmering white flowers; however many times darkness covers the earth, and thick darkness the people, they have the power to bring back the dawn again. This is suggested by the "trailing" of the verse, the sound of *bakari to nari ni keri*. There is some similarity between this verse and Morris's *Summer Dawn:*

> The summer night waneth, the morning light slips,
> Faint and gray 'twixt the leaves of the aspen.

This verse of Buson's is said to be his death-verse, 辭世. It shows a stage of enlightenment to which even the word "self-less" is inapplicable. He died in the serenity of natural beauty in which he had lived. This was not possible for either Bashō or Issa, who lived and died in the beauty of human life, a beauty that is not grown, but growing, continually born and reborn in travail of spirit.

手鼻かむ音さへ梅の盛り哉   芭 蕉
Tebana kamu   oto sae ume no   sakari kana

The sound of someone
Blowing his nose with his hand;
The plum-blossoms at their best.   Bashō

The sound, short and conclusive, sharpened Bashō's sense of smell for the moment, so that he was suddenly aware of what he had been doing for some time, smelling the scent of plum-blossoms and absorbing the faint yet deep white colour. On thinking it over, what struck Bashō was the fact that the blowing of the nose with the hand had not seemed to him a dirty or ungentlemanly thing, but had been taken as it was, an action, a sound, a phenomenon of nature, not separated in its essence from the sight and odour of the plum-blossoms.

There is a verse by Issa which goes beyond the above by Bashō:

畠打や手涕をねぢる梅の花
Hatauchi ya   tebana wo nejiru   ume no hana

Tilling the field,
He wipes his snotty hand
On the plum-flowers.

To do this on a fine cambric handkerchief is all right, but not on the overhanging spray of flowers. Truly Wordsworth says,

And custom lie upon thee with a weight
Heavy as frost, and deep almost as life.

梅 の 花 爰 を 盗 め と さ す 月 か   一 茶
Ume no hana   koko wo nusume to   sasu tsuki ka

"Steal this one,"—
The moonlight seems to say,—
"This branch of flowering plum-tree!" Issa

There is no doubt, of course, that on this particular occasion
Issa did not break off the branch that the moonlight picked out
for him.

紅 梅 や 入 日 の 襲 ふ 松 か し は   蕪 村
Kōbai ya   irihi no osou   matsu kashiwa

Red plum-blossoms:
The setting sun assails
Pines and oak trees.   Buson

The level rays of the sun strike on the oaks and pines above
the plum-tree, and flood them with a strength and depth of
colour that surpasses that of the obscurely red blossoms. There
is here no attempt on the part of the poet to unite himself with
nature, to live his own life into nature. Buson makes himself
a *tabula rasa* upon which to portray the scene which somehow
or other disturbs him. It is true that we can find subjective
elements here, as everywhere, the contrast of the masculine
pines and oaks with the feminine plum-tree, the use of the word
"assail" which really expresses the poet's own feeling of being
overwhelmed by the rich colour of the rays of the setting sun.

阿 古 久 曾 の 心 は 知 ら ず 梅 の 花   芭 蕉
Akokuso no   kokoro wa shirazu   ume no hana

The inner mind of Akokuso
I do not know,—
But these plum-flowers!   Bashō

Bashō is here thinking of a poem of Tsurayuki, 883–946,
whose name as a child was Akokuso;

人 は い さ 心 も 知 ら ず ふ る さ と は
花 ぞ 昔 の 香 に 匂 ひ け る

The hearts of people I know not;
　　But the cherry-blossoms
Of my native place,—
　　Their scent is that of long ago.

The minds and hearts of men are always changing. Friends grow cold and leave us; men are fickle and uncertain. But Bashō's feeling is not of this rather misanthropic flavour. He says he does not know, and does not care to know, what was in Tsurayuki's mind when he uttered the words of his poem. All Bashō knows, and all he needs to know, is that the plum-blossoms have the beauty of form and colour and scent that they always had.

文 は 跡 に 梅 さ し 出 す 使 か な　　　　　　其 角
Fumi wa ato ni　ume sashiidasu　tsukai kana

The messenger;
He offers the branch of plum-blossom,
　　Then the letter.　　　　　　　　　　Kikaku

Usually the (descending) order of importance of these three elements would be, the letter, the flowering branch, the messenger. Here, however, we have the messenger, the flowering branch, the letter. The beauty of the flowers is greater than the importance of the letter, but the mind of the messenger is more charming than even the flowers he offers.

梅 ち り て 淋 し く な り し 柳 か な　　　　　無 村
Ume chirite　sabishiku narishi　yanagi kana

The plum-blossoms having fallen,
How lonely
　　The willow-tree!　　　　　　　　　　Buson

While plum-blossoms were blooming, the willow-tree seemed to share in their life and colour, but now the flowers have fallen, the willow-tree stands sad and solitary.

白梅や垣の内外にこぼれ散る　　　　　樗　良
Shiraume ya　kaki no uchisoto ni　koborechiru

White plum-blossoms;
Outside and inside the hedge,
They fall and spill.　　　　　　　　Chora

Compare Browning's lines in *Home Thoughts from Abroad:*

My blossomed pear-tree in the hedge
Leans to the field and scatters in the clover
Blossoms and dewdrops.

散るたびに老行く梅の梢かな　　　　　蕪　村
Chiru tabi ni　oi-yuku ume no　kozue kana

With every falling petal,
The plum branches
Grow older.　　　　　　　　　　　Buson

When all the blossoms are out, the plum-tree has a youthful
aspect that hides its age, but as each petal falls more of the
black branch becomes visible, and the years are seen in the
branches of the tree. At each moment, as each petal falls for
ever to the ground, a vast and irrevocable extent of time passes.
Each moment is felt as an age.

梅散るや草堂に火をともしゆく　　　　暁　臺
Ume chiru ya　sōdō ni hi wo　tomoshiyuku

Going to light the candles
In the thatched temple,
Plum-blossoms falling.　　　　　　　Gyōdai

We have here the harmony of the weak light in prospect,
the soft outlines of the straw-thatched Hall, the silent fall of
the white petals.

夕月や梅ちりかゝる琴の上   子 規
Yūzuki ya   ume chirikakaru   koto no ue

The moon of evening;
Plum-blossoms fall
On the lute.   Shiki

In this verse Shiki has imitated Buson's imitation of Chinese
poetry,—or it may be a painting or a screen that he is looking
at. In any case, it is not a verse of direct experience, but
indirect experience may be deeper than direct, as we see, for
example, in the painful stories of Hardy's novels.

紅梅の落花燃らむ馬の糞   蕉 村
Kōbai no   rakka moyuramu   uma no fun

The fallen flowers of the red plum
Seem to be burning
On the horse manure.   Buson

Freshly dropped horse manure lies on the ground, and upon
it fall deep red petals that seem to burn as the horse-droppings
steam in the cold morning air. What is striking here is the
way in which the burning red colour of the fallen flowers takes
away all our feeling of disgust at the droppings of the horse.
The indifference of the flowers, their *burning indifference*, in-
duces this same feeling in us.

Buson does not attempt to enter into the inner being of so-
called ugly things and bring out the beauty of their real nature.
Here, the beauty of the blossoms takes away the odiousness of
the dung, and we are left ourselves to live in the life of both.

商人を吼える犬ありももの花   蕉 村
Akindo wo   hoeru inu ari   momo no hana

A dog barks
At a pedlar:
Peach-trees are blooming.   Buson

This is a picture of a small village in spring. A pedlar makes as if to go into a house, and the dog asleep in the entrance suddenly begins to bark at him. The question is, what is the (undoubted) connection between the dog barking at the pedlar, and the peach-blossoms that are hanging over the walls everywhere? Are the flowers also in their colourful way, barking at all and sundry? Is the dog blossoming into sound as he expresses his part of the "stream of tendency" by which we fulfil the law of our being? There is a passage in the *Saikontan*[1] which strongly resembles Buson's verse:

桃源犬吠、桑間鶏鳴。

The barking of a dog in a village of peach-blossoms;
The crowing of a cock among the mulberry-trees.

There is another passage in the same book, which gives a kind of hint at the feeling which Buson had in writing his verse:

竹籬下忽聞犬吠鶏鳴、恍似雲中世界。

The barking of dogs and crowing of cocks inside the bamboo fences transports me to a realm up in the clouds.

喰ふて寢て牛にならばや桃の花　　　　蕪村
Kūte nete　ushi ni narabaya　momo no hana

Having eaten, to fall asleep,
And become an ox,
Under the peach-blossoms!　　　Buson

There is a saying that if you fall asleep immediately after eating you will become an ox, (in the next life, perhaps.) Buson takes this adage and through it expresses his feeling about the peach-flowers. To eat one's fill, to lie down like an ox under the flowering tree and sleep,—this is the real poetic life, where all wants are satisfied, all is natural, the poetry taken for granted, absorbed unconsciously, unintellectually, a spiritual life as serene as the life of animals.

There may be here a recollection in Buson's mind of the Cow-herding Pictures well-known in Zen. In fact there is a picture by Buson accompanying the above verse, with a passage

[1] See page 74.

from the *Tsurezuregusa*, the 93rd section. This tells the story
of a man who was going to sell an ox to another man the next
day. That night, however, the ox died, and it seemed to be a
loss for the seller. "Not so," said someone; "when we consider
this as a warning of the ephemeral nature of things, the death
of the ox was very profitable to the owner." All the other
people laughed and said, "What you say is true enough, but it
is not limited to the owner of the ox."

あけぼのやことに桃花の鶏の聲　　　　其角
Akebono ya　koto ni tōka no　tori no koe

Dawn,—
And the voice, above all,
Of the peach-blossom cock.　　　Kikaku

Henderson says of this verse,

> Kikaku's chief interest seems to have been to paint a
> "Symphony in Reds,"

and translates the verse:

The dawn is here!
And ho!—from peach-blossoms the voice
Of Chanticleer!

The rosy hue of the sunrise, the red jowl and comb of the cock,
the pink of the peach-flowers,—these are no doubt here. But
there other ways of taking Kikaku's verse. The dawn is at
hand with the promise of new life. From the village of peach
blossoms comes the thrilling voice of the cock. Life is at tiptoe.

But I feel somehow rather worried about 桃花, *tōka*. This
is a Chinese expression; it is not 桃の花, *momo no hana*. And
looking around in dictionaries and commentaries, it seems that
tōka may be the name of a kind of fighting-cock. Cock-fighting,
cultivated especially among the Chinese, took place on a clear,
cloudless day, and the fighting-cock is himself announcing the
good weather of his day of gory combats.

Further, in an old book, *Genjuki*, 玄中記, it says:

> There is a certain mountain in the south-east of China
> on which there is a huge peach-tree. Three thousand

leagues it stretches out its branches, and above it there is a Heavenly Cock. When the sun rises first on this peach-tree, the Heavenly Cock crows, and all the cocks over the land repeat its cry.

We should therefore perhaps translate this verse:

> Dawn,—
> The voice, above all,
> Of the peach-coloured fighting-cock.

古 寺 の 桃 に 米 ふ む 男 か な   芭 蕉
Furudera no　momo ni kome fumu　otoko kana

> By the old temple,
> Peach-blossoms;
> A man treading rice.   Bashō

A man belonging to the temple is treading a kind of wooden machine that hulls the rice in an outhouse. Over it hang the white flowers of the peach. The age of the temple, the youth of the flowers, the thud of the pestle with its rustic music have an inexplicable harmony of colour and sound and sentiment.

船 頭 の 耳 の 遠 さ よ 桃 の 花   支 考
Sendō no　mimi no tōsa yo　momo no hana

> Peach-blossoms!
> But the ferryman
> Is deaf . . .   Shikō

The poet is being ferried across a river, and as he gazes at the flowering peach-trees on the banks, reflected in the smooth surface of the water, he speaks to the old man who is rowing him across, feeling a desire to share with someone the beauty of the world before his eyes. The old man is hard of hearing, and does not hear or heed him.

梨 の 花 月 に 文 讀 む 女 あ り   蕪　村
Nashi no hana   tsuki ni fumi yomu   onna ari

　　A pear-tree in bloom:
　In the moonlight,
　　A woman reading a letter.   Buson

　One is reminded of Whistler's *A Symphony in White*, and of
the description of the pear-tree in Katherine Mansfield's *Bliss*.
Meisetsu thinks of Seishōnagon or Murasaki Shikibu, poetesses
of Old Japan. Shiki suggests a Chinese lady leaning out of the
window to read a love-letter.

梨 さ く や い く さ の あ と の 崩 れ 家   子　規
Nashi saku ya   ikusa no ato no   kuzure-ie

　　By a house collapsed,
　A pear-tree is blooming;
　　Here a battle was fought.   Shiki

　The house has fallen down for no apparent reason, from disuse
and lack of repair perhaps. Near it, thousands of human beings
gouged one another's eyes out, and slit open stomachs, enjoyed
themselves after the fashion of their animal forbears. But this
too time can change into something of pathos and faint splen-
dour. A pear-tree stands there, its white blossoms quite still.
What has it to do with battles long ago, or this tumble-down
hut?

菜 畑 や 二 葉 の 中 の 虫 の 聲   尚　白
Nabatake ya   futaba no naka no   mushi no koe

　　A field of rape:
　In the seed-leaf
　　An insect is chirping.   Shōhaku

　The crying of the insect, a single tiny insect, seated on one
of the green shoots of the rape plants, in a large field, has a
singularly penetrating meaning. It is as if the green sprouts
of the young plants themselves had, like the stones that Christ

spoke of, broken into voice.

菜 の 花 や ひ と も と 咲 き し 松 の 下   宗 因
Na-no-hana ya   hitomoto sakishi   matsu no shita

A head of rape-flowers
Has bloomed
Beneath the pine-tree.   Sōin

This verse is like the rape-flowers themselves, like Keats'
Grecian Urn, that can tease us out of thought

As doth eternity.

These seventeen syllables are worth the whole of *Paradise
Regained*.

菜 の 花 の 中 を 淺 間 の け ぶ り 哉   一 茶
Na-no-hana no   naka wo asama no   keburi kana

Amid the rape-flowers,
The smoke
Of Mount Asama.   Issa

Mount Asama is an active volcano in Shinano. There was a
terrible eruption in 1783, when Issa was twenty years old.
    What is the connection between the distant smoke of the
volcano, and the yellow flowers at our feet? This is the mystery
that will never be solved, for it is of the very nature of man
that in him alone all things have their form of union or sepa-
ration. What man hath joined, let not God put asunder.

菜 の 花 や 月 は 東 に 日 は 西 に   蕪 村
Na-no-hana ya   tsuki wa higashi ni   hi wa nishi ni

A field of rape-flowers:
The sun in the west,
The moon in the east.   Buson

Between the moon on the one hand and the sun on the other,
lies stretched out a great field of flowers. As far as the eye
can see, a vast expanse of yellow rape-flowers; in the still bright
west, the red sun; in the darkening east, the silver moon. In
other verses Buson expresses the feeling of vastness and peace
that a field of rape gave him;

菜 の 花 や 晝 一 と し き り 海 の 音
Na-no-hana ya   hiru hitoshikiri   umi no oto

An expanse of rape-flowers:
For a time, at noon,
The sound of the sea.

When we compare Buson's verse with the corresponding waka
in the *Manyōshū*, we are struck with the difference between the
two worlds of poetic life:

ひ ん が し の 野 に か ぎ ろ ひ の 立 つ 見 え て
か へ り み す れ ば 月 傾 き ぬ

Over the eastern moor,
The light of dawn
Is seen;
Looking back,
The moon is sinking.

菜 の 花 の 中 に 城 あ り 郡 山   許 六
Na-no-hana no   naka ni shiro ari   kōriyama

Kōriyama;
Amidst the rape-flowers,
A castle.   Kyoroku

This is a real castle in Kōriyama of Yamato Province, but it
is also a fairy castle, like those we see in dreams. No road
leads in or out, there is no voice of drum or trumpet. In the
silence, the white walls rise from the golden flowers. In the
blue sky of spring, white clouds are sailing.

菜畠に花見顔なる雀かな   芭 蕉
Na-batake ni   hanami-gao naru   suzume kana

> Sparrows
> In the fields of rape,
> With flower-viewing faces.   Bashō

This reminds us of Wordsworth's experience expressed in
Lines Written in Early Spring;

> The birds around me hopped and played,
> Their thoughts I cannot measure:—
> But the least motion which they made,
> It seemed a thrill of pleasure.

菜の花や鯨もよらず海暮れぬ   蕪 村
Na-no-hana ya   kujira mo yorazu   umi kurenu

> Flowers of rape;
> No whale approaches;
> It darkens over the sea.   Buson

Rape-flowers extend down to the edge of the cliff, beyond
which stretches out to infinity the boundless ocean. All the
long spring day, no spume-spouting whale approaches the shore,
nothing of strange aspect or meaning appears, and day darkens
on rape-blossoms and sea waves. This whale belongs to those
that Arnold speaks of, in the ocean

> Where the sea-snakes coil and twine,
> Dry their mail and bask in the brine;
> Where great whales come sailing by,
> Sail and sail with unshut eye,
> Round the world for ever and aye.

菜の花の小村豊かに見ゆる哉   子 規
Na-no-hana no   ko-mura yutaka ni   miyuru kana

> What a rich village it looks,
> There in the midst
> Of the rape-flowers!   Shiki

However difficult it may be we must look upon this verse as a picture, and not allow it to fall into didacticism, and make it a text for meditation upon the truth that

> Distance lends enchantment to the view,

that

> All that glisters is not gold,

and that

> Fine feathers do not make fine birds.

The village looks affluent just as ice *looks* cold, though we do not touch it. In other words, the sensation is of richness; it is perceived immediately, not deduced or inferred from anything. It is this very absence of intellectuality *per se* that gives the verse its poetic value.

Other verses of Shiki in which he uses the rape-flowers to add magnificence or increase it are the following:

菜 の 花 や 金 蓮 光 る 門 徒 寺
Na-no-hana ya   kinren hikaru   montodera

> Rape-flowers,
> And golden lotuses shining
> In a Shin temple.

菜 の 花 や あ ち ら こ ち ら に 七 大 寺
Na-no-hana ya   achira kochira ni   shichi-dai-ji

> Flowers of rape;
> The Seven Great Temples[1]
> Far and near.

山 か げ や 菜 の 花 さ き ぬ 春 過 ぎ ぬ   大 魯
Yamakage ya   na no hana sakinu   haru suginu

> In the shade of the hill,
> Rape-flowers have bloomed;
> Spring is over.   Tairo

The pathos of nature,—not human pathos, or the pathetic

---

[1] In Nara.

fallacy—is brought out in this verse as indirectly and quietly
as in nature itself. The plants grow in the shadow and have
budded and bloomed as they may, but the spring also in which
they flowered is as transient.

雨 風 の 荒 き ひ ま よ り 初 櫻   樗 良
Ame-kaze no   araki hima yori   hatsu-zakura

In the intervals
Of rough wind and rain,
The first cherry-blossoms.   Chora

The two aspect of this verse, the poet's sympathy for the
cherry-flowers, and the eagerness of things to live, even of such
frail, ephemeral blossoms,—what is the connection between
them? Here, as always, the more we can see the identity of
the subjective and objective aspects, the closer we get to the
same life that runs through poet and flowers. That is to say,
we must sink down deeper and deeper into that region where
our life and that of other things is subsumed under one activity.

谷 水 や 石 も 歌 よ む 山 ざ く ら   鬼 貫
Tani-mizu ya   ishi mo utayomu   yama-zakura

The wild cherry:
Stones also are singing their songs
In the valley stream.   Onitsura

The clear tones of the trickling streams of spring water
harmonize with the purity of the wild cherry-blossoms. The
hardness of stones, the softness of water, the tender texture of
the flower petals are one.

The singing of the stones may seem a mere figure of speech,
or literary convention; it goes farther in Wordsworth's

To the loose stones that lay upon the highway,
I gave a moral life;

and is most profound in Christ's words:

"I tell you that if these should hold their peace, the stones would immediately cry out!"

But they are all the same stones.

海手より日は照つけて山ざくら   蕉 村
Umite yori   hi wa teritsukete   yama-zakura

From the direction of the sea,
The sun shines
On the mountain cherry-blossoms.   Buson

This looks almost foolishly simple, vacant and meaningless,
and this feeling is somewhere near the truth, for it is the
simplicity of the sea, the vacancy of the sunshine, the mean-
ingless beauty of the cherry-blossoms that Buson is expressing.
Over the boundless ocean there is not a sail to be seen; only
the sun shines from over the sea onto the expanse of pink
blossoms that sweep up from the shore to the sky.

湯も浴びて佛をがんで櫻かな   一 茶
Yu mo abite   hotoke ogande   sakura kana

Having bathed in hot water,
And worshipped before the Buddha,—
The cherry-blossoms!   Issa

To feel clean in the body, and purified and simple in spirit,
then to gaze at the purity and simplicity of the cherry-blossoms,
—if we have done this in the morning, we may die without
regret in the evening.

鶏の聲も聞ゆるやま櫻   凡 兆
Niwatori no   koe mo kikoyuru   yama-zakuru

The cry of a cock
Is heard too,—
Wild cherry-blossoms!   Bonchō

This is a rather simple verse, but a young poet might easily miss the chance to compose it. Among the mountains, Bonchō stands gazing at the blossoms that stand out against the dark boughs and leaves of other trees. Nature alone is felt in its silent beauty. At this moment, a cock crows in the distance, and everything is humanized. The cry of the cock, so vociferous and revealing, is like the triumph of the flowers that bloom with such abandon.

是は是はとばかり花の吉野山　　　　　　貞 室
Kore wa kore wa to bakari hana no yoshino-yama

"Ah!" I said, "Ah!"
It was all that I could say—
The cherry-flowers of Mt. Yoshino! Teishitsu

This is often criticized on the ground that the cherry-blossoms of the last line could be replaced by any other superlatively beautiful thing. This may be so, and as haiku, it may be defective, but from the point of view of Zen, this "Ah!" is what is to be uttered, the only thing to be done, when we really see *anything* for the first time. Bashō himself refers to this verse with approval in speaking of Yoshino.[1]

The following verse by Kubutsu may be compared and contrasted with that of Teishitsu:

口あいて落花眺むる子は佛
Kuchi aite rakka nagamuru ko wa hotoke

A child gazing at the falling flowers
With open mouth,
Is a Buddha.

A verse on a different subject but with a similar attitude to that of Teishitsu by Shōhaku:

星月夜空の廣さよ大きさよ
Hoshizukiyo sora no hirosa yo ōkisa yo

A starlit night;
The sky,—the size of it,
The extent of it!

---

[1] かの貞室が是は是はと打ちなぐりたるに我れ言はん言葉もなくて云云，笈の小文

花 の 雲 鐘 は 上 野 か 淺 草 か   芭 蕉
Hana no kumo   kane wa ueno ka   asakusa ka

A cloud of cherry-blossoms;
The temple bell,—
　　Is it Ueno, is it Asakusa?   Bashō

It is early afternoon. The air is warm and hazy. As Bashō
sits in his hut at Fukagawa, he can see, when he wishes, the
cloud-like masses of cherry-blossoms in the direction of Ueno
and Asakusa. The boom of a great temple bell comes sounding
across the fields; it must be from one of these two places.

The poem is not an alternative question. It belongs to the
same realm as that of Dōgo in the 55th Case of the *Hekiganroku*.

道吾與漸源、至一家弔慰。源拍棺云、
生邪死邪。吾云、生也不道、死也不道。
源云、爲什麼不道。吾云、不道不道。

Dōgo and Zengen went to a house to offer their condo-
lences. Knocking on the coffin, Zengen said, "Dead or
alive?" Dōgo answered, "I won't say alive and I won't
say dead." Zengen asked, "Why won't you tell me?" Dōgo
replied, "I simply won't say."

Bashō is in that poetic state where all things are one, yet retain
their individuality. This was caused in him and conveyed to
us by the haze, the spring heat, the cloudy mist of flowers, the
vague swelling sound of the bell from the unknown to the
unknown.

大 名 を 馬 か ら お ろ す 櫻 か な   一 茶
Daimyō wo   uma kara orosu   sakura kana

The cherry-blossoms!
They have made a daimyō
　　Dismount from his horse.   Issa

This is perhaps reminiscent of Kikaku's poem of Kusunosuke's
taking off his armour to see the peonies. The verse is found
in Vol. 3, Summer. Man's being subservient to Nature is *the*
great example of

He who would be master must be servant of all.

明星や櫻さだめぬ山かつら   其　角
Myōjō ya   sakura sadamenu   yama-katsura

The morning star,
The cherry-blossoms distinguished
Among trailing clouds.   Kikaku

This verse has the vastness of early morning in spring on
the mountains of Yoshino.   The trailing clouds are almost in-
distinguishable from the cherry-blossoms that cover the hills,
and above all still glows in the dark sky the star of dawn.   But
soon the poet discerns the flowers clearly.

さくらさくらと唄はれし老木かな   一　茶
Sakura sakura to   utawareshi   oiki kana

"Cherry-flowers, cherry-flowers . . ."
It was sung of,
This old tree.   Issa

This is another example of those verses which Issa has com-
posed from folk-songs or fables or proverbs.   "Sakura, sakura,"
comes in a naga-uta called *Dōjōji*, 道成寺, which was composed
in 1753.   Issa died in 1827.

ぶらんどや櫻の花をもちながら   一　茶
Burando ya   sakura no hana wo   mochinagara

The child sways on the swing,
In his hand a flowering branch
Of cherry-blossom.   Issa

This must be one of the most objective verses that Issa ever
wrote.   It is a picture as if by Buson, but the child,—this be-
longs to the world of Issa.

櫻さくころ鳥あし二本馬四本　　　　　　鬼 貫
Sakura saku koro　tori ashi nihon　uma shihon

> When cherry-blossoms are blooming,
> Birds have two legs,
> Horses four.　　　　　　　　　　　　Onitsura

This verse may be taken in two ways; first, in praise of the cherry-blossoms and their supreme and overwhelming beauty. When the cherry-flowers bloom, all other things lose their interest temporarily, and are like the number of the legs of birds and horses, unremarkable and prosaic things. The other explanation is that when cherry-blossoms come, our senses and sensations become abnormally stimulated, and the most ordinary things are seen as full of meaning, full of their "thusness."

At the moment, I find either interpretation equally interesting, but I do not think the verse to be great poetry. Onitsura almost certainly meant the verse to be taken in the latter way, and this is confirmed by another verse of his:

目は横に鼻は堅なり春の花
Me wa yoko ni　hana wa tate nari　haru no hana

> Eyes horizontal,
> Nose vertical;
> Flowers of spring.

This has the prescript 孝行, Filial Piety, and means that obedience to one's parents is a natural thing, just like the blooming of the cherry-blossoms in spring.

順ふや音なき花も耳の奥　　　　　　　　鬼 貫
Shitagau ya　oto naki hana mo　mimi no oku

> Silent flowers
> Speak also
> To that obedient ear within.　　　　　Onitsura

This has the prescript: 大心禪師六十賀, "Congratulating the Zen Teacher Daishin on his 60th birthday."

The sixtieth year is called 順耳, Obedient Ear, from Confucius' words in *Rongō*, Chapter IV:

六十而耳順

At sixty, my ear was obedient.

Onitsura takes this "obedient ear" not in the Confucian sense of obedience to the moral laws of the universe, but in the sense of obedience to Nature. This verse is not, in the strict sense, haiku, but expresses the state of mind in which haiku are composed. The confusion of the senses of hearing and sight is a matter of experience, and is also one of the qualities ascribed to a Buddha. (See Bashō's verse, page 608.)

見かへればうしろを覆ふ櫻かな　　　樗良
Mikaereba   ushiro wo ōu   sakura kana

Looking over my shoulder,
All behind was covered
In cherry-blossoms.　　　　Chora

The poet had a feeling of exultation, of luxuriousness, as though bathing in cherry-flowers. Like the Jabberwocky,

He chortled in his glee.

Another by the same author :

四方の花に心さわがしき都かな
Yomo no hana ni   kokoro sawagashiki   miyako kana

Their hearts
And the capital a-bustle,
With cherry-blossoms everywhere.

Here it is not the poet who feels his relation to Nature through the flowers, but man as a whole. The individual is swallowed up in the body poetic. There is the same feeling in another verse of his :

諸人や花をわけ入り花を出づ
Morobito ya   hana wo wakeiri   hana wo izu

Everyone going into
Cherry-blossoms, coming out of
Cherry-blossoms.

世 の 中 は 三 日 見 ぬ 間 に 櫻 か な   蓼 太
Yo no naka wa   mikka minu ma ni   sakura kana

The world,
Unseen for three days,—
And cherry-blossoms!   Ryōta

This verse is almost devoid of poetry, yet its very common-placeness may make us suspect an experience that humanity has every spring. We feel the tremendous power of nature that can transform the world in such a short time. There is nothing of interest or joy around us, but after a few days, cherry-blossoms are everywhere, and the minds of men are renewed. We feel too the secret, silent, unceasing working of nature. Its sameness and faithfulness always comes as a shock of surprise.

花 の 陰 あ か の 他 人 は な か り け り   一 茶
Hana no kage   aka no tanin wa   nakari keri

Under the cherry-blossoms,
None are
Utter strangers.   Issa

This poem, like many of Tennyson's, hides its profundity under a veil of ease and ordinariness. Men have no relation to men.

> Now I can be alone, and leave all things to themselves, and the fig-tree may be barren if it will, and the rich may be rich. My way is my own alone.[1]

Each man is related only to God, to Reality; but when he and this Reality, even for a moment, are one, he feels his inseparability, his original inseparateness from his fellows. There is the same thought in

One touch of nature makes the whole world kin.

Or to put it in another way, when a man through beauty becomes aware of the Original Nature which is common to all things, but cloudy and obscure in mankind, the flowers and

[1] *The Man who Died*, D. H. Lawrence.

other people and himself, all things, are like clear mirrors
reflecting one another.

工夫して花にランプを吊し鳬   子 規
Kufa shite   hunu ni rampu wo   tsurushi keri

> What pains I took,
> Hanging the lamp
> On the flowering branch!   Shiki

This seemingly subjective, ego-centric verse is really not so.
The intense absorption with which he was hanging the lamp
upon the blossoming cherry-tree is not only purely objective,
but is used to praise the beauty of the flowers.

人聲にほつとしたやら夕櫻   一 茶
Hitogoe ni   hotto shita yara   yūzakura

> At people's voices,
> The cherry-blossoms
> Have flushed a little.   Issa

This is a remarkable example of personification. Issa thinks
of the cherry-blossoms as if they were a young, bashful girl,
who at the voices of visitors would become pink and embarrassed.
This verse is different from the conceits of the metaphysical
poets. It represents the tenderness of colour, the youthfulness
of blooming, the delicacy of the attraction and grace of the
cherry-flowers.

釣鐘の雲にぬれたる櫻かな   子 規
Tsurigane no   kumo ni nuretaru   sakura kana

> Cherry-blossoms,
> Wet by the clouds
> Round the temple bell.   Shiki

The combination here of the wet, pink cherry-blossoms, the

massive, black, cold bell, the vague, soft, enfolding mist, is
worthy of Shiki, who is more of an artist in words than a poet
of the emotions. The poetic brevity of the original verse super-
imposes each of the three things upon the others, without,
however, any loss of distinctness.

世にさかる花にも念佛申しけり　　　芭　蕉
Yo ni sakaru　hana nimo nenbutsu　mōshi keri

Even to cherry-blossoms
At their height in this world,
We murmur, "Namuamidabutsu!"　Bashō

This verse has more poetry in it than appears on the surface,
but we may take it as representative, in a way, of the older
haiku as distinct from the modern.　In earlier haiku, that is,
up to the time of Shiki, 1866–1902, there was always a certain
religious foundation which occasionally becomes obvious, as in
the above verse.　Modern haiku, however subtle or poetic it
may be, seems shallow and rootless by comparison.　In the
present verse, Bashō expresses his feeling of the all-applicableness
of the spirit of the *nenbutsu*, a feeling of gratitude, and of the
ephemeral nature of the greatest and most beautiful things of
this world.　Even to the perfection of the cherry-blossoms we
must repeat once more, "Namuamidabutsu."　It is a kind of
habit, but so is poetry, so is life itself.

There is a verse by Issa, much shallower, but in which also
the fundamentally religious nature of haiku is apparent:

観音のあらんかぎりは櫻かな
Kannon no　aran kagiri wa　sakura kana

Wherever Kwannon is,
Everywhere,
There are cherry-blossoms.

天からでも降つたるやうに櫻かな　　　　　一　茶
Ten kara de mo　futtaru yō ni　sakura kana

> Ah, these cherry-flowers,
> As though wafted down
> From heaven! Issa

We may compare Bridges' *Nightingales*:

> Beautiful must be the mountains whence ye come,
> And bright in the fruitful valleys the streams, wherefrom
> Ye learn your song:

> Where are those starry woods? O might I wander there,
> Among the flowers, which in that heavenly air
> Bloom the year long!

On other occasions also, Issa used heaven to describe the beauty of the cherry-blossoms:

夜櫻や美人天から下るとも
Yozakura ya　bijin ten kara　kudaru tomo

> Cherry-blossoms at night!
> Just like angels
> Come down from heaven.

夜櫻や天の音楽聞し人
Yozakura ya　ten no ongaku　kikishi hito

> Blossoms at night!
> People after hearing
> Heavenly music.

肌の好き石に眠らん花の山　　　　　路　通
Hada no yoki　ishi ni nemuran　hana no yama

> A hill of cherry-blossoms;
> I will slumber
> On a smooth stone. Rotsū

Spring is the sleepy season and the poet looks for a comfortable flat stone upon which he may sleep and imbibe the warmth and meaning of the season.

雲 を 呑 ん で 花 を 吐 く な る 吉 野 山   蕪 村
Kumo wo nonde   hana wo haku naru   yoshino yama

Swallowing the clouds,
Vomiting forth the cherry-blossoms,
Mount Yoshino!

Buson

The clouds are low, and mingle with the cherry-blossoms, so that they look like the breathing in and breathing out of the mountains of Yoshino. "Swallowing" and "vomiting" are violent expressions, not perhaps so strong in the original, that express the billowy, foaming flowers and mist that rise, wave upon wave, all over the hills of Yoshino.

鐘 消 え て 花 の 香 は 撞 夕 か な   芭 蕉
Kane kiete   hana no ka wa tsuku   yūbe kana

The temple bell dies away.
The scent of flowers in the evening
Is still tolling the bell.

Bashō

The sound of the bell has ceased, but its reverberations are continued in the scent of the flowers. This interchange of the senses is one of the marks of a Buddha.

此 や う な 末 世 を 櫻 だ ら け か な   一 茶
Kono yō na   masse wo sakura   darake kana

In these latter-day,
Degenerate times,
Cherry-blossoms everywhere!

Issa

According to Buddhism, the world has been growing more corrupt since the death of Buddha. Yet even in such a hell on earth as this present world, every spring paradisal flowers bloom in profusion everywhere. There is a trace here of Browning's feeling in

> God's in his heaven,
> All's right with the world!

That is to say, Issa feels and expresses some doubt of his own creed of The Pure Land Sect, that all is vanity, this world a dewdrop world, and the life after death the all-important thing. He has the thought of a line or two of one of Spenser's Sonnets (from *Amoretti*):

That is true beauty, that doth argue you
To be divine and born of heavenly seed:
Derived from that fair Spirit, from whom all true
And perfect beauty did at first proceed.

There is another verse of Issa's, in *Ora ga haru*, of similar meaning:

今 の 世 も 鳥 は ほ け 經 鳴 き に け り
Ima no yo mo   tori wa hokekyō   naki ni keri

Even in this present world,
Birds sing
"Hokekyō!"[1]

行 き 暮 れ て 雨 漏 る 宿 や 糸 櫻 　　　　　蕪 村
Yukikurete   amemoru yado ya   ito-zakura

Overtaken by evening,
The roof of the inn leaks;
A drooping cherry-tree.　　　　　Buson

The poet had taken refuge in a wayside inn, for it had begun to rain early in the evening. It was a very miserable lodging-place, the roof leaking with a monotonous drip, drip. But looking out of the window, he saw a beautiful *ito-zakura*, its long slender branches hanging down like a weeping willow, with cherry-blossoms and raindrops glistening palely in the evening light. This haiku is very close to waka in its lyrical spirit, and in fact probably derives from the celebrated waka of Tadanori:

[1] The name of one of the most famous Buddhist sūtras, especially prized by the Nichiren Sect.

行き暮れて木の下かげを宿とせば
花やこよひのあるじならまし

Darkness o'ertakes me;[1]
The shadow of this tree
My inn,
Its flowers my host,
This night.

さまざまの事おもひ出す櫻かな   芭　蕉
Samazama no   koto omoidasu   sakura kana

How many, many things
They call to mind,
These cherry-blossoms!   Bashō

Bashō renounced the world on the death of Sengin, 蟬吟, that
is, Tōdō Yoshitada, son of Tōdō Shinshiro, who was in charge
of Ueno Castle.   Twenty years later, in 1687, he was invited
by his former master Tōdō Shinshiro, and the above verse was
the result.   Looking at the same flowers in the same garden
when he had spent his youth with his friend, Bashō felt what
Wordsworth says in the mouth of the Wanderer:

I see around me here
Things which you cannot see; we die, my Friend,
Nor we alone, but that which each man loved
And prized in his peculiar nook of earth
Dies with him, or is changed.[2]

There is a similar verse by Shiki:

我病んで櫻に思ふこと多し
Ware yande   sakura ni omou   koto ōshi

The cherry-blossoms:
Being ill, how many things
I remember about them.

[1] Literally, "walking, getting dark."
[2] *Excursion*, 469–74.

花さいて思ひ出す人皆遠し   子 規
Hana saite   omoidasu hito ' mina tōshi

The cherry-blossoms blooming,
Those I remember
All far away.   Shiki

This becomes poetry only when we keep our eye steadily on
the cherry-flowers. All the poetic feeling that we can truly
ascribe to them belongs to them intrinsically. And the wish to
enjoy this intrinsic meaning (of affection and longing) is based
on the same state of mind as that of Yuima, who was ill
because all human beings are ill. We are to apprehend the
meaning of things to be "saved" not individually, but as mem-
bers one of another.

辛崎の松は花よりおぼろにて   芭 蕉
Karasaki no   matsu wa hana yori   oboro nite

The pine-tree of Karasaki,
More dim and vague
Than the cherry-blossoms.   Bashō

There is a colour print by Hiroshige of this famous tree. It
is shown in the rain, and it is in truth more poetical, in the
sense of romantic and lyrical, than the cherry-blossoms of
Yoshino. The flowers under the hazy moon are not more
beautiful, not more in harmony with each other, than this
ancient pine-tree in the faint moonlight.

Karasaki is on the south-western shore of Lake Biwa, and
this verse was composed at a distance from the tree, (湖水の
眺望).

Seisensui quotes a waka of the Emperor Gotoba, Eighty-
second Emperor, 1184–98:

辛崎の松の緑をおぼろにて
花より續く春の曙

The green
Of the pine-tree of Karasaki
Is indistinct also,
Continuous with the cherry-blossoms,
In the spring morning.

人
も
一
茶

迎
た

さ
い
た

さ
く
ら
が
咲
ば

苦
の
娑
婆
や

家
も
一
茶

子
が
這
へ
ば

と
び

は
へ
ば

と
ぶ

に
は
の
蝶

Left

Niwa no chō   ko ga haeba tobi   haeba tobi

In the garden, a butterfly:
The baby crawls, it rises;
She crawls, it rises again.   *Issa*

To his verse and sketch the poet has added the words, "The house and Issa too". Note that the verse given in the text is a variant. (The above form is slightly different from that given in the text, p. 549.)

Right

Ku no shaba ya   sakura ga sakeba   saita tote

A world of grief and pain,
Even when cherry-blossoms
Have bloomed.   *Issa*

To this verse (the *haiga* is also by the poet) is added the words, "The people, and Issa, too."

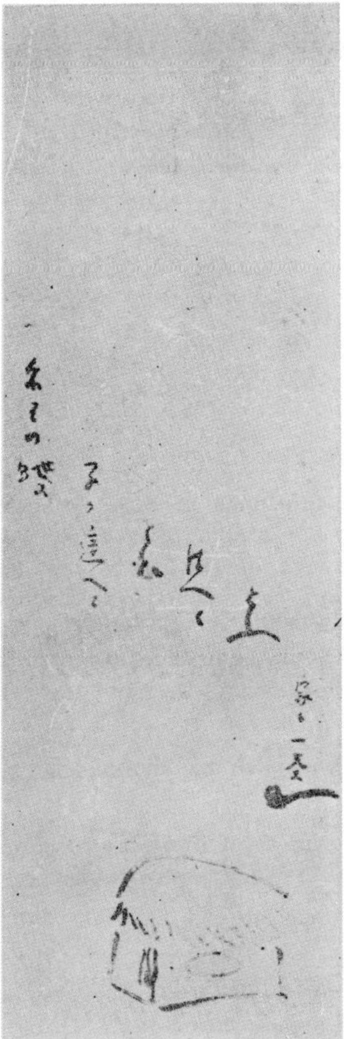

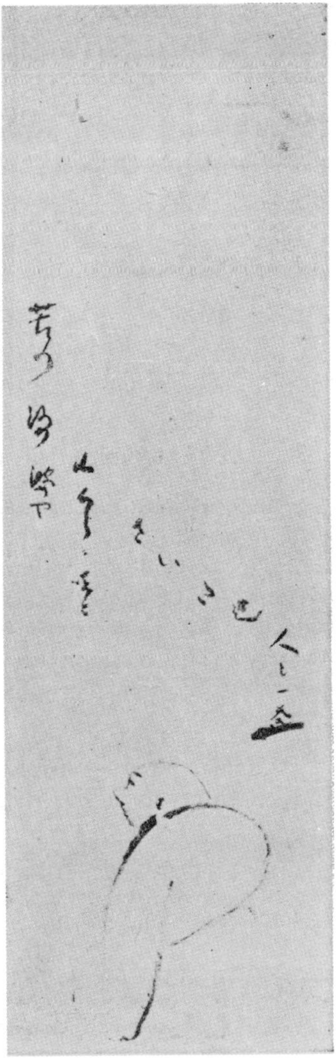

From this, some commentators think that Bashō's verse should be understood as:

> The pine-tree of Karasaki,
> Hazy and indistinct
> From the cherry-blossoms.

This view may well be the correct one, but the ordinary interpretation gives us a more poetical meaning.

斯う活て居るも不思議ぞ花の陰　　　　一 茶
Kō ikite   iru mo fushigi zo   hana no kage

> What a strange thing,
> To be thus alive
> Beneath the cherry-blossoms!　　　Issa

Of all the multitude of strange things in this mysterious world of ours, the strangest is the simple fact of our own existence. When we become aware of this, it is not self-consciousness of the ordinary kind, it is not the intellectual, ego-centric experience expressed in "cogito ergo sum," but an interpenetration of ourselves with the faint blue sky and the tender pink blossoms, in which I am I and they are they and yet we are one.

> Life is a pure flame, and we live by an invisible sun within us,

and whenever we catch even a glimpse of it we are consumed with the wonder and mystery of the suchness of things.

苦の娑婆や櫻が咲けばさいたとて　　　　一 茶
Ku no shaba ya   sakura ga sakeba   saita tote

> A world of grief and pain,
> Even when cherry-blossoms
> Have bloomed.　　　Issa

The relation between pain and beauty is the major problem, not only of poets, but of all men. From the common "O for a thousand years at the age of thirty," to Keats'

> All is cold beauty,
> Pain is never done,

this insoluble problem is felt at all stages and degrees. But *in the insolubility of the problem lies the meaning.*

花咲いて死ともないが病かな   來 山
Hana saite   shinitomo nai ga   yamai kana

The cherry-flowers are blooming;
I do not wish to die,
But this illness . . .   Raizan

In this verse the whole problem of practical life is stated. It is answered by being stated. All solutions are false, Christian and Buddhist alike. Only the question, the dilemma, the contradiction is true and eternally valid.

Contrast Raizan's haiku with Saigyō's waka:

> 願はくは花の下にて春死なむ
> その二月の望月のころ

> My earnest desire
> Is that I may die
> Beneath the cherry-blossoms,
> In spring, the second month,
> At the full moon.

There is a direct contrast of feeling about death, and there seems to be a vast difference between the poet who seeks to avoid the inevitable, and he who accepts it. But both verses are poetry, both have Zen; both are human and both are divine. Our desire to live, live on and on, more abundantly,—this is of the essence of our Buddha nature.

さく化の中にうごめく衆生かな   一 茶
Saku hana no　naka ni ugomeku　shujō kana

We human beings,
Squirming about among
The flowers that bloom.

Issa

This is one of a series of six poems of The Six Ways, 六道,
or six directions of reincarnation, 六趣, as follows:

地　獄

夕月や鍋の中にて鳴く田にし
Yūzuki ya　nabe no naka nite　naku tanishi

Hell
The evening moon:
The pond-snails crying
In the saucepan.

餓　鬼

化ちるや呑たき水を遠霞
Hana chiru ya　nomitaki mizu wo　tōgasumi

The Hungry Ghosts
Flowers are scattering:
The water we wish to drink,
In the mist far away.

畜　生

散る花に佛とも法ともしらぬ哉
Chiru hana ni　butsu tomo hō tomo　shiranu kana

Animals
In the falling of the flowers,
They see no Buddha,
No Law.

修　羅

聲々に花の木陰のばくち哉
Koegoe ni　hana no kokage no　bakuchi kana

Malevolent Nature-Spirits
Under the shade of the cherry-blossoms,
Voice against voice,
The gamblers.

人　間

咲く花の中にうごめく衆生哉
Saku hana no naka ni ugomeku shujō kana

Men

We human beings,
Squirming among
The flowers that bloom.

天　上

かすむ日やさぞ天人の御退屈
Kasumu hi ya sazo tennin no gotaikutsu

Gods

A day of haze:
Even the Dwellers of Heaven
Find it tedious, surely.

花にくれて我が家遠き野道かな　　　　蕪　村
Hana ni kurete waga ie tōki nomichi kana

Among the blossoms, it grows late,
And I am far from home,—
This path over the moor. 　　　Buson

It is a question which has the more meaning for the poet,
the cherry-flowers that have delayed him with their beauty and
gaiety, and this silent, deserted road. The truth is that one
is nothing without the other, just as the flowery kimono and
gorgeous sash, and the severe simplicity of a Japanese room
demand each other.

夕ざくらけふも昔に成りにけり　　　　一　茶
Yū-zakura kyō mo mukashi ni nari ni keri

Evening cherry-blossoms:
Today also now belongs
To the past. 　　　Issa

The feeling of the cherry-blossoms at night and in the day-

time is different. In the dusk, with lanterns glimmering here
and there, the trees no longer trees but blossoms suspended in
the air above and around us, we realize that as it is born, each
moment dies, belonging as it does equally to the past and the
present. Meeting is the beginning of parting, and in the pres-
ence of such beauty this feeling of time is intensified until each
moment under the cherry blossoms is a painful pleasure, not
only instantaneously realized, but one emotion with two names.
And in the verse above, today and the past are also two names
of one thing, something that has no name, something that we
know in the evening under the cherry-trees.

月 光 西 に わ た れ ば 化 影 東 に 歩 む 哉 　　　蕪 村
Gekkō nishi ni watareba　kaei higashi ni　ayumu kana

The moon passes westward,
The shadow of the flowers
Moves eastward. 　　　　　　　　　　　　　　　Buson

The original is unusually irregular, being 11, 7, 5. Buson
must have used this form to express slow movement. This
verse has no possible pictorial meaning, but requires a spreading
out of the mind in time that is not intellectual but poetical,
akin to the working of the historical imagination.

There is here, in the realm of the inanimate, with its deep
causal necessity and the Destiny in nature that lies below it,
an analogy with the animate realm, in which

> practical requirements, so-called, are merely the mask of
> a profound inner compulsion.[1]

What seems mechanical in the world of light and shadow, what
seems to happen in human life for purely utilitarian reasons,—
all these things are perceived by the poetical mind as expres-
sions of free life.

---

[1] Spengler, Arts of Form. VI.

花に來て花にいねぶるいとまかな　　蕪　村
Hana ni kite   hana ni ineburu   itoma kana

I came to the cherry-blossoms;
I slept beneath them;
This was my leisure.　　Buson

When we see that cherry-blossoms are something to sleep
under, we have attained a state beyond that of the average
artist or poet. Beauty and significance are to be imbibed without
strain or affectation. A life of art, like that of goodness, is to
be lived as the normal, the ordinary thing, without letting the
right hand know or care about what the left hand does. All
aesthetic and ethical pleasure must be spontaneous, without
meaning or gain, just like the fish in the water and the bird in
the air.

花を踏みし草履も見えて朝寝かな　　蕪　村
Hana wo fumishi   zōri mo miete   asane kana

He sleeps late;
There are his straw sandals,
That trod the fallen petals.　　Buson

The poet goes to see his friend, somewhat late in the morning.
He is still in bed, his wife says, and the poet sees his straw
sandals, perhaps with petals of the cherry-blossoms still adher-
ing to the soles.
The subject of the poem is the cherry-blossoms, and in the
very indirectness with which their beauty is praised lies the
value of this verse.

春の夜は櫻に明けて仕舞ひけり　　芭　蕉
Haru no yo wa.   sakura ni akete   shimai keri

The spring night
Has come to an end,
With dawn on the cherry blossoms.　　Bashō

The delicacy of the poetical feeling makes explanation difficult here. Bashō has spent the night under the cherry-flowers with his friends and pupils, drinking and eating and writing poetry. Dawn comes, and the cherry-blossoms of evening are now the cherry-blossoms of day, the same yet different, different yet the same.

筏士の蓑やあらしの花ごろも　　　　　　　蕪　村
Ikada-shi no　mino ya arashi no　hana-goromo

The straw coats of the raftsmen,—
The storm makes them
Flowery robes.　　　　　　　　　　　Buson

One day of wind and rain, Buson ascended Arashi Yama, and from there saw the above scene. The raftsmen in *mino* and *kasa*, both of straw or reeds, are standing on the raft made of a series of logs bound together. The river winds swiftly between the hills, and the wind blows down into it the petals of the falling cherry-blossoms. These stick to the wet straw-coats of the raftsmen, giving them robes of flowers.

花を得ん使者の夜道に月を哉　　　　　　　其　角
Hana wo en　shisha no yomichi ni　tsuki wo kana

To bring me the flowers,—
Oh, that the evening path of the messenger
May be moon-lit!　　　　　　　　　　Kikaku

Kikaku wants the messenger to come early, before the moon ceases to shine. Also he wishes the messenger to come on a moon-lit night, so that the flowers may retain, in his mind, that journey along the road with the moon shining down on them. Every year Kōrokō, 行露公, had sent flowers from his own garden, but this year he was later than usual.

落花枝に歸ると見れば胡蝶かな   守 武
Rakka eda ni kaeru to mireba kochō kana

A fallen flower
Flew back to its branch!
No, it was a butterfly.   Moritake

This is an ancient verse, famous, and much discussed as to
its poetic merit. There was a momentary mistake, with disil-
lusionment, expressed in the third line, and as such, this is not
poetry. Nevertheless, we feel that Moritake, like Alice, has
peeped into the garden he could not enter.

歌書よりも軍書にかなし吉野山   支 考
Kasho yorimo gunsho ni kanashi yoshino-yama

More than the songs,
The annals of war moved me to grief,
On Mount Yoshino.   Shikō

Man is the poetical animal. He is the only poetical thing in
the world. The flowers of the mind, above all, the flowers of
action, these are the best. The plain, grim statements of the
histories of the lives of those ancient warriors are more moving
than the lyrics of feeling and sentiment. The real cherry-
blossoms of Mt. Yoshino are the men who fought and died there.

木のもとは汁も膾も櫻かな   芭 蕉
Ki no moto wa shiru mo namasu mo sakura kana

Under the cherry-trees,
On soup, and fish-salad and all,
Flower petals.   Bashō

This is a picture rather than a poem, but there is also per-
haps a feeling of the way in which all things are blended with
one another through some particular agency.

苗代の水に散り浮く櫻哉   許 六
Nawashiro no   mizu ni chiri-uku   sakura kana

   Cherry-blossoms
Fall and float on the water
   Of the rice-seedlings.   Kyoroku

It is a picture of pale pink, the young green of the rice-plants,
enclosed in a rectangular frame of water, blue with the sky.

静かさや散るにすれあふ花の音   樗 良
Shizukasa ya   chiru ni sureau   hana no oto

   Stillness:
The sound of the petals
   Sifting down together.   Chora

The sound of the scattering petals, like that of the falling
snow, is very near to silence. The original actually says, "the
sound of the flowers rubbing against one another as they fall."
The verse is more of the inner mind than of sensation.

咲くからに見るからに花のちるからに   鬼 貫
Saku-karani   miru-karani hana no   chiru-karani

   The cherry-flowers bloom;
We gaze at them;
   They fall, and . . .   Onitsura

There is nothing beyond what is said here, in spite of the
"and . . ." Pilate asked Christ, "What is truth?" The answer
is given here. The answer is,

      The cherry-flowers bloom;
   We gaze at them;
      They fall, and . . .

This "and . . ." is the human element in Nature. It is the
peasant or sage somewhere visible in a Chinese landscape.

人戀し灯ともし頃を櫻散る   白　雄
Hito koishi   hitomoshi goro wo   sakura chiru

My heart is full of yearning,
The candles being lit,
  Cherry-blossoms falling.   Shirao

There is a deep and almost painful harmony among these
three so apparently unrelated things, the longing soul, the fall-
ing flowers, the lighting of a candle.   At this moment of life-
in-death, death-in-life, the candle, the blossoms and the yearning
heart are three names of one thing: the burning, flowering,
desiring are only aspects of one activity.

  Far or forgot to me is near;
  Shadow and sunlight are the same.[1]

There are some lines at the end of Goethe's *Nahe des Geliebten*,
which portray the feeling of the unreality of space, but ending,
rightly enough, with the assertion of its objectivity.

  Ich bin bei dir, du seist auch noch so ferne,
    Du bist mir nah!
  Die Sonne sinkt, bald leuchten mir die Sterne.
    O wärst du da!

花散るやおもたき笈の後より   蕪　村
Hana chiru ya   omotaki oi no   ushiro yori

Behind me,
Old and weak,[2]
  Flowers are scattering.   Buson

This "behind me" may have the meaning of Marvell's

  But, at my back, I always hear
  Time's winged chariot hurrying near.

The poet sits old and dejected, heavy-hearted; and behind him
the cherry-tree in the garden steadily and remorselessly scatters
its blossoms.

[1] Emerson, *Brahma*.
[2] For 'Old and weak' read 'Heavy travelling altar.' See Blyth,
History of Haiku, Vol. I, p. 286.

只たのめ花もはらはらあの通り   一 茶
Tada tanome   hana mo hara-hara   ano tōri

Simply trust:
Do not also the petals flutter down,
Just like that?   Issa

Towards separate things, Issa is full of Zen, but this poem
has a different flavour, for it expresses Issa's attitude towards
the universe as a whole, his religion. However much we may
say that Zen and the Nenbutsu have the same object, the way
of each is radically different, and appeals to different types of
mind. Explaining the difference intellectually, we may say that
in Shin, we are nothing, in Zen we are everything. The emo-
tional difference is still greater. Issa's poem mentions neither
Amida nor Kwannon, it does not compare us with the flowers.
But it leaves us with a sense of *lachrimae rerum;* this is never
the case with Zen. In Shin, the evanescence of things is
pointed to, as here, to remind us of our powerlessness, to
remind us of the compassion of Amida, of the world to come.
In Zen, impermanence, like the Emptiness of things, is empha-
sized as a means of getting us to give up the illusion of an
eternal separate, impermeable self, so that we may be filled
with all things and act in and through them, and they in us.

水鳥の胸に分け行く櫻哉   浪 化
Mizu-tori no   mune ni wake-yuku   sakura kana

The water-fowl swims,
Parting with her breast
The cherry petals.   Rōka

The moving picture is most beautiful. The petals floating on
the surface of the water are not submerged, but divided by the
breast of the water-bird. The petals part as the bird moves,—
as though by self-motion.

花散りて木の間の寺となりにけり 蕪 村
Hana chirite ko-no-ma no tera to nari ni keri

The cherry-blossoms having fallen,
The temple belongs
To the branches.

Buson

There is a very delicate, almost unexplainable meaning here.
It is not that the cherry-blossoms and the branches are person-
ified and spoken of as possessing the temple one after the other.
There is some deeper and more intangible relation between the
temple and them.

花ちりて静かになりぬ人心 古友尼
Hana chirite shizuka ni narinu hito-gokoro

The blossoms have fallen:
Our minds are now
Tranquil.

Koyū-ni

Not that this tranquillity is superior to the excitement of our
hearts while the cherry-blossoms were blooming. It is neither
better nor worse. It is simply inevitable, like the blooming,
like the falling of the cherry-blossoms themselves. There is a
waka of Narihira,[1] 業平, which may well have been the original
of this haiku:

世の中にたえて櫻のなかりせば
春の心はのどけからまし

Were there no cherry-blossoms
In this world of ours,
The hearts of men in spring
Might know serenity.

A humorous verse, by Bashō, of the same import, is the
following:

花に寝ぬこれもたぐひか鼠の巣
Hana ni nenu kore mo tagui ka nezumi no su

[1] 825–880.

        Is it not like a mouse's nest,—
    This being unable to sleep
        For the flowers?

That is to say, the poet is unable to sleep at night because of
the excitement of the cherry-blossoms, and compares his heart
to the nest of the mice who are squeaking and scuffling all
night long.

One more, by Shadō, 洒堂:

        花散て竹見る軒のやすさかな
        Hana chitte   take miru noki no   yasusa kana

        The flowers having fallen,
    Looking at the bamboos,
        It is restful under the eaves.

        花散つて又しづかなり園城寺   鬼 貫
        Hana chitte   mata shizuka nari   enjōji

        The cherry-blossoms having fallen,
    Enjōji Temple
        Is quiet again.   Onitsura

    The peace that has returned after the merry crowds that
thronged the temple precincts have departed, is not more
poetical than the bustle and confusion while the cherry-flowers
were blooming. Even from the ordinary, rational point of view,
we can see the compensation in it all—cherry-blossoms and
noise; bare or half-leafy branches and peace.

    We have in this poem a sensation of the passage of time, yet
it is felt as an eternal moment. This corresponds in a temporal
way with the Buddhist doctrine of cosmic interrelationship of
space, and identity of existence.   Of course, such ideas are in
no way involved in the above poem, much less hinted at.   It
is simply the temple, the blooming of the cherry-blossoms, their
falling, the chattering and the silence, all in one, *all as one.*

    Another of Onitsura's on the same subject, theoretically at
least better than the former:

        梅散つてそれよりのちは天王寺
        Ume chitte ̇soreyori nochi wa   tennōji

After the plum-blossoms
Have fallen,
Tennōji Temple.

氣に入つた櫻のかげもなかりけり　　　　一 茶
Kiniitta　sakura no kage mo　nakari keri

That cherry-blossoms,
That pleased me so much,
Have vanished from the earth.　　　Issa

The flowers that "caught his fancy,"—not a trace of them
remains. It is just as though they had never existed, a tremen-
dous cause, aesthetically, with no effect whatever. There is
something akin to the feeling of

Full many a flower is born to blush unseen,
And waste its sweetness on the desert air.

草臥れて宿かるころや藤の花　　　　芭 蕉
Kutabirete　yado karu koro ya　fuji no hana

O'er wearied,
And seeking a lodging for the night,—
These wistaria flowers!　　　Bashō

After walking all day, from morning to night, on his way
to Yoshino, Bashō and Tokoku, 杜國, reached the outskirts of
a village and were looking for the cheapest and poorest inn to
stay at. Suddenly they came across the pale purple festoons of
the wistaria. Their colour was both the colour of a spring
evening, and in some way the colour of their weariness which
was swallowed up in them. Man's extremity is God's op-
portunity:

When the half-gods go,
The gods arrive.

The appropriateness of evening to the wistaria flowers has
always been felt. Hakurakuten has the following poem:

三月三十日題慈恩寺

慈恩春色今朝盡、　終日徘徊倚寺門。
惆悵春歸留不得、　紫藤花下漸黄昏。

The Last Day of the Third Month[1]
at Jionji Temple[2]

That morning, spring was at an end in Jionji;
All day long I wandered near the temple gate.
However we grieve, spring will not tarry or return;
Yellow twilight was falling under the purple wistaria flowers.

There is also a waka by Shiki:

瓶にさす藤の花ぶさ花垂れて
病の牀に春暮れんとす。

Clusters of wistaria in the vase;
    The flowers hang down,
In the sick room;
    Spring begins to darken.

藤の花あやしき夫婦休みけり   蕪　村
Fuji no hana   ayashiki fūfu   yasumi keri

Wistaria flowers;
Resting under them,
    A strange couple.   Buson

The word "ayashiki" implies something questionable, suspicious, here in the sense of the pair's not being what they purport to be, an ordinary married couple on a journey. There is something in the way they sit, the way they address each other, that suggests they have run away, the man from his master's shop, the woman from her home or from more unlovely surroundings.

But what is noteworthy here is the wistaria, whose purple blossoms hanging down over the heads of the unconscious pair, have some deep concord in their transient beauty and grace with the fate of the two beneath them.

[1] Lunar Calendar.
[2] Near Chōan.

藤 の 花 た ゞ う つ ぶ い て 別 哉　　　　　越 人
Fuji no hana　tada utsubuite　wakare kana

Flowers of the wistaria;
Only hanging down their heads
At the parting.　　　　Etsujin

It is not clear whether this parting took place in the evening or early morning, but there is here a comparison between the flowers and the people that goes deep because it is not merely one-sided. It brings out the beauty of dejection of both.

There is a verse by Issa which has a similar feeling:

は る の 日 の 入 所 な り 藤 の 花
Haru no hi no　iru tokoro nari　fuji no hana

Where the spring sun
Sinks down,—
The wistaria flowers.

山 吹 の う つ り て 黄 な る 泉 か な　　　　嵐 雪
Yamabuki no　utsurite ki naru　izumi kana

Catching the reflection
Of the yamabuki,
The spring is yellow.　　　　Ransetsu

This is a very simple verse, but it is somehow difficult to omit it. The reason is perhaps the relation of the *yamabuki* or yellow rose, to water. The *yamabuki* has flowers very similar in colour and shape to the buttercup, but it is a bush with long sprays that bend over. The yellow is somewhat glittering, and its reflection in water is very strong. The water appears to come out yellow from the earth, and flows away in yellow waves.

There is a verse by Bashō which has a similar subject of flower and water:

ほ ろ ほ ろ と 山 吹 散 る か 滝 の 音
Horo-horo to　yamabuki chiru ka　taki no oto

The petals of the yellow rose,—
Do they flutter down
At the sound of the rushing water?

芭蕉桃青

ほろ〳〵と
山吹ちるか
たきのおと

Horohoro to yamabuki chiru ka   taki no oto

  The petals of the yellow rose,—
Do they flutter down
  At the sound of the waterfall?

The verse is by Bashō, the picture by his disciple Kyoroku. Bashō says in *Saimon no Ji* (柴門辞) of Kyoroku: "In painting he was my teacher; in æsthetics, my pupil."

  Bashō composed the *haiku* in the spring of 1688 by the water-fall of Nishigo in Yoshino.

SPRING

The flowers are falling and scattering on the banks of the Nishigō Rapids. The question form of the verse represents a feeling in the mind of the poet that there is some profound relation between the small, yellow petals and the force of the swirling waters.

紫 の 夕 山 躑 躅 家 も な し　　　　　　子　規
Murasaki no　yūyama tsutsuji　ie mo nashi

Purple the mountains of evening,
The azaleas;
Not a house to be seen.　　　　　　Shiki

Our feelings swings backwards and forwards between man and nature. There is perhaps some regular systole and diastole in this, could we perceive it, in correspondence with some inner or outer physical occurrences. In the blood, in the glands, in the moon, in the stars there is, it may be, some deep and pervasive influence which sways us to this attraction and repulsion. Sometimes we feel as Shiki did when he wrote the above verse, that nature is complete in itself without man. The infinite blue sky, or one single leaf is enough. The hills with the purple that seems part of their very being, the faintly purple pink of the azaleas in the gloom of the grove, these are enough, without the feeling of space, without the slightest tinge of human thought or feeling. Indeed, the very absence of all signs of habitation is what brings out the meaning of the purple colour, of flower and mountain, just as an empty road is more expressive of humanity than the busiest thoroughfare.

つ つ じ 生 け て そ の 陰 に 干 鱈 さ く 女　　芭　蕉
Tsutsuji ikete　sono kage ni hidara　saku onna

A woman
Under the azaleas placed in the pot,
Tearing up dried cod.　　　　　　Bashō

This is a splendid example of the creation-discovery of harmony among apparently unrelated and discordant things. In a rather rough and simple vessel, someone, probably the woman herself, has arranged a few branches of flowering azaleas. She crouches beside them tearing up pieces of dried cod. What is it that brings together the aesthetic and the domestic? What is the affinity between the beauty of the purple flowers, and the dry, stringy strands of salt fish?

むしつてはむじつては捨て春の草　　　來　山
Mushitte wa　mushitte wa sutete　haru no kusa

Plucking it, plucking it,
Throwing it away,—
The grass of spring.　　　Raizan

This is the essence of triviality, but the *essence*, and therefore of infinite meaning and importance. This verse is similar in its unconsciousness to that of Sono-jo, a poetess, pupil of Buson :

手をのべて折行く春の草木かな
Te wo nobete　ori-yuku haru no　kusaki kana

As I go along,
Stretching out my hand and plucking
The grasses and leaves of spring.

So soft and pleasant to the touch, so acridly fragrant are the plants and bushes in spring-time, that the poetess unthinkingly, almost wantonly, breaks off twigs and branches, sprays and leaves, coming into bodily contact with spring through the feel of things.

いろいろの名もむづかしや春の草　　　洒　堂
Iroiro no　na mo muzukashi ya　haru no kusa

All the various
Difficult names,—
Weeds of spring.　　　Shadō

The expression "difficult names" suggests the infinite variety of shapes and colours of the grasses and plants that grow up under the spring sun. It implies also the mystery of nature that we pretend to understand, hiding our ignorance under many and lengthy words. Yet these very circumlocutions express the infinite multitude of forms that Nature takes in spring.

よく見れば薺花咲く垣根哉　　　　芭　蕉
Yoku mireba   nazuna hana saku   kakine kana

Looking carefully,—
A shepherd's purse is blooming
Under the fence.　　　　Bashō

In early spring the *nazuna* has a small, white, four-petaled flower. The point here is the "looking carefully," which does not mean with an inquisitive, pelmanised, or scientific eye, but with Wordsworth's eye, Goethe's Augenbegabung.

While with an eye made quiet by the power
Of harmony, and the deep power of joy,
We see into the life of things.

What is this "harmony" which quietens our eye? It is the humanity of the flower and the floweriness of our own nature. But the really important thing is the way in which this "looking carefully" has come down through the poets. Shiki evidently remembered Bashō's verse when he wrote:

よく見れば木瓜の蕾や草の中
Yoku mireba   kiuri no tsubomi ya   kusa no naka

Looking carefully,—
The buds of a cucumber flower
In the grass.

This "looking steadily at the object" has penetrated into the very soul of the Japanese.

垢爪や薺の前もはづかしき　　　　一　茶
Akazume ya   nazuna no mae mo   hazukashiki

Before my shepherd's purse gruel,
I am ashamed,—
These dirty nails!　　　　Issa

This verse is entitled 人の日, "Day of Man." According to
an ancient Chinese tradition, each of the first seven days of the
year is consecrated to the following: the fowl, the dog, the pig,
the sheep, the cow, the horse, and last, the seventh day, to
man. On this day, the 7th of January, is the Feast of the
Seven Herbs of Health, 七草の祝, when the seven herbs, parsley,
shepherd's purse, etc., are boiled with rice gruel.

Issa knew that

日 日 是 好 日 、

Every day is a good day,

and that dirty nails or clean nails are of no account whatever,
but he knew also that

人 日 是 好 日 、

The day of man is a good day,

and that this particular day was special, unique, a day on which
dirty nails are out of place, when a man is to separate himself
from the horse and the cow and the dog.

古 寺 や 炮 烙 す て る 芹 の 中   蕪 村
Furudera ya hōroku suteru seri no naka

The old temple:
A baking-pan
    Thrown away among the seri.   Buson

Seri is one of the Seven Herbs of spring. It grows in damp
soil, both the root and the leaves being eaten. It has a small,
white flower in spring. It is sometimes translated "parsley."

The harmony between the old temple, the broken piece of
crockery, and the *seri* is subtle but real, because experienced.
The *seri*, a kind of rank parsley, is growing in an old pond or
ditch. Half-seen among the *seri* is a broken earthenware pot.
This pot is in the same world, not by its symmetry, nor by
its historical associations, nor by any poetical glamour thrown
over it, but by Buson's realization of its absolute, infinite,
eternal value. The strange thing is that it is the setting of
the broken pot that arouses Buson to a sense of its significance.

The greenness of the *seri* in space, the age of the temple that exists in time, lift it beyond time and space into the world of meaning.

これきりに徑盡きたり芹の中   蕪　村
Kore kiri ni komichi tsukitari   seri no naka

This is all there is:
The path comes to an end
Among the seri.   Buson

Following a narrow path that he thought would lead in the direction he wished to go, Buson found that it only led to a patch of *seri*, a small plot that someone had cultivated. When a path dwindles away to nothing, we have a peculiar feeling of of frustration and helplessness. In the following verse also, this feeling of impotence issues into a poetic experience.

路たえて香にせまり咲く茨かな
Michi taete ka ni semari saku ibara kana

The path ending,
Approaching the scent,
Wild roses blooming!

Paths and roads have a very deep and ancient significance to mankind and almost all animals, which Buson felt strongly. A very large number of his verses succeed or fail in giving expression to what a path meant to him.

五月雨に見えずなりぬ徑かな
Samidare ni   miezu narinuru   komichi kana

In the summer rains,
The path
Has disappeared.

うらがれの中に路ある照葉かな
Uragare no   naka ni michi aru   teruha kana

Through the withered copse,
A path;
The yellowing leaves.

三徑の十歩に盡きて蓼の花
Sankei no　juppo ni tsukite　tade no hana

> After ten paces,
> The garden[1] ends:
> Flowers of the knotweed.

蕎麥刈てゐるるや我ゆく道の端
Soba katte　iru ya ware yuku　michi no hata

> Cutting the buckwheat,
> At the side
> Of the road I walk.

近道に出てうれし野の躑躅かな
Chikamichi ni　dete ureshi no no　tsutsuji kana

> Going by a short cut,
> The azaleas on Ureshi[2] Moor:
> What happiness!

我歸る道幾筋ぞ春の草
Ware kaeru　michi ikusuji zo　haru no kusa

> On the road back,
> How many lines
> Of spring grass!

道のべや手よりこぼれて蕎麥の花
Michi no be ya　te yori koborete　soba no hana

> On the road-side,
> Spilled from someone's hand,
> Flowers of buckwheat.

古道と聞てゆかしき雪野かな
Furumichi to　kiite yukashiki　yukino kana

> Hearing this was an ancient road,
> It was pleasant
> Over the snowy moor.

眞直に道あらはれて枯野かな
Massugu ni　mich arawarete　kare no kana

> Over the withered moor
> The road stretches out
> Straight.

[1] *Sankei* means "three paths," i.e. a hermit's garden.　[2] Happy.

細道になりゆく聲や寒念佛
Hosomichi ni   nariyuku koe ya   kannembutsu

Chanting mid-winter *nenbutsu*,
The voices of the devotees fainter,
The path narrower.

細道をうづみもやらぬ落葉かな
Hosomichi wo   uzumi mo yaranu   ochiba kana

The narrow path,
Not entirely covered
In fallen leaves.

山路來てなにやらゆかし菫草   芭 蕉
Yamaji kite   naniyara yukashi   sumire-gusa

Coming along the mountain path,
There is something touching
About these violets.   Bashō

Naniyara expresses Bashō's unwillingness to notice the violet,
to make a verse on it. Somehow or other it compels him to
notice it, importuning him like a weeping infant;

A violet by a mossy stone
Half hidden from the eye.

This flower and the heart of Bashō have some deep affinity.
Contrast the objectivity of Buson:

すわりたる舟を上れば菫かな
Suwaritaru   fune wo agareba   sumire kana

Getting off the boat
That had grounded,—
The violets!

Bashō's verse is extended and "explained" by Gyōdai:

菫つめばちいさき春の心かな
Sumire tsumeba   chiisaki haru no   kokoro kana

Picking a violet,—
The slender
Heart of Spring!

摘むもをしつまぬもをしき菫かな　　　直 女
Tsumu mo oshi tsumanu mo oshiki sumire kana

　　　To pluck it is a pity,
　　To leave it is a pity,
　　　　Ah, this violet!　　　　　　　Naojo

This is like Meredith's

　　Love that so desires would fain keep her changeless,
　　Fain would fling the net, and fain have her free,[1]

but goes beyond it, for the poetess solves her *mondō* by finding
pleasure in the very dilemma itself. Emily Dickinson has the
same thought, intellectually expressed:

　　　　　　In insecurity to lie
　　　　　　Is joy's insuring quality.

手にとれば猶うつくしき菫かな　　　孤 舟
Te ni toreba nao utsukushiki sumire kana

　　　The violet:
　　Held in the hand,
　　　　Yet more lovely.　　　　　　Koshū

One is reminded of those enlargements of portions of Sesshū's
paintings. The more they are enlarged, the more marvellous
the technique, the more masterly, the more significant every
line and stroke is seen to be. Further, when the violet is held
in the hand, it seems almost an extension of one's own body,
giving a feeling of intimacy beyond the power of the eye.

早淋し朝顔蒔くといふ畠　　　一 茶
Haya sabishi asagao maku to yū hatake

　　　A flower-bed
　　Where morning-glories are being sown,—
　　　　Loneliness already!　　　　　　Issa

How delicate the mind of man is, especially that of a poet,

---

[1] *Love in the Valley.*

elated and cast down with the veriest trifles and mere fancies. By the association of ideas, morning-glories—autumn—loneliness —the planting of the seeds in spring brings up the recollection of their fated decline and withering so soon as bloomed.   So with our children, when they say "Look papa! I can reach to this place now!" our pleasure is a sadder one than theirs, for it is tinctured with the feeling of time, the friend and enemy of mankind.

骨柴の刈られながらも木の芽哉   凡 兆
Honeshiba no   karare nagara mo   ki-no-me kana

> The brushwood,
> Though cut for fuel,
>   Is beginning to bud.   Bonchō

    Nature will have "her perfect work" under all conditions, however unfavourable and unnatural.